Introduction

KIM WATTY,* BEVERLEY JACKLING** and RICHARD M. S. WILSON***

**Deakin University, Melbourne, Australia, **Victoria University, Melbourne, Australia, ***Loughborough University, UK*

The skills set and competencies required by accounting graduates have changed significantly over the past 50 years. Global markets, technology and a heightened focus on the public interest imperative of accounting information are but some of the driving influences. Not surprisingly, research and discussion about personal transferable skills (also referred to as generic skills, soft skills, employability skills, attributes and/or competencies) in higher education generally, and in accounting education specifically, have received increased attention in the literature. In an environment of increasing accountability which exists in higher education, various stakeholders have voiced their concerns about accounting graduates who lack many of the personal transferable skills necessary for employment as accounting professionals in a global workforce. As a consequence, those involved in accounting education have often been criticised for failing to provide opportunities for accounting students to develop these important personal transferable skills within the curriculum.

It is often noted, however, that these criticisms have also been levelled at graduates from other practice-related disciplines, including engineering, architecture, law, medicine, economics and finance. Whether personal transferable skills are best defined in a discipline-specific or trans-disciplinary context is a debate which continues in the literature.

Given the vocational nature of the accounting discipline, the views of future employers and professional accounting bodies are important in the design of current and future accounting programs and courses. While some undergraduate students may elect to continue their formal academic studies following graduation, most will seek full-time employment, and some will continue studying for professional accounting qualifications to achieve professional status. Given this approach following graduation, a focus in accounting programs is the provision of work-ready graduates thus highlighting the links between accounting education, skills and employment. Stated differently, the development of personal transferable skills provides an opportunity to bridge the gap between education and employment. We are not suggesting here that accounting graduates should *be* accounting professionals upon graduation; however, we are acknowledging that they should have the technical ability and a personal transferable

skill set to *become* professional accountants, if that is to be their chosen occupational field.

Increasingly, professional accountants are required to exercise high-level skill development and application in their judgement, decision-making, problem-solving, communications and critical thinking. This list is not exhaustive but it is indicative of the personal transferable skills expected in an increasingly complex global market. In accounting education, the global movement toward the use of International Financial Reporting Standards (IFRS) (a principles-based standards framework) provides a recent example of the heightened need for graduates who are learned in more than the technical aspects of the discipline. A principles-based approach requires well-developed critical thinking and problem-solving skills as financial statements which conform to IFRS are based on estimates and judgements. This approach contrasts with a rules-based approach in which students of accounting as well as practitioners have traditionally relied on a set of prescriptive rules to be applied to a specific financial reporting situation.

The development of personal transferable skills in accounting education has been discussed in various contexts and this has raised many interesting questions. For example: should personal transferable skills be embedded within the accounting curriculum? How do we assess the attainment of personal transferable skills? What role do employers play in identifying the personal transferable skills most relevant for accounting graduates?

Together, the contributions that follow provide additional insights which address these questions and, in so doing, raise further questions and identify future challenges.

The initial chapter by Anna Jones challenges the assumption that personal transferable skills are trans-disciplinary and that they cannot be defined separately from their educational and professional context. Using in-depth interviews with Australian academics across five discipline areas, evidence is provided which highlights the unique, discipline-specific conceptualisations of three generic attributes—problem-solving, critical thinking, and communication. The chapter concludes by recognising that personal transferable skills are shaped by the fact that their professional and disciplinary context assists academic staff with the concept of embedding their development and assessment as part of curriculum design.

The next four chapters focus on changes in practice designed to enhance the development of personal transferable skills in accounting programs.

Identifying the dimensions of a hypothesised structure of the expectation-performance gap of accounting education in a New Zealand setting is the focus of the chapter by Bui and Porter. Based on a review of the literature, a framework to identify the unique components of the expectations-performance gap is proposed, tested and evaluated. Semi-structured interviews with key stakeholder groups—graduate employers, recent graduates, accounting educators, and final year students—were undertaken to test the framework. The authors conclude that, by identifying the components of the expectations-performance gap, educators are better placed to narrow the gap by focussing on causes which are linked to each component.

The next chapter by Gracia adds valuable insights into students' experience of and orientation to workplace learning. Using student interview data from the U.K., Gracia reports on the impact of students' expectations and conception of workplace learning on their transition to an extended (48 weeks) supervised period of work experience. Reporting on the students' conceptions of supervised work placements provides

important insights into an area of the curriculum in accounting education which is receiving much attention in the personal transferable skills discussion. The findings indicate that students with a 'technical' conception view the supervised work placement as an opportunity to develop their technical competence, while those who display an 'experiential' conception are more likely to view the placement as an opportunity to develop personal skills and abilities beyond the technical.

Willcoxson, Wynder and Laing provide readers with an extensive discussion of a 'whole-of-program' mapping process designed to review the teaching of personal transferable skills in an Australian university accounting program. This chapter incorporates templates which may be modified or adapted should others wish to undertake a similar mapping process. This may be particularly useful given the global focus on assurance of learning outcomes. Importantly, the changes that occurred as a result of the mapping process are of interest given the increased focus on the ability of students to interact, collaborate and initiate resulting from the project. The authors refer to the 'lively discussions' among academics which occurred as part of the process—an aspect of program improvement to which many readers will relate.

Focussing on students at the graduate level, the chapter by Fortin and Legault reports the implementation and evaluation of the usefulness of a mixed teaching approach in developing/improving personal transferable skills in Canada. The views of accounting students regarding the usefulness of the mixed teaching model in the graduate program were investigated. The findings reveal that the students found the activities to be useful in developing the competencies investigated. These findings were validated by the responses to a questionnaire by the students' workplace supervisors who indicated that students had very good or excellent competency levels. Furthermore, results on the CA Uniform Evaluation attest to the high level of academic and professional skills possessed by the students participating in the program.

Using student focus groups, the research conducted by Stoner and Milner in the U.K. analyses the effects on students of a project to integrate personal transferable skills in two first year subjects—Management Accounting and Business Statistics. This chapter reports on the students' voice and informs readers of the importance of understanding how the authors' efforts to embed the development and assessment of employability skills are perceived and interpreted by this critical stakeholder group. Further, the authors remind us of the complexity of integrating personable transferable skills into the curriculum and, in a refreshing evaluation of their project, they note that 'difficulties were expected, but not to the extent encountered'.

The chapter by Awayiga, Onumah and Tsamenyi examines employers' perceptions of the adequacy of the knowledge and skills (specifically professional and information technology skills) of accounting graduates entering the profession in Ghana. Research of this nature considers the importance of contextualising accounting education at different stages of political and social development occurring throughout the world. The findings of this chapter inform the development of accounting education in Ghana and, potentially, in other developing countries. Interestingly, the research concludes that the skills and knowledge requirements of accounting graduates from Ghana are no different from those required in other, more economically-advanced, countries. In particular, this chapter highlights the international perspective of personal transferable skills required by accountants in meeting the requirements of the global economic community.

The final chapter by Keneley and Jackling examines the acquisition of personal transferable skills by culturally-diverse student cohorts studying accounting in Australia. The study is motivated by the increased proportion of international students studying accounting in Australia and the concerns expressed that the personal transferable skills of these students have not met the expectations of employers. The study investigates the extent to which students perceive that their undergraduate accounting degree studies have contributed to the development of their personal transferable skills with a focus on the differences between local and international students. The findings illustrate that perceptions of the development of many of these skills in the accounting curriculum differ between local and international students. Of significance is the finding that, when compared with local students, international students view the academic environment as an important source of personal transferable skill development. The study provides the impetus for the further extension of inquiry by educators to capture a more complete picture of skill integration in the accounting curriculum. In particular the study highlights the need to develop educational practices which embed personal transferable skill development in the curriculum in a way that maximises the opportunities for culturally-diverse student cohorts to enhance their employment outcomes on graduation.

Consistent with the world-wide level of interest and focus on personal transferable skills in accounting education, as noted above, we have contributions in this volume from academics located in a variety of countries—specifically Australia, Canada, Ghana, New Zealand and the U.K.

In summary, these contributions provide a broad range of perspectives on a topic of interest to all in accounting education. Together they add to our understanding of the many issues and challenges faced in the development of personal transferable skills in accounting education. Not surprisingly, and given the nature of personal transferable skills, many of these contributions will resonate with colleagues from disciplines other than accounting.

Generic Attributes in Accounting: The Significance of the Disciplinary Context

ANNA JONES

University of Melbourne, Australia

ABSTRACT *Generic skills and attributes are a significant issue in accounting education as a consequence of the changing business environment and a perception that graduates are not equipped for the workforce of the twenty-first century. Until recently, generic attributes have been poorly theorised and defined and have been viewed as separate from the disciplinary context. This paper examines the nature of generic attributes and presents a conceptual overview for theorising generic attributes. It reports the findings of a qualitative study which investigated the relationship between disciplinary culture and generic attributes. This study found that academics' conceptualisation of generic attributes is influenced by the culture of the discipline in which they are taught. This has profound implications for accounting education as this paper argues that generic attributes must be understood as part of the professional and scholarly practice of accounting and so taught as integral to disciplinary practice.*

Introduction

Over the last 15 years there has been an increasing focus on generic skills and attributes and a considerable body of research in this area (AC Nielsen Research Services, 2000; Assiter, 1995; Australian Council for Educational Research, 2001b; Barrie, 2006; Beckett and Hager, 2002; Bennett *et al.*, 2000; Bowden *et al.*, 2000; Clanchy and Ballard, 1995; De La Harpe *et al.*, 2000; Dearing Commission, 1997; Department of Education Science and Training, 2005; Drummond *et al.*, 1998; The Association of Graduate Recruiters, 1995). However, despite the interest in generic skills and attributes there remains disagreement about how they can best be understood, defined, situated, taught and assessed. This paper argues that generic attributes in accounting are shaped by disciplinary and professional knowledge and skills. In arguing this, the paper draws on a recent study which examined the ways in which academic staff conceptualised

generic skills (Jones, forthcoming). The study found that the ways in which generic attributes are constructed are profoundly influenced by the disciplines in which they are taught. This conceptualisation of generic skills situates them as part of the professional and scholarly practice of the discipline rather than external to it (and hence imposed upon it). While this study did not include accounting directly, this paper draws on the accounting literature to inform the disciplinary perspective. The paper argues that the ways in which the subject is conceptualised influences what is taught and how. This has serious implications for accounting as it points to the importance of conceptualising generic attributes in relation to the context in which they are taught and the context of the future professional needs of graduates.

While the term *generic skills* is used in much of the literature, the term *attributes* is used here, as it used in much of the more recent literature (c.f. Barrie, 2006), because of the problems with the term *skill*, which suggests clear, definable and measurable outcomes. These definitional problems will be discussed in detail.

Much of the literature has outlined the need for accounting graduates to be employable, which requires both knowledge and skills. The concern regarding deficiencies in the education of graduates entering business employment, including accounting, was voiced a decade ago in the UK by the Dearing Commission for the National Committee of Inquiry in Higher Education (Dearing Commission, 1997) and was echoed in the USA (The Secretary's Commission on Achieving Necessary Skills, 2000). The importance to employers of both content knowledge and more generic 'capabilities' was emphasised (The Association of Graduate Recruiters, 1995) with a focus on skills such as problem-solving, communication and teamwork. However, the identification of generic attributes and the associated question of their transferability from the university to the workplace is not a simple one (Atkins, 1999).

This emphasis on generic attributes remains current in higher education policy in Australia. The policy paper *Our Universities: Backing Australia's Future, Assuring Quality* (2005) argues for the promotion and testing of generic attributes through the *Graduate Skills Assessment* (Australian Council for Educational Research, 2001a). The assumption underlying this is that generic skills (the term 'skills' is used in the Graduate Skills Assessment project) are transdisciplinary, identifiable and measurable. It is assumed that key generic skills can be identified, defined, tested and measured in isolation from the disciplinary context. This paper challenges this assumption that generic skills are transdisciplinary and so can be defined separately from their educational and professional context.

Underlying these broad descriptions of graduate outcomes are a number of unexamined assumptions. While governments, university policy makers and employer groups argue for the importance of generic attributes and, while there may be some agreement as to the attributes which are important, if one closely examines the ways in which these attributes are defined, there is a distinct lack of clarity. Barnett (1994, p. 80) argues that the language and objectives around generic skills used by industry and by the university are not necessarily congruent:

> Questions are also begged in the view that the transferable skills required for a successful economy are the same metacognitive skills sought by the genuine higher education. We may use terms like communication skills, analytical skills and so forth to describe what we are up to in programmes of study in universities and they may be terms that are in use to describe skills felt not to be appropriate in the world of work. But are they, in fact, all the same terms?

More recently, this has been emphasised in the *Precision Consultancy Report on Graduate Employability Skills in Australia* (Business Industry and Higher Education Collaboration Council, 2007).

Recent research finds that generic attributes are intrinsically complex and there is a range of ways of defining and conceptualising these attributes. The idea that there can be one defining term *generic skills* that encapsulates all the aspirations of both the academy and employers should be shelved in favour of an understanding of generic attributes that takes into account their relationship with context. What is required by employers will vary from industry to industry and what is taught in universities may also vary across universities and between disciplines. Levels of communication between stakeholders can be increased through an exploration of how generic skills and attributes are defined and conceptualised in a given context. The aim is to move towards a shared understanding without guaranteeing consensus.

This paper does not assume that generic attributes are utterly context-dependent nor that they exist only relative to their context. Rather, it assumes that, although there is the possibility for abstraction and generalisability, the way in which the attributes are conceptualised cannot be understood in isolation from the social and cultural context within which they exist.

The Study

The study referred to in this paper is based on in-depth interviews with academic staff in two large, research-intensive Australian universities. In addition to the interviews, documents were collected. These included copies of assessment tasks, subject outlines, lists of generic skills and/or attributes included in subject objectives and departmental versions of university graduate attributes. These were collected to inform the ways in which staff described their teaching. Five disciplines (history, physics, economics, law and medicine) were selected. These five were chosen because they had clearly established disciplinary cultures and so conclusions regarding the relationship between the discipline and the construction of generic attributes could be established. The generic attributes focused upon in this study were problem-solving, critical thinking and communication. These attributes were chosen because they were the focus of interest across the literature and because they were seen as being important both within the higher education sector and the by employer groups.

Academic staff in each discipline were selected to allow for a broad range of specialisation or area of interest. Further, in selecting participants, the aim was also to have a range of age, experience and position level. Initially six people from each discipline were selected (three from each institution). Further interviews were then conducted when necessary until saturation was achieved, which is the point at which no new themes are observed in the data or when the same ideas keep reoccurring from participants (Miles and Huberman, 1994). Six participants were interviewed in history, seven in physics, eight in economics; seven participants were interviewed in law and nine in medicine. In medicine, two of the participants were not medical practitioners but were the key to medical education in their respective schools. Each interview was between 50 and 90 min in length. Interviews were semi-structured to allow for exploration of individual thinking. Interviews were audio-recorded and transcribed in full. Analysis was emergent and coding involved re-reading and validation through cross-checking across all transcripts. From this coding, themes or patterns were identified and refined. Hypothetical relationships identified in the initial coding were confirmed, modified or rejected on the basis of this process. In addition to the formal interviews, the researcher had a number of informal conversations with a range of people from each of the disciplines to gain some background into the culture of the disciplines and into the educational issues that were pertinent to each area.

Findings from investigations into the nature of generic attributes have shown that there is a wide range of ways of conceptualising them (Barrie, 2006; Jones, forthcoming). The present study demonstrated that generic attributes are highly context-dependent and are shaped by the disciplinary context in which they are taught (Jones, forthcoming). This study found that attributes such as critical thinking and problem-solving were understood very differently between disciplines. For example, in physics, problem-solving is understood as the use of abstract modelling, using mathematics as the tool of analysis to solve physical problems, using either theoretical or experimental processes. In law, however, problem-solving was based upon an understanding of legal principles and conventions while in medicine, problem-solving was based upon the nexus between biomedical knowledge, the clinical relationship and diagnostic reasoning to ascertain therapeutic outcomes. In economics, problem-solving was understood as the use of economic tools and reasoning. In all disciplines investigated, the ways in which problem-solving was understood was influenced by the particular conceptual tools and desired outcomes of the particular discipline. Therefore, the disciplinary or 'content' knowledge was of the utmost importance in shaping the ways in which problem-solving was understood and in the tools used in the process of problem-solving.

In the case of critical thinking, this study also found that the disciplinary context is also important in influencing the ways in which critical thinking is understood. For example, in history, critical thinking is the examination of evidence (both primary and secondary sources), understanding the social context, acknowledging ambiguity and the multiple perspectives inherent in history and understanding the role of the historian in constructing a historical argument. In physics, by contrast, critical thinking requires an examination of the logic and accuracy of a model and for experimental physicists, the rigour of experimental technique. In economics, critical thinking is the use of the theoretical toolkit of the discipline to examine economic questions. In law, critical thinking involves the use of evidence and assumptions, questions of professional and social ethics, an awareness of the social context and a historical perspective. In medicine, critical thinking requires clinical reasoning that also utilises an understanding of medical evidence and an awareness of the complex ethical issues associated with medical practice.

Even skills such as communication are understood in quite different ways in different disciplines. For example, the skills required to write up a laboratory report in physics are quite different from the skills required to write a legal paper or a historical review essay or an economic report. Oral communication skills in each discipline are also quite different. For example, the skills required to present a legal argument are different from those required to engage in historical debate or to communicate effectively with a patient (Jones, forthcoming). Furthermore, and very importantly, the skills used in the context of the university may not be the same as those required by employers, although this was not investigated in detail in this study.

A further issue in the teaching of generic attributes is that their complexity means they are difficult to assess (Jones, 2007). Thus there may not be alignment between statements of support for generic attributes and the assessment of them. Although generic attributes are valued, what tends to be assessed is the more 'concrete' content knowledge. In addition, the emphasis upon disciplinary knowledge means that generic attributes are implicit. There is a substantial body of literature showing that assessment drives learning of content (Biggs, 1999; Brown and Knight, 1994; Entwistle, 1997; Ramsden, 1992) and more recently, skills (Haigh and Kilmartin, 1999). As Leggett *et al.* (2004) point out, the relative importance of skills and the possibility of a gap between espoused theory and practice can be explained by the assessment framework.

Generic Attributes in Accounting

The disciplinary culture of accounting is important in shaping the conceptualisation and teaching of generic skills. The notion of accountants as small business or personal tax agents has changed and now many accountants are working as strategic management consultants, organisational advisors or systems analysts. Increasingly, those in the accounting profession work as part of a team in a global business environment where the skills of communication, innovation, analysis and team work are valued. They are also operating in a world of increasing uncertainty and complexity and so accountants need the skills to deal with ambiguity and with problematic situations. Accountants must have an understanding of the global context, the economic environment, the internal workings of organisations, group dynamics, the positions of various stakeholders, interpersonal and group dynamics, information technology, the professional role and an understanding of ethics (Carr *et al.*, 2006; De Lange *et al.*, 2006). In short, accounting is a discipline that requires flexibility of thinking, analytical and critical skills, interpersonal skills and an understanding of business in both a local and global world.

Changes in technology, the increase in globalisation and the growth of the knowledge economy have caused changes in the business environment (Candy *et al.*, 1994; Drucker, 1969; Drummond *et al.*, 1998) and a commensurate need to focus on skills development (Bailey, 1997). Albrecht and Sack (2000) identified a number of changes which are of significance to the accounting profession. These include: an increased pace of change; shorter product life-cycles and shorter competitive advantage; the requirement for more decisive actions by management; the emergence of new industries and new professional services; increased uncertainty; increasingly complex business transactions; changes in financial reporting and relationships with financial markets; increased regulatory activity and an increased focus on customer satisfaction. Within the accounting profession there is a growth in the importance of finance, strategy, information technology and e-commerce. Accounting professionals are no longer restricted to accounting departments but increasingly perform a consulting role (Christensen and Rees, 2002). These changes have meant that there is a greater need for graduates to have the attributes of flexibility, initiative, creativity, analytic and critical skills and the ability to work with others both in a local and global context. Along the same lines the Institute of Management Accountants (cited in Jackson *et al.*, 2006) identified the need to restructure accounting education to meet the needs of industry, taking into account the increasing demand for a range of flexible conceptual and interpersonal skills required in the accounting profession. The *SCANS Report* (The Secretary's Commission on Achieving Necessary Skills, 2000) identified the importance of higher order thinking, problem-solving, interpersonal skills, and the ability to take initiative. Stowers and White (1999) identified the important communication skills among professional accountants as being oral presentations, writing, interpersonal skills, listening and interviewing. Paul McDonald, executive director of Robert Half Management Resources (cited in Jackson *et al.*, 2006), outlined the importance of communication skills (written and oral), organisational, analytical, research and problem-solving abilities. Within accounting there is a clear need for communication, problem-solving and critical thinking skills (De La Harpe *et al.*, 2000). Gabric and McFadden (2001) point to the importance of problem-solving and communication and found that both employers and students judged the importance of these skills were significantly higher than the value of technical skills (which are albeit still important). Moreover, there is a concerning trend for a growing gap between higher education and the accounting profession (Broome and Morris, 2005).

There is already a considerable body of research into the ways in which generic skills and attributes are taught in the context of accounting and business studies (Boyce *et al.*, 2001; De La Harpe *et al.*, 2000; Hill and Milner, 2006; Humphreys *et al.*, 1997; Monks, 1995). However, some of these studies consider that generic skills/attributes are externally devised and must be integrated into the discipline so are, therefore, to some extent in competition with it. This notion that generic attributes are separate from disciplinary knowledge and from the scholarly pursuits of higher education has led to a fear that an emphasis on skills will be in competition for space in the 'content' of the curriculum and hence, in many cases, a resistance to generic attributes becomes apparent amongst teachers in higher education (Jones, 2007).

There is another body of literature in accounting which acknowledges the significance of the disciplinary context (Carr *et al.*, 2006; De Lange *et al.*, 2006; Lucas *et al.*, 2004; Tempone and Martin, 2003; Watty, 2007; Watty *et al.*, 1998). While the importance of broad-based or 'generic' skills such as critical thinking, problem-solving and communication are central, there is a concern to investigate the ways in which these operate in a disciplinary context and this has resulted in more specific accounting-focused competencies. For example, Sin and Jones' (2003) analysis of the discourse of accountants provides a detailed description of the interactions, communication strategies and thinking skills that enable accountants to solve problems successfully, based on that published by CPA Australia and the Institute of Chartered Accountants in Australia (ICAA). A small selection of this literature has been summarised in Table 1 below to illustrate the generic attributes required in accounting.

In summary, the skills of critical thinking, problem-solving and communication in accounting require a connection between theory and practice, an understanding of the business environment both global and local, and the ability to transfer skills across business contexts. Critical thinking requires an ability to analyse and evaluate, construct an argument, think independently and be conscious of both professional responsibilities and an ethical dimension. Problem-solving requires a good conceptual understanding in order to understand the nature of a problem by identifying and analysing its components. Communication requires the ability to communicate via letters memos and reports the interpretation of both financial and non-financial data within a professional or business context. Furthermore, there is an important ethical dimension which requires the ability to apply ethical reasoning and behaviour to all aspects of one's professional life.

What is clear from this is that the skills which accounting graduates need are an integration of so called 'generic' skills and accounting knowledge. In other words, the ways in which generic skills are conceptualised in accounting are very much shaped by the professional and conceptual disciplinary context.

Leveson (2000) argues that there are definitional differences between employers and academics in perceptions of generic and workplace skills. She challenged the assumption of the transferability of skills, and the assumption that the skills studied in university will be immediately relevant to the required workplace skills. She concluded that 'the identification of skills developed by graduates needs to be understood and articulated by the individual graduate and secondly understood by employers' (p. 162).

Clearly generic skills or attributes are one of the key issues in contemporary accounting education and yet, as Barrie (2002) remarked, there is a lack of coherence in the underlying theoretical and conceptual basis of generic attributes. This inconsistency in understanding is one of the many impediments to the systematic curriculum development and teaching of generic attributes. Thus it is essential for accounting educators to develop a thorough theoretical and empirical understanding of generic skills, their conceptual underpinnings, development and teaching. This paper provides a conceptual framework within which

Personal Transferable Skills in Accounting Education

The development of generic skills (often referred to as 'soft skills') in accounting education has been a focus of discussion and debate for several decades. During this time employers and professional bodies have urged accounting educators to consider and develop curricula which provide for the development and assessment of these skills. In addition, there has been criticism of the quality of accounting graduates and their ability to operate effectively in a global economy. Embedding generic skills in the accounting curriculum has been acknowledged as an appropriate means of addressing the need to provide 'knowledge professionals' to meet the needs of a global business environment.

Personal Transferable Skills in Accounting Education illustrates how generic skills are being embedded and evaluated in the accounting curriculum by academics from a range of perspectives. Each chapter provides an account of how the challenge of incorporating generic skills in the accounting curriculum within particular educational environments has been addressed.

The challenges involved in generic skills development in higher education have not been limited to the accounting discipline. This book provides examples which potentially inform a wide range of discipline areas. Academics will benefit from reading the experiences of incorporating generic skills in the accounting curriculum from across the globe.

This book was originally published as a themed issue of *Accounting Education: an international journal.*

Kim Watty is Professor of Accounting in the School of Accounting, Economics and Finance at Deakin University, Australia. She has published widely and completed major research projects in accounting education, both nationally and internationally, and is an Associate Editor of *Accounting Education: an international journal.*

Beverley Jackling is Professor of Accounting in the School of Accounting and Finance at Victoria University, Australia. Her research interests include the educational aspects of business and accounting education. She has published widely in accounting education and been the recipient of numerous national and internationally competitive research grants and awards. She is an Associate Editor of *Issues in Accounting Education.*

Richard M. S. Wilson is Emeritus Professor of Business Administration & Financial Management in the Business School, and Visiting Professor in the Department of Information Science, at Loughborough University, UK. He is the founding editor of *Accounting Education: an international journal.* He has published widely and holds two Lifetime Achievement Awards - one being specifically for his work in the field of accounting education.

Contents

First published 2012
by Routledge
2 Park Square, Milton Park, Abingdon, Oxfordshire OX14 4RN

Simultaneously published in the USA and Canada
by Routledge
711 Third Avenue, New York, NY 10017

First issued in paperback 2014

Routledge is an imprint of the Taylor & Francis Group, an informa business

This book is a reproduction of *Accounting Education: an international journal*, volume 19, issue 1. The Publisher requests to those authors who may be citing this book to state, also, the bibliographical details of the special issue on which the book was based.

British Library Cataloguing in Publication Data
A catalogue record for this book is available from the British Library

ISBN 13: 978-0-415-69920-4 (hbk)
ISBN 13: 978-1-138-81830-9 (pbk)

Typeset in Times New Roman
by Taylor & Francis Books

Publisher's Note
The publisher would like to make readers aware that the chapters in this book may be referred to as articles as they are identical to the articles published in the special issue. The publisher accepts responsibility for any inconsistencies that may have arisen in the course of preparing this volume for print.

Personal Transferable Skills in Accounting Education

Edited by
Kim Watty, Beverley Jackling and Richard M. S. Wilson

Routledge
Taylor & Francis Group
LONDON AND NEW YORK

Table 1. Generic attributes in accounting

Carr *et al.* (2006)

- Functional competencies such as decision-making, risk analysis, measurement, reporting and research;
- Personal competencies such as professional demeanour, problem-solving, decision-making, interaction, leadership, communication, project management; and
- Business competencies such as strategic/critical thinking, industry perspective, global perspective legal perspective, client focus.

De Lange *et al.* (2006)

- Communication, such as oral expression, listening and writing;
- Analytical skills such as software skills, problem-solving, experience with business information systems and information system design skills; and
- Ethical decision-making, which includes solving ethical and social problems.

Sin and Jones (2003)

Analytic and design skills

- Identify, find, evaluate, organise and manage information and evidence
- Research skills
- Analyse, reason and logic, conceptualise
- Solve problems
- Construct arguments
- Interpret data
- Ethical reasoning

Appreciative skills

- Evaluate and react to new ideas
- Make judgements
- Think and act critically
- Know what questions to ask
- Recognise one's own strengths and limitations
- Appreciate ethical dimensions
- Appreciate professional behaviour

Personal and interpersonal skills

- Ethical behaviour
- Thinking and acting independently
- Toleration of ambiguity
- Creative thinking

Interpersonal skills

- Listening
- Present and discuss
- Negation skills (with people from different backgrounds)
- Understanding group dynamics
- Collaboration skills

generic attributes in accounting can be understood and so provides the basis for further research into the framing and teaching of generic attributes in accounting.

Barrie (2006) has identified four distinct understandings of generic skills/attributes in higher education: the precursory, complementary, translation and enabling conceptions. The first or precursory understanding sees generic skills as the attributes to which disciplinary knowledge can be added; the second sees them as a complement to the discipline-specific understandings but not part of the discipline; the third views generic attributes as enabling the translation of university learning into other settings; and the fourth is the most complex understanding of generic attributes, viewing them as the aptitudes that lie at the heart of scholarly knowledge and which can both support the creation of new knowledge and transform the individual. Barrie's study points to the importance of considering that generic attributes are part of disciplinary practice and hence not in competition with content but part of the process of learning and, in the case of accounting, part of the process of apprenticeship into the profession.

Difficulties in the Definition of Generic Attributes

There are at least three problems associated with notions of generic attributes. These are: first, questions of definition; second, questions regarding the level of complexity of the attributes under consideration; and third, the notion of transferability. All these questions raise doubts as to what it is to which the term 'generic skill' refers, and how much commonality there is amongst the various stakeholders in their understanding of the term. This section will examine these three issues associated with the definition of generic attributes.

As the above sample of lists of accounting graduate attributes attest, there are a number of different descriptors of the key generic attributes in accounting. Definitions of generic skills vary in their emphasis on the centrality of the workplace, on the emphasis on skills or on more general 'attributes' and in their assumption of transferability. The problems inherent in these definitions are outlined below. Golding *et al.* (1996) define generic skills as those common to more than one occupation or field of knowledge. Bennett *et al.* (2000) define generic skills as those skills which can support study in any discipline and which can potentially be transferred to a range of contexts, in higher education or in the workplace. The emphasis in this definition is on supporting study in any discipline and, only secondarily, on the skills needed by employers.

Although generic skills and attributes are central to higher education, there is uncertainty as to precisely which skills can be identified as 'generic' and even more uncertainty as to how those skills are defined and whether, indeed, 'skill' is the most appropriate term. One of the central problems in discussing generic skills is that there are a number of terms used in the literature to describe similar phenomena. These terms include generic skills, transferable skills, personal transferable skills, core skills, key skills, graduate attributes, generic attributes or other permutations of these terms. Further adding to the confusion is the seemingly interchangeable use of terms such as competences, capabilities, attributes, skills or outcomes (Bennett *et al.*, 1999). Barnett (1994) questions the meaning of the term *skills*. He argues that the term has no substantive content outside of a definite setting. In addition, he argues that the way in which the skill is acquired will affect the character of that skill. Barnett's argument calls into question the whole notion of generic or context-flexible skills, since each skill is developed and performed in and arising from a particular context and so may be dependent upon that context.

The term 'generic skills' is invested with a considerable degree of ambiguity. Leveson (2000) sees this definitional confusion as being one of the central problems, arguing that it has created an expectation gap between educators and employers in accounting. Universities may claim that they are teaching generic skills and mean one thing while employers may be expecting something different. Marginson (1993) points out that academic lists of generic skills may not be the same as work-related generic skills, even if there are many terms that are common to both lists. This, he points out, is because the terms arise out of differing contexts and thus take on different meanings. Marginson suggests that one important difference is that, in higher education, generic skills are understood in terms of knowledge. The disciplinary context is of the utmost importance because it forms the knowledge-base out of which these skills arise and from which these skills are defined. Employers may have yet another knowledge base (or series of bases) which they assume to be universal.

Thus, there is no shared language amongst stakeholders, and as Lucas *et al.* (2004) suggest, because of the tacit nature of generic attributes there is a need for a shared understanding of the nature of these skills. One of the key stakeholders are students and yet, as Lucas *et al.* (2004) point out in an investigation of the meaning that students attach to skills within accounting degree program, students do not have a clearly articulated understanding of the nature of skills, nor one that corresponds with subject or degree objectives. They argue that students view skills as being context specific and tacit rather than generic.

A number of lists of skills and or attributes have been produced by educators (see for example, Drummond *et al.*, 1998; Fallows and Stevens, 2000; Gibbs, 1994; Gibbs and Habeshaw, 1989; Thorley, 1994) and employers (Harvey *et al.*, 1997; The Association of Graduate Recruiters, 1995). These lists include concepts such as communication, numeracy, teamwork, technical/multimedia skills, problem-solving, critical thinking and analysis. Bennett *et al.* (1999, p. 76) argue that these lists have been developed pragmatically and that this is characteristic of the atheoretical approach to this field. They state that what the different sets of skills have in common is that they are 'theoretically threadbare'. Moreover, although a number of skills an attributes are claimed by universities as that to which they aspire for their graduates, practical necessity dictates that universities will continue to prepare students for professional accounting accreditation examinations at the expense of greater generic skills development (De Lange *et al.*, 2006).

The notion of the transferability of skills across context is problematic and the assumption that skills learnt in one context can be easily transferred to another context is questionable (Tempone and Martin, 2003). Further, there is little evidence to suggest that students will easily transfer skills developed in the classroom to a professional context nor apply theoretical concepts to practical applications without well-structured guidance and scaffolding. As discussed above, there is confusion between notions of 'generic' and 'transferable'. Since the terms are frequently used interchangeably, there is an assumption that generic attributes, by their nature, can be transferred between disciplines and from a university context to non-academic context (either professional or personal). However, the evidence that these attributes are actually transferable, and the nature of this transferability is problematic. Perkins and Salomon (1994) argue that the conditions for the transfer of learning cannot be taken for granted but require stringent conditions. Indeed, Golding *et al.* (1996) point out that the notion that generic attributes can necessarily be transferred from one context to another is problematic because there is an important context specific element to learning.

An Operational Definition of Generic Attributes

In the following section, the key features of generic attributes are described with a view to producing a workable definition. It is proposed that generic skills or attributes have a number of features. The first element of generic attributes in higher education is that they are taught within the disciplines and appear to be embedded within the content; the second is their limited transferability; the third is that they are often tacit and hence not clearly articulated or explicitly taught; and the final feature is that generic skills/attributes are organic, so while it is common to speak of critical thinking, problem-solving or analysis as being separate attributes, each is intertwined with the other and so not easily disentangled.

The Embedded Nature of Skills and Attributes

The importance of generic attributes as embedded cannot be assumed. For example, there is an influential and long running debate in the literature regarding the generalisability of critical thinking (Ennis, 1992; McPeck, 1981; Norris, 1992). Ennis and Norris are proponents of the view that critical thinking is a generic skill and can be taught independently of content. McPeck (1990), in contrast, argues that disciplinary knowledge already contains what is central to critical thinking. Smith (1992) argues that one of the key elements of critical thinking is knowledge. He points out that one cannot think critically unless one has knowledge of the topic, so one must think analytically or critically *about something*. One must solve problems using a particular body of knowledge and all the conventions accompanying it. This is particularly the case in higher education since, without an understanding of the theoretical or technical knowledge; it is difficult to imagine how one could think critically or analytically or in a problem-solving manner. This paper argues that disciplinary knowledge and higher order generic attributes are intertwined.

There is a considerable body of evidence, both empirical and theoretical, to suggest that generic attributes exist within, and are best taught from within, the disciplines. For some time, research that has pointed to the importance of the relationship between discipline specific knowledge and skills such as critical thinking and problem-solving (Alexander and Judy, 1988; Baron and Sternberg, 1987; Nickerson *et al.*, 1985). What is important is the interaction between knowledge and the skills and attributes of reasoning (critical thinking, analysis and problem-solving) and the ways in which this is then communicated to others. This research demonstrates that there is a network of interconnections between disciplinary knowledge and of how that is structured; between reasoning skills and attributes and between the skill of communicating the knowledge and reasoning. Generic attributes arise out of the dynamic interplay between disciplinary knowledge and reasoning skills.

Limited Transferability of Skills/Attributes

The idea of transferability is taken to mean that the skills and attitudes learned in one context can be used in another context (Misko, 1995). There is much evidence to suggest that the transferability of generic skills is limited (Barnett, 1994; Lilly, 1995; Lohrey, 1995; Marginson, 1994; Misko, 1995; Perkins and Salomon, 1994). Misko (1995) clearly points to the failures of the transfer of skills from education to the workplace. She argues that, if the transfer is to take place, the skills of transfer must be explicitly taught. Further, she points to the importance of content specific knowledge and discipline-based learning. Referring to the literature on expert and novice learners, Misko argues that content specific knowledge is one of the major factors in producing expertise. This expertise requires the integration of content knowledge with reasoning, interpersonal and communication skills.

The Tacit Nature of Skills/Attributes

The tacit nature of generic attributes can be explained in part by their embeddedness in the disciplines. Although they are often seen as being skills that are extraneous to the disciplines, nevertheless they are taught within the discipline and so often assumed to be learnt by 'osmosis' through the teaching of disciplinary knowledge. As Atkinson (1997, p. 74) points out with reference to teaching, 'academics, normally considered masters of precise definition seem almost unwilling or unable to define critical thinking'. Fox (1994) argues that academics find it very difficult to define analysis or critical thinking even though the terms are used interchangeably in discussing students' work and the reason for this is that critical thinking is cultural, learned intuitively and hence recognised but difficult to explain.

Organic Nature of Skills/Attributes

Generic skills are organic, interconnected networks rather than discrete skills. That is, they are entities which are interwoven with the discipline and with each other. In other words it is very difficult to disentangle meaningfully critical thinking from problem-solving, from analysis and from the communication of these ideas. This can be seen clearly in the lists of attributes in accounting (Table 1) and the ways in which these attributes are meaningfully intertwined in a complex conceptual web.

Part of the complexity of generic skills and attributes is the relationship between them. Bloom *et al.* (1956), in devising his taxonomy, argued that higher order skills are separable and form a developmental hierarchy. Bloom *et al.'s* Taxonomy identifies six levels in the area of learning: knowledge, comprehension, application, analysis, synthesis and evaluation. His analysis is open to question as there are doubts regarding the separate and hierarchical nature of these skills (Nodrvall and Braxton, 1996). So while higher order generic attributes are frequently referred to as being separate entities, it may actually be more useful to understand them as overlapping or clustering. Hager *et al.* (2002) point out that, in practice, they overlap and interweave like the threads in a carpet. So while at one level higher order generic skills such as analysis, problem-solving, critical thinking and communication, for example, can be regarded as separate, in reality they are interconnected and interdependent. It may not be possible to think critically without analytical skills, nor to solve problems without elements of analysis or critical thinking and not possible to do any of these without the ability to communicate the outcomes of one's reasoning.

Importance of Disciplinary Context

Another influential body of higher education literature has examined disciplinary culture, with the seminal work being Becher's (1989) study of academic research cultures. While there is a considerable body of work in this area (Becher, 1989; Becher and Trowler, 2001; Braxton and Hargens, 1996; Donald, 2002; Hativa and Marincovich, 1995; Kolb, 1985; Lattuca and Stark, 1994; Lenze, 1995; Lodahl and Gordon, 1972; Neumann *et al.*, 2002; Smeby, 1996), this has been contested by the argument that disciplinary boundaries are becoming increasingly fluid (Brew, 2001; Gibbons *et al.*, 1994; Scott, 1995). Although acknowledging this change in the authority of disciplinary epistemology, the present paper considers that disciplines remain a powerful influence on academic staff identity (Henkel, 2000) and on teaching practice (Neumann *et al.*, 2002), and hence an important starting point for any investigation of generic skills.

The problem with a duality between content and skills is that it prevents a unified understanding of this aspect of teaching and learning. The current assumptions about generic attributes suggest that there is disciplinary ('content') knowledge and there are skills or attributes that can be bolted onto disciplinary knowledge or, at best, be embedded in it. In contrast, this paper argues that generic skills and attributes are part of the epistemology and culture of the disciplines. They exist within the content knowledge of the disciplines. As a consequence, skills and attributes will be shaped by the discipline of which they are a part. This means that they will not exist in identical form in each discipline. While there may be meta-disciplinary skills that transcend disciplinary contexts, this is by no means certain:

> ... the doubt is whether skills, at any serious level, can be independent of the context, the forms of life, the traditions and expectations in which they are embedded (Barnett, 1994).

As a newer discipline, accounting derives its knowledge base from more traditional disciplines and from the imperatives of its particular professional practice. It has a unique disciplinary and professional culture and with this comes particular knowledge creation and verification practices as well as professional ethics and practices. It is evident from the literature on generic skills in accounting that skills, conceptual knowledge and the professional context are integrated. For example, solving a problem may require the ability to identify information, analyse and interpret it using particular accounting concepts, make recommendations or evaluations and communicate the findings either orally or in writing in an appropriate format, all within an ethical framework.

From the Perspective of Educational Theory

A discussion of generic attributes incorporates a number of overt or implicit assumptions regarding learning. The fundamental assumption underpinning this study is that learning is situated and learners involve themselves in a community of practice or inquiry (Brown *et al.*, 1989; Lave and Wenger, 1991). Learning is a process of both individual and social knowledge construction. Learners engage with knowledge in their own epistemological context and in the social context since meaning-making is both an individual and a social practice. It follows then, as part of teaching and learning, that conceptualisations of generic attributes are similarly situated. The implication is that any serious understanding of the nature of generic attributes needs to be framed within the disciplinary context and this paper points to the influence of disciplinary cultures on the construction of generic attributes.

In much of the current educational research knowledge is conceived of as being situated, in that it arises from particular contexts and relationships. It can also be viewed as being partial since each individual perspective cannot be a complete version of what is known. Given that truth emerges from an individual perspective in a social context, knowledge is also multiple since there is no single position that can be arrived at. Knowledge is a product of the activity and situations in which it is produced and thus a concept is always under construction because it is negotiated between the learners and the social situation (Brown *et al.*, 1989). The learner does not gain a discrete body of knowledge but engages in a process which emerges from particular settings and relationships and so meaning is not a self-contained structure but is defined relative to its context. This is not to suggest that there are no cognitive structures, but rather that these structures may be reconceptualised by the context. This is of great relevance in a discussion of the place of generic attributes in accounting education as it points to the importance of the disciplinary and departmental culture in shaping teaching and learning practices, a proposition which has been discussed in detail by Trowler and Cooper (2002).

The Implications for Accounting Education

There are a number of implications for accounting education raised by this paper. First, there is a need for accounting educators to identify and define the skills and attributes which are valued in accounting both within the academy and within the profession and to acknowledge that these may not necessarily be the same attributes or articulated in exactly the same ways. As discussed previously, there has been considerable work already completed identifying the generic attributes valued within the accounting context, both professional and educational. Thus it is important to build on the literature which explores generic skills in accounting to consider with precision, how each of these attributes is defined and hence where the potential for miscommunication regarding expectations, either within higher education or between higher education and the profession, may exist. Furthermore, it may be necessary to acknowledge that there may not be a single teaching and learning context as accounting has a number of sub-disciplines. However, while an attempt at definition and description of particular generic attributes in the accounting context is very important, at the same time this process must acknowledge the complexity and integrated nature of these skills. Second, it is necessary to identify how these skills and attributes can best be taught when conceptualised as integral to disciplinary knowledge, how they can be actively rehearsed by students and then assessed. Third and finally, it is necessary to identify the potential barriers to the teaching of generic attributes. These can include, as discussed earlier, the fear that these attributes are separate from the disciplinary culture and externally imposed and so in competition with 'content'. Other factors that can be barriers to the teaching of generic attributes include a lack of confidence that arises because these attributes are not clearly defined in ways that are relevant to the disciplinary culture (Jones, 2007). Furthermore, there is uncertainty as to how generic attributes can be adequately assessed, particularly in the context of the large classes that are increasingly a feature of modern higher education.

Knight and Page (2007) investigated competencies such as critical thinking, problem-solving, team-work, ethical practice, creativity and project management in a number of areas, including accounting education. They acknowledge the difficulties in assessing these competencies and recommend:

- Relevant, planned assessment activities
- Clear reasoning behind the design of activities and their implementation
- Relevant assessment criteria and feedback
- Reporting in terms of target outcomes

Furthermore, in terms of the teaching and assessment of these competencies, attributes or skills, Knight and Page suggest consideration of target competencies across the whole degree program so that the patterns of consistency, continuity and progression are examined.

Lucas *et al.* (2004) recommend not just an accounting-based approach to generic skills but recommend the adaptation of intellectual and key skills descriptors to the subject content (i.e. a very fine-grained contextualisation) and an acknowledgement that these skills may manifest themselves differently within different subject contexts. Jackson, Watty and Yu (2006) recommend the alignment of assessment and generic skill development and outline a detailed model for the conceptualisation and mapping of generic skills in accounting across an undergraduate program and provide a set of accompanying resources. The emphasis in modern accounting on analysis, critique and evaluative skills, the need for ethical reasoning, an understanding of the economic and social context of business and the ability to communicate these understandings with colleagues and clients requires an understanding of the integration between 'soft' or generic attributes and content knowledge in accounting.

Conclusion

Accounting, like other disciplines, belongs to a community of practice (Wenger, 1998) and so shares a set of interests, knowledge, values and skills with others in this particular community. Thus there are specialised ways of structuring, interpreting information and a specialised language for discussing the information and practices. In other words, accounting has its own discourse and hence particular ways of negotiating meaning and communicating that with others. Therefore, while there are skills which are shared with other disciplinary areas, they are infused with the language, structures, knowledge and practical skills of accounting. What is clear is the interdependence of knowledge, skill and language.

This paper has challenged the assumption that generic attributes are transdisciplinary and argued that they are profoundly influenced by the disciplinary context in which they are taught. Further, in the case of accounting education, they are also influenced by the accounting profession and the needs of employers. This paper has outlined some of the difficulties in understanding and defining generic attributes and has proposed a working description of generic attributes which can then be refined according to the disciplinary culture. It has outlined findings from a recent study into generic attributes which found that attributes such as critical thinking, problem- solving and communication were conceptualised and taught in very different ways in each discipline.

This paper argues for the centrality of disciplinary accounting knowledge, and the incorporation of this in an understanding of generic attributes. It recommends planning for the teaching and assessment of generic attributes across the accounting curriculum which acknowledges these attributes to be part of the scholarly and professional knowledge of the field. This is not to advocate disciplinary isolationism as there is much which can be learnt from the conversations between disciplines, but rather to argue that attributes such as problem-solving, critical thinking, communication, and teamwork (to name but a few) are part of scholarly practice and part of professional practice and need to be taught in this way.

References

AC Nielsen Research Services (2000) *Employer Satisfaction with Graduate Skills: Research Report* (Canberra: Evaluations and Investigations Programme, Higher Education Division, Department of Education, Training and Youth Affairs).

Albrecht, W. S. and Sack, R. J. (2000) *Accounting Education: Charting the Course through a Perilous Future* (Sarasota, Florida: The American Accounting Association).

Alexander, P. A. and Judy, J. E. (1988) The interaction of domain-specific and strategic knowledge in academic performance, *Review of Educational Research*, 58(4), pp. 375–404.

Assiter, A. (Ed.) (1995) *Transferable Skills in Higher Education* (London: Kogan Page).

Atkins, M. J. (1999) Oven-ready and self-basting: taking stock of employability skills, *Teaching in Higher Education*, 4(2), pp. 267–280.

Atkinson, D. (1997) A critical approach to critical thinking in TESOL, *TESOL Quarterly*, 31(1), pp. 71–94.

Australian Council for Educational Research (2001a) *Graduate Skills Assessment* (Canberra: Department of Education, Training and Youth Affairs).

Australian Council for Educational Research (2001b) *Graduate Skills Assessment: Summary Report* (Canberra: Higher Education Division, Department of Education, Training and Youth Affairs).

Bailey, T. (1997) Changes in the nature of work: the implications for skills and assessment, in: H.F.J. O'Neil (Ed.) *Workforce Readiness: Competencies and Assessments* (Mahwah, NJ: Erlbaum).

Barnett, R. (1994) *The Limits of Competence: Knowledge, Higher Education and Society* (Buckingham: The Society for Research into Higher Education and Open University Press).

Baron, J. and Sternberg, R. (1987) *Teaching Thinking Skills: Theory and Practice* (New York: W. H. Freeman and Company).

Barrie, S. (2002) *Understanding Generic Graduate Attributes*. Paper presented at the 10 OESD Conference: Improving Student Learning Symposium, Brussels 4th–6th September.

Barrie, S. (2006) Understanding what we mean by the generic attributes of graduates, *Higher Education*, 51(2), pp. 215–241.

Becher, T. (1989) *Academic Tribes and Territories: Intellectual Enquiry and the Cultures of Disciplines* (Buckingham: Society for Research into Higher Education & Open University Press).

Becher, T. and Trowler, P. (2001) *Academic Tribes and Territories: Intellectual Enquiry and the Culture of Disciplines* (second ed.) (Buckingham: The Society for Research into Higher Education and Open University Press).

Beckett, D. and Hager, P. (2002) *Life, Work and Learning: Practice in Postmodernity* (London: Routledge).

Bennett, N., Dunne, E. and Carre, C. (1999) Patterns of core and generic skill provision in higher education, *Higher Education*, 37(1), pp. 71–93.

Bennett, N., Dunne, E. and Carre, C. (2000) *Skills Development in Higher Education and Employment* (Buckingham: The Society for Research into Higher Education and Open University Press).

Biggs, J. (1999) *Teaching for Quality Learning at University* (Buckingham: SRHE and Open University Press).

Bloom, B., Englehart, M., Furst, E., Hill, W. and Krathwohl, D. (1956) *Taxonomy of Educational Objectives: Cognitive Domain* (New York: David McKay).

Bowden, J., Hart, G., King, B., Trigwell, K. and Watts, O. (2000) Generic Capabilities of ATN University Graduates. Retrieved November, 2003, from http://www.clt.uts.edu/ATN.grad.cap.project.index.html

Boyce, G., Williams, S., Kelly, A. and Yee, H. (2001) Fostering deep and elaborative learning and generic (soft) skill development: the strategic use of case studies in accounting education, *Accounting Education: an international journal*, 10(1), pp. 37–60.

Braxton, J. and Hargens, L. L. (1996) Variation among academic disciplines: analytical frameworks and research, in: J. Smart (Ed.) *Higher Education: Handbook of Theory and Research*, (Vol. xi) (New York: Agathon Press).

Brew, A. (2001) *The Nature of Research: Inquiry in Academic Contexts* (London: Routledge Falmer).

Broome, O. W. and Morris, M. H. (2005) Multi-entity partnering in accounting education: narrowing the gap between the profession and academia, in: B. N. Schwartz and J. E. Ketz (Eds) *Advances in Accounting Education: Teaching and Curriculum Innovations, 7* (New York: Elsevier).

Brown, J. S., Collins, A. and Duguid, P. (1989) Situated cognition and the culture of learning, *Educational Researcher*, 18(1), pp. 32–42.

Brown, S. and Knight, P. (1994) *Assessing Learners in Higher Education* (London: Kogan Page).

Business Industry and Higher Education Collaboration Council (2007) *Graduate Employability Skills* (Canberra: Precision Consultancy for the Department of Education, Science and Training, Commonwealth of Australia).

Candy, P., Crebert, G. and O'Leary, J. (Eds) (1994) *Developing Lifelong Learners through Undergraduate Education* (Canberra: National Board of Employment, Education and Training).

Carr, S., Chua, F. and Perera, H. (2006) University accounting curricula: the perceptions of an alumni group, *Accounting Education: an international journal*, 15(4), pp. 359–376.

Christensen, D. and Rees, D. (2002) An analysis of the business communication skills needed by entry-level accountants. Available at: http://www.mountainplains.org/articles/2002%20articles/communication%20skills4MPJ.pdf (accessed March 2008).

Clanchy, J. and Ballard, B. (1995) Generic skills in the context of higher education, *Higher Education Research and Development*, 14(2), pp. 155–166.

De La Harpe, B., Radloff, A. and Wyber, J. (2000) Quality and generic (professional) skills, *Quality in Higher Education*, 6(3), pp. 231–243.

De Lange, P., Jackling, B. and Gut, A. (2006) Accounting graduates' perceptions of skills emphasis in undergraduate courses: an investigation from two Victorian universities, *Accounting and Finance*, 46, pp. 365–386.

Dearing Commission (1997) *Higher Education in the Learning Society. Report of the National Committee of inquiry into Higher Education* (London: HMSO).

Department of Education Science and Training (2005) *Our Universities: Backing Australia's Future, Policy Paper 10 Assuring Quality* (Canberra: Common Wealth of Australia).

Donald, J. (2002) *Learning to think: Disciplinary perspectives* (San Francisco: Jossey-Bass).

Drucker, P. (1969) *The Age of Discontinuity; Guidelines to Our Changing Society* (New York: Harper and Row).

Drummond, I., Nixon, I. and Wiltshire, J. (1998) Personal transferable skills in higher education: the problems of implementing good practice, *Quality Assurance in Education*, 6(1), pp. 19–27.

Ennis, R. (1992) The degree to which critical thinking is subject specific: clarification and needed research, in: S. Norris (Ed.) *The Generalizability of Critical Thinking* (New York: Teachers College Press).

Entwistle, N. (1997) Contrasting perspectives on leaning, in: F. Marton, D. Hounsell and N. Entwistle (Eds) *The Experience of Learning* (Edinburgh: Scottish Academic Press).

Fallows, S. and Steven, C. (Eds) (2000) *Integrating Key Skills in Higher Education: Employability, Transferable Skills and Learning for Life* (London: Kogan Page).

Fox, H. (1994) *Listening to the World: Cultural Issues in Academic Writing* (Urbana: National Council of Teachers of English).

Gabric, D. and McFadden, K. T. (2001) Student and employer perceptions of desirable entry-level operations management skills, *Mid-American Journal of Business*, 16(1), pp. 51–59.

Gibbons, M., Limoges, C., Nowotny, H., Schwarzman, S., Scott, P. and Trow, M. (1994) *The New Production of Knowledge: The Dynamics of Science and Research in Contemporary Societies* (London: Sage).

Gibbs, G. (1994) *Developing Students' Transferable Skills* (Oxford: The Oxford Centre for Staff Development).

Gibbs, G. and Habeshaw, T. (1989) *Preparing to Teach: An Introduction to Effective Teaching in Higher Education* (Bristol: Technical and Educational Services).

Golding, B., Marginson, S. and Pascoe, R. (1996) *Changing Context, Moving Skills: Generic Skills in the Context of Credit Transfer and the Recognition of Prior Learning* (Canberra: National Board of Employment, Education and Training).

Hager, P., Holland, S. and Beckett, D. (2002) *Enhancing the Learning and Employability or Graduates: The Role of Generic Skills* (Melbourne: Business/Higher Education Round Table).

Haigh, M. J. and Kilmartin, M. P. (1999) Student perceptions of the development of personal transferable skills, *Journal of Geography in Higher Education*, 23(2), pp. 195–206.

Harvey, L., Moon, S. and Geall, V. (1997) *Graduates' Work: Organisational Change and Students' Attributes* (Birmingham: The University of Central England, Centre for Research into Quality).

Hativa, N. and Marincovich, M. (Eds) (1995) *Disciplinary Differences in Teaching and Learning: Implications for Practice* (San Francisco: Jossey Bass).

Henkel, M. (2000) *Academic Identities and Policy Change in Higher Education* (London: Jessica Kingsley Publishers).

Hill, W. Y. and Milner, M. M. (2006) The placing of skills in accounting degree programmes in higher education: Some contrasting approaches in the UK. (Electronic Version), *Social Science Research Network*. Available at: http://www.papers.ssrn.com/so13/papers (accessed May 2008).

Humphreys, P., Greenan, K. and McIlveen, H. (1997) Developing work-based transferable skills in a university environment, *Journal of European Industrial Training*, 21(2), pp. 63–69.

Jackson, M., Watty, K., Yu, L. and Lowe, L. (2006) *Final Report to the Carrick Institute for Learning and Teaching in Higher Education: Assessing Students Unfamiliar with Assessment Practices in Australian Universities* (Strawberry Hills, Australia: The Carrick Institute for Learning and Teaching in Higher Education).

Jackson, M., Watty, K. and Yu, X. (2006) *Inclusive Assessment: Improving Learning For All. A Manual for Improving Assessment in Accounting Education* (Strawberry Hills, Australia: The Carrick Institute for Teaching and Learning in Higher Education).

Jones, A. (2007) Generic skills as espoused theory. *ISSOTL Conference, University of New South Wales*, Sydney 2nd–5th July.

Jones, A. (2009) Re-disciplining generic attributes: the disciplinary context in focus, *Studies in Higher Education*, 34(1), pp. 85–100.

Knight, P. and Page, A. (2007) *The Assessment of 'Wicked' Competencies: Report to the Practice-based Professional Learning Centre* (Milton Keynes: Open University).

Kolb, D. A. (1985) Learning styles and disciplinary differences, in: A.W. Chickering (Ed.) *The Modern American College* (San Francisco, CA: Jossey Bass Publishers).

Lattuca, L. and Stark, J. (1994) Will disciplinary perspectives impede curricular reform? *Journal of Higher Education*, 65(4), pp. 401–426.

Lave, J. and Wenger, E. (1991) *Situated Learning: Legitimate Peripheral Participation* (Cambridge: Cambridge University Press).

Leggett, M., Kinnear, A., Boyce, M. and Bennett, I. (2004) Student and staff perceptions of the importance of generic skills in science, *Higher Education Research and Development*, 23(3), pp. 295–312.

Lenze, L. F. (1995) Discipline-specific pedagogical knowledge in linguistics and Spanish, in: N. Hativa and M. Marincovich (Eds) *Disciplinary Differences in Teaching and Learning: Implications for Practice* (San Francisco: Jossey-Bass).

Leveson, L. (2000) Disparities in perceptions of generic skills: academics and employers, *Industry and Higher Education*, 14(3), pp. 157–164.

Lilly, M. (1995) *Key Competencies and the AVTS, Issues Paper No 1* (Melbourne: National Centre for Competency Based Assessment and Training).

Lodahl, J. B. and Gordon, G. (1972) The structure of scientific fields and the functioning of university graduate departments, *American Sociological Review*, 37(1), pp. 57–72.

Lohrey, A. (1995) Transferability in relation to the key competencies. Occasional Paper No. 16: Centre for Workplace Communication and Culture, UTS/James Cook University.

Lucas, U., Cox, P., Croudace, C. and Milford, P. (2004) Who writes this stuff? Students' perceptions of their skills development, *Teaching in Higher Education*, 9(1), pp. 55–68.

Marginson, S. (1993) *Arts, Science and Work* (Canberra: Australian Government Publishing Service).

Marginson, S. (1994) The problem of 'transferable' skills, *Melbourne Studies in Education*, 35(1), pp. 4–28.

McPeck, J. (1981) *Critical Thinking and Education* (New York: St Martin's).

McPeck, J. (1990) *Teaching Critical Thinking: Dialogue and Dialectic* (New York: Routledge).

Miles, M. B. and Huberman, A. M. (1994) *Qualitative Data Analysis: An Expanded Sourcebook* (second ed.) (Thousand Oaks: Sage Publications).

Misko, J. (1995) *Transfer: Using Learning in New Contexts* (Leabrook, South Australia: National Centre for Vocational Education Research).

Monks, K. (1995) Combining academic rigour and transferable skills: a business degree for the 1990s, *Education and Training*, 37(1), pp. 17–23.

Neumann, R., Parry, S. and Becher, T. (2002) Teaching and learning in their disciplinary contexts: a conceptual analysis, *Studies in Higher Education*, 27(4), pp. 405–415.

Nickerson, R. S., Perkins, D. N. and Smith, E. E. (1985) *The Teaching of Thinking* (Hillsdale, NJ: Lawrence Erlbaum Associates).

Nodrvall, R. and Braxton, J. (1996) An alternative definition of quality of undergraduate college education: toward usable knowledge for improvement, *Journal of Higher Education*, 67(5), pp. 483–498.

Norris, S. (1992) *The Generalizability of Critical Thinking: Multiple Perspectives on an Educational Ideal* (New York: Teachers College Press).

Perkins, D. N. and Salomon, G. (1994) Transfer of Learning, in: T. Husen and T. N. Postlethwaite (Eds) *The International Encyclopedia of Education* (second ed., Vol. 11) (Oxford: Pergamon).

Ramsden, P. (1992) *Learning to Teach in Higher Education* (London: Kogan Page).

Scott, P. (1995) *The Meanings of Mass Higher Education* (Buckingham: Society for Research into Higher Education & Open University Press).

Sin, S. and Jones, A. (2003) *Generic Skills in Accounting: Competencies for Students and Graduates* (Frenchs Forest, NSW: Perrson Education Australia).

Smeby, J. (1996) Disciplinary differences in university teaching, *Studies in Higher Education*, 21(1), pp. 69–79.

Smith, F. (1992) *To Think: In Language, Learning and Education* (London: Routledge).

Stowers, R. H. and White, G. T. (1999) Connecting accounting and communication: a survey of public accounting firms, *Business Communication Quarterly*, 62(2), pp. 23–40.

Tempone, I. and Martin, E. (2003) Iteration between theory and practice as a pathway to developing generic skills in accounting, *Accounting Education: an international journal*, 12(3), pp. 227–244.

The Association of Graduate Recruiters (1995) *Skills for Graduates in the 21st Century* (Cambridge: The Association of Graduate Recruiters).

The Secretary's Commission on Achieving Necessary Skills (2000) *Skills and Tasks for Jobs: A SCANS Report for America* (Washington D.C.: US Department of Labor).

Thorley, L. (1994) Personal transferable skills, in: D. Saunders (Ed.) *The Complete Student Handbook* (Oxford: Blackwell).

Trowler, P. and Cooper, A. (2002) Teaching and Learning Regimes: implicit theories and recurrent practices in the enhancement of teaching and learning through educational development programmes, *Higher Education Research and Development*, 21(3), pp. 221–240.

Watty, K. (2007) Quality in accounting education and low English standards among overseas students: is there a link, *People and Place*, 15(1), pp. 22–29.

Watty, K., Cahill, D. and Cooper, B. (1998) Graduate attributes: perceptions of accounting academics, *Asian Review of Accounting: Special Education Issue*, 6(1), pp. 68–83.

Wenger, E. (1998) *Communities of Practice. Learning, Meaning and Identity* (Cambridge: Cambridge University Press).

The Expectation-Performance Gap in Accounting Education: An Exploratory Study

BINH BUI and BRENDA PORTER

Victoria University of Wellington, New Zealand

ABSTRACT *Since the mid-1980s, professional accounting bodies, employers of accounting graduates and academics alike have lamented the failure of universities to equip accounting graduates with the competencies required for the modern business environment. Changes to accounting education have been made but the gap between the competencies which employers expect—and perceive—accounting graduates to possess has not previously been examined holistically. Based on a review of the literature, a framework of accounting education's expectation-performance gap (comprising an expectation gap, a constraints gap and a performance gap) is proposed. The paper also reports an exploratory study designed to test the proposed framework. Following a document study of the accounting programme of a New Zealand university, interviews were conducted with students, academics, graduate trainees and employers associated with the programme. The research provides support for the proposed framework and resulted in identifying ways in which the gap may be narrowed.*

1. Introduction

Since the mid-1980s, professional accounting bodies, employers of accounting graduates and academics alike have criticised accounting programmes for failing to equip graduates with the competencies (knowledge, skills and personal attributes) required by members of the accounting profession in the modern, technologically-astute, rapidly changing business environment. They have also called for accounting education to change to rectify the perceived deficiencies (for example, American Accounting Association (AAA), 1986; Arthur Andersen *et al.*, 1989; Thompson, 1995; Brown and McCartney, 1995; American Institute of Certified Public Accountants (AICPA), 1998; Institute of Management Accountants (IMA), 1994; 1996, 1999; Albrecht and Sack, 2000).

The perceived mismatch between the competencies which the profession[1] expects—and perceives—graduating accounting students to possess gives rise to an expectation-performance gap in accounting education. Various factors have been identified as contributing to this gap, including differences in the views of the profession and academics regarding the competencies which accounting graduates should possess, and the appropriate programme to develop these competencies (Stout and Schweikart, 1989; Armitage, 1991; Simons and Higgins, 1993). More fundamentally, while employers appear to believe that universities should prepare students to become competent members of the workforce, most academics consider that universities have a key role in developing students' intellectual capability and ability to 'challenge conformity and convention' and 'think for themselves' (Camp, 1997; Inglis and Dall'Alba, 1998; Polster, 2000; Craig and Amernic, 2001).

Students' perceptions of accountants, accounting work, and accounting courses also contribute to the gap. Millard (2003), for example, found that students characterise accountants as mere bean-counters and accounting work as being dull and laborious. Along similar lines, Haigh (1994) found that accounting students expect accounting courses to provide knowledge and skills that are readily applicable to their future careers, and they tend to react negatively to educators who deviate from this goal. Such perceptions may discourage bright, creative students from pursuing accounting degrees and joining the profession (Saemann and Crooker, 1999).

Universities' promotion and tenure structure also contributes to the gap; it ranks research productivity above teaching excellence (Schultz *et al.*, 1989; Tang and Chamberlain, 1997; Porter and Carr, 1999) and provides little incentive to lecturers to develop new accounting programmes. As Kerr (1975, p.773) observed more than 30 years ago, while universities 'hope' that academics do not neglect their teaching responsibilities, they 'reward' their performance primarily based on their research and publications. This inevitably leads academics to concentrate on research rather than teaching activities.

Reviewing these factors, it seems that accounting education's expectation-performance gap has a number of components—each reflecting a different cause. However, although prior studies have investigated individual factors contributing to the failure of accounting education to provide graduates with the competencies expected of them by the profession, none has examined the gap holistically. This paper proposes a comprehensive framework—comprising an expectation gap, a constraints gap (subdivided into institutional and student constraints), and a performance gap—for accounting education's expectation-performance gap. Each component reflects a causal factor identified in the extant literature. The paper also reports the results of an exploratory study of the accounting programme of a New Zealand (NZ) university which was designed to explore the validity of the hypothesised structure of the expectation-performance gap. The findings provide support for the proposed framework and suggest that the outcomes of tertiary level accounting education could be better aligned with the expectations of the profession by recognising the gap's constituent parts and targeting measures to narrow each component.

In the next section of the paper, relevant literature is reviewed and the hypothesised structure of accounting education's expectation-performance gap is proposed. This is followed by a description of the methodology adopted for the exploratory study and the study's findings. In the concluding section of the paper, the contribution and limitations of the research are outlined, and opportunities for further research are identified.

2. Review of Relevant Literature

An early study highlighting accounting education's failure to equip students to meet the changed needs of the accounting profession is that of the Bedford Committee

(AAA, 1986). This identified three major changes that had affected the profession, namely:

- accounting services had become both broader and more specialised in nature;
- management advisory services, requiring specialised expertise, had developed; and
- the emergent competitive accounting market required accountants to have a broadly-based education, and knowledge of both accounting information systems and the role of the accounting function within an organisation.

The Bedford Committee noted that accounting education had been slow to respond to these changes and was critical of the static nature of both accounting curricula and teaching methods.

A *White Paper* issued by the (then) Big Eight accounting firms (Arthur Anderson *et al.*, 1989) concurred with the Bedford Committee's views but, while the latter concentrated on accounting education's scope, content and teaching, the *White Paper* focused on the skills and knowledge required by accountants in public practice. It identified, in particular: communication, intellectual and interpersonal skills; and accounting, auditing, organisational and general business knowledge. The *White Paper* urged accounting academics, university administrators, professional organisations and accrediting bodies to collaborate to effect appropriate changes in accounting education so as to secure a positive future for the profession.

Along similar lines, a study by the American Institute of Certified Public Accountants (AICPA, 1998) found that certified public accountants (CPAs) believed that, in order for the profession to remain competitive in the changing business environment, in addition to traditional accounting and auditing services, it needed to provide services that rely on professional judgment and be able to enhance the client's value. The study concluded that CPAs' competencies need to include skills such as communication, leadership, strategic thinking and client focus (AICPA, 1998, p. 22). Studies by the Institute of Chartered Accountants in England and Wales (ICAEW, 1996) and the Institute of Chartered Accountants of Australia (ICAA, 1998a, b, 2001), similarly identified a need for accounting education to respond to changes in the business environment. Primarily using interviews and surveys to derive inferences (though with smaller samples than studies in the USA)[2] they concluded that, if the profession is to remain relevant to the business community, it needs to move from traditional and information-based services to knowledge-based services (see ICAA, 2001 for a summary of these studies' findings).

Rather than focusing on why accounting education should change, Albrecht and Sack (2000), in a study jointly sponsored by the AICPA, the American Accounting Association (AAA), the USA-based Institute of Management Accountants (IMA) and the (then) Big 5 accounting firms, highlighted difficulties facing accounting education. Warning that 'accounting education today is plagued by many serious problems', the researchers drew attention to three in particular, namely:

- declining enrolments in accounting programmes;
- the 'broken' and obsolete nature of the accounting education model; and
- practitioners and accounting academics indicating that they would not major in accounting if they were to choose their degree programme again.

They concluded: 'if those problems are not seriously addressed and overcome, they will lead to the demise of accounting education' (Albrecht and Sack, 2000, p. 1).

A study by the AICPA (2004) and Fielding (2005) support Albrecht and Sack's conclusion. The AICPA, noting that the current business and regulatory environment is conducive to an expansion of the accounting profession,[3] observed that the supply of qualified accountants does not appear to match the demand. Similarly, Fielding (2005) noted that, in a study in the UK by Robert Half International (RHI, 2001), 40% of respondents reported that their audit firm had experienced difficulty in recruiting staff with the right skills to satisfy the increased workload.

Reviewing the studies outlined above, questions arise as to:

(i) What are the 'right skills' (or competencies) of accounting graduates?
(ii) Why is accounting education not producing graduates with these competencies?

(i) The Desired Competencies

Professional accounting bodies in, for example, Australia and NZ, the UK and the USA have sponsored studies designed to identify the desired competencies of professional accountants (Birkett, 1993;[4] ICAEW, 1996; AICPA, 1999). They concluded that professional accountants require functional competencies (technical accounting expertise), broad business competencies (a broad business perspective and general business skills), and personal competencies (including strategic thinking and management; communication, leadership, and interpersonal skills; and an ability to adapt to change and to work in global markets).

Standard setting and accrediting bodies, such as the (then) Education Committee of the International Federation of Accountants (IFAC, 2002) and the UK's Quality Assurance Agency for Higher Education (QAA, 2007),[5] respectively, have similarly recognised the importance of accounting graduates possessing technical accounting competencies, organisational and business competencies and personal competencies—including, in the last case: interpersonal, communication and teamwork skills; numerical and computing skills; critical thinking, research and analytical skills; and an ability to learn independently.

The attributes of accounting graduates most valued by employers have also been investigated. Kim *et al.* (1993), for example, surveyed 750 public and private sector employers in Singapore to determine the criteria they use to select graduates for accounting jobs. They found that job interest and motivation are the most highly rated attributes. Hassall *et al.* (2005) similarly surveyed 214 employers of management accountants in Spain and the UK; they found the most highly-valued generic skills for accounting graduates to be teamwork, organisational, computing and communication skills, and time management. In the USA, Simons *et al.* (1995) surveyed 167 employers and found that drive and motivation were the most desired attributes, followed by teamwork, oral communication and numeric skills, enthusiasm, and interpersonal sensitivity; least important were a relevant degree and performance in university studies. In contrast, Ahadiat and Smith (1994), in their survey of 357 organisations in different industries (including accounting firms) in the USA, found that, although personality and social characteristics (such as reliability) were rated the most important of 'twelve most important competencies', academic achievement also ranked highly. They also found that large CPA firms accord greater importance to academic achievement and advancement potential than do smaller firms.

The desired competencies from the perspective of accounting graduates have been studied by researchers such as De Lange *et al.* (2006) and Carr *et al.* (2006). De Lange *et al.* surveyed 310 graduates from two universities in Victoria (Australia) to determine their views on the skills required of accountants, and the emphasis placed on the development of those skills in the accounting curriculum. The respondents noted a lack of emphasis on most of the generic skills desired by the profession, especially interpersonal, oral communication and computing/information technology skills. Carr *et al.* surveyed 236 alumni from Massey University (NZ) who graduated in Accounting between 1995 and 2003 to ascertain their views on the most important competencies required for graduates to excel in the profession. The skills and personal attributes identified were: accounting techniques; communication, problem-solving and critical thinking; professionalism and global and local perspectives.

Studies investigating the perceived strengths and weaknesses of accounting graduates entering the workforce include a survey by the ICAA (1994) of 325 Australian accounting firms. This found that accounting graduates are considered to be deficient in communication, computing and interpersonal skills. However, in 1995, a study by the Australian Society of Certified Practicing Accountants (ASCPA) found that Australian university courses were adjudged to be largely successful in providing accountancy graduates with the information technology skills required for entry-level positions (ASCPA, 1995). In the UK, a survey of 214 employers of management accountants found that graduates entering the profession were perceived to be deficient in stress management skills, the ability of organise and delegate tasks, and in their knowledge of the accounting profession (Arquero *et al.*, 2001).

(ii) Reasons for Accounting Education not Producing Graduates with Desired Competencies

Prior researchers have identified a number of reasons for accounting education failing to provide graduates with the desired competences. These fall into four broad categories, namely:

(a) differences in the expectations of accounting academics and employers;
(b) students' perceptions of accounting programmes and the profession, and their ability and aptitude;
(c) institutional constraints;
(d) the ineffectiveness of university teaching.

(a) Differences in the expectations of accounting academics and employers. Studies by Armitage (1991), Novin *et al.* (1997), Theuri and Gunn (1999), and Francis and Minchington (1999) all found significant differences the views of academics and practitioners about the subject-matter taught in universities. Armitage (1991), for example, found that, while academics teaching advanced financial accounting courses believed they should focus on fairly narrow technical topics, practitioners preferred a wider coverage of topics. Similarly, Francis and Minchington (1999) discovered significant differences in the level and type of quantitative skills taught at universities and those used in practice: educators placed emphasis on mathematical skills that are now largely performed by technology.

Adopting a broader approach, the Administrators of Accounting Programs Group of the Practice Involvement Committee of the AAA highlighted the distance between accounting academics and practitioners (cited in Bullock *et al.*, 1995). It reported that, while practitioners believe accounting educators are not interested in teaching, have easy work demands and are out of step with practice, accounting educators perceive entry-level accounting work to be boring. This implies that educators may under-assess the level of knowledge, skills and attributes required of accounting graduates. Differences of opinion are also implied in the findings of a study by Watty (2005). She surveyed accounting academics at 30 Australian universities and found that accounting educators considered that accounting education to be compliance-driven and largely prescribed by the requirements of the profession and university administrators. The respondents signalled that, in their view, accounting education should be aimed at empowering students and helping them to achieve high academic standards.

In the USA, studies by May *et al.* (1995) and the Accounting Education Change Commission (AECC, 1995) (each of which surveyed approximately 1000 accounting academics in the USA) similarly found that accounting academics believe there is a need for change (albeit by only a small majority—56%—in May *et al.'s* study) but they disagree widely about the required extent and form of the change.

(b) Students' perceptions of accounting programmes and the profession, and their ability and aptitude. Most studies of the reasons for students deciding to pursue an accounting degree have found that students are attracted to a career in accounting primarily because of job security, a high salary, an opportunity to use special abilities and aptitudes, high ethical standards, excellent training and mentoring, and a friendly working environment (Shivaswamy and Hanks, 1985a, b; Kochanek and Norgaard, 1985; Felton *et al.* 1994). However, once at university, students' positive attitude towards accounting both as a discipline and as a profession seems to decline. Marriott and Marriott (2003), investigating the attitude of accounting students in both their first and final year at two UK universities, found that students in their final year perceive accounting as a degree programme, and a career, to be much less enjoyable, less satisfying and less challenging than they expected when they entered university. Along similar lines, Kochanek and Norgaard (1985) found that more than 67% of the 393 accounting students they surveyed across the USA, view a career in accounting (especially in the large accounting firms) as daunting, entry work as being dull and stressful, and competition for advancement as stiff. Approaching the issue from a different angle, Ahmed *et al.* (1997), from a survey of 295 students from five NZ universities, found that accounting students perceive significant costs attach to an accounting career, including a heavy workload and low earnings during the early years, and view accountants as being dull. Nevertheless, the study also found that students who choose accounting as a career consider the resulting benefits, such as financial security and job-related opportunities, outweigh the costs involved.

Other studies have investigated accounting students' intellectual ability. Adams *et al.* (1994), for example, conducted a longitudinal study of 238 students enrolled in an introductory accounting course at a university in the USA. They found that students exiting the accounting degree programme upon completion of the introductory course had, on average, a higher Grade Point Average (GPA) than those who did not transfer out. Based on this finding, the researchers suggest that accounting programmes deter bright students from entering the profession. By contrast, Riordan *et al.* (1996), in a longitudinal study of 4800 students in two state institutions in the USA between 1989 and 1993, found that the GPA of students entering the accounting degree programme upon completion of the introductory course was, on average, higher than that of students exiting the programme. Along similar lines, Sander and Reding (1993), investigating the cognitive abilities of 113 accounting students and 192 liberal arts/social sciences majors in the USA, found that, in general, accounting students scored more highly than did students from the other disciplines. Further, empirical evidence obtained by Simons *et al.* (1995) and Ameen *et al.* (2002) suggests that accounting students demonstrate a higher level of communication skills than their business student counterparts.

Notwithstanding their ability, students' motivation and attitude to learning may influence their academic performance and, thus, the competencies with which they graduate. A survey by Wooten (1998) of 271 students in an introductory accounting course in the USA revealed that motivation (rather than inherent ability) is a key factor in explaining academic performance. Sharma (1997) investigated the conceptions of 165 second year accounting and finance students in an Australian university about the purpose of learning in accounting and finance degree programmes. He found that 76% of his respondents indicated that memorising is of primary importance in accounting, and that accounting education is a means of acquiring knowledge and/or of learning how to apply that knowledge in the future.

(c) Institutional constraints. A number of constraints within universities have been identified as contributing to the failure of accounting education to provide accounting graduates with the competencies expected of them by the profession. However, the key constraint usually identified is the conflict between teaching and research. Nevertheless, research by Street *et al.* (1993), Manakyan and Tanner (1994), and Lindsay and Campbell (1995) indicates that the impact of this factor varies between institutions. Using the Carnegie classification of the missions of Accounting Schools in the USA[6] and the responses of 153 Deans and 162 Heads of Accounting Departments in the USA, Street *et al.* (1993) found that teaching, research and service were assigned different ratings in the tenure and promotion decisions of schools with different missions. At Research I and II type schools, research was given greater emphasis than in the other schools but, in comprehensive schools, teaching was ranked more highly than research. Manakyan and Tanner (1994) and Lindsay and Campbell (1995) studied the relationship between research productivity and teaching effectiveness. From their survey of 226 accounting academics in the USA, Manakyan and Tanner found a small but significant negative correlation between the number of publications and teacher ratings. However, 47% of their respondents indicated that research helps to improve teaching, 29% suggested that it hampers teaching, and 24% expressed the opinion that teaching and research efforts do not conflict. Lindsay and Campbell's (1995) study found that research productivity was positively associated with teaching effectiveness in comprehensive schools but not in doctoral granting schools.

Other researchers have examined the impact of class size on learning effectiveness but with varied results. For example, Hill (1998), in a study of 120 accounting students in two introductory accounting courses in the USA, after controlling for instructor and delivery modes, found no significant correlation between class size and student performance. In contrast, Murdoch and Guy (2002), investigating the relative performance of students taught in large ($n = 280$) and small classes ($n = 39$), found that students taught in small classes performed better in the final examination than those taught in large classes. Similarly, interviews conducted by Hill and Milner (2007) with 13 academics in six UK universities indicated that large class size is a constraint on teaching students softer skills.

The impact of external factors on teaching effectiveness has been another area of research interest. Dominelli and Hoogvelt (1996), for example, studied the effect, in the UK, of a shift in university funding from a teaching- to a research-based structure, and the establishment of an external body to evaluate research productivity and determine the allocation of research funding. They concluded, *inter alia*, that the shift to research-based funding, and the external evaluation of research performance, are primary causes of an apparent decline in teaching quality. Porter and Carr (1999) reported on the development and implementation of a new accounting programme at a university in NZ, designed to better align the outcomes of the programme with those identified as being desirable by the Accounting Department's key stakeholder groups. The 'ideal' programme design was modified significantly as a consequence of: (i) the lack of the teaching resources and facilities required to support the proposed programme; (ii) the university's reward system that emphasised research productivity over teaching excellence; and (iii) pressure from other departments in the Business Faculty to retain the 'core' papers of the business degree (especially those taught by them—and thus their student enrolments and associated funding).[7] Along similar lines, Craig and Amernic (2001) contended that the primary cause of accounting education not responding to calls for change is the prevalent 'audit culture' in university administration, which emphasises quantity and revenue (i.e. student enrolments and fees) at the expense of teaching quality.

Duncan and Schmutte (2006) examined the relationships between changes to accounting programmes and (a) two external forces (AECC's recommendations and the AICPA's 150-hour accounting education requirement) and (b) two institutional constraints (institution size and AACSB accreditation). They surveyed 231 Department Heads in the USA and found that larger and AACSB-accredited schools implement more changes to their accounting programmes than do smaller and non-AACSB accredited schools. If the schools are perceived to be primarily affected by the AECC's recommendations, the changes involve broadening the scope of the curriculum (in particular, incorporating more liberal subjects); if they are more affected by the AICPA's 150-h requirement, the changes involve introducing more technical accounting courses.

(d) The ineffectiveness of university teaching. The perceived ineffectiveness of teaching in accounting programmes exacerbates the impact of institutional constraints on accounting education. Wolk *et al.* (1997) used Adaptation-Innovation (AIK) Theory to study the relationship between academics' problem-solving instructional style and (a) their perceptions of accounting pedagogy; and (b) their teaching methods. They found that only 41% of the 82 accounting educators they surveyed were 'innovators'; the other 59% were 'adaptors'. Based on their findings, the researchers suggested that a majority of accounting educators prefer to adopt traditional teaching styles rather than introduce new ones.

Swain and Stout (2000) investigated the teaching development of accounting educators in the USA that was designed to effect the recommendations of the AECC. They found that the 109 recent doctoral graduates they surveyed held the view that teaching development depends primarily on personal effort, even though responsibility for the development of appropriate teaching should be shared between academic employers, educators and individual students. Some support for Swain and Stout's findings was provided by Stice and Stocks (2000) who sought to identify the determinants of teaching effectiveness. They asked 87 accounting educators to rate the relative importance of 52 factors that affect teaching effectiveness: instructor enthusiasm was consistently rated as being the foremost determinant.

3. Hypothesised Structure of Accounting Education's Expectation-Performance Gap

From the above review of extant literature it is evident that significant research has been conducted into the existence and causes of accounting education's failure to adequately equip accounting graduates with the competencies (knowledge, skills and attributes) desired/expected by the accounting profession—a failure that has prompted calls for accounting education to change. However, no prior study has explored the issue holistically or developed a comprehensive framework within which its contributing factors may be examined.

Based, *inter alia*, on the studies outlined above, a hypothesised structure of the gap between the competencies which accounting graduates are (i) expected; and (ii) perceived, to possess by the profession (or, more specifically, employers) was developed. As may be seen from Figure 1, its components reflect the contributory causes identified in the literature. These are as follows:

(i) differences in the expectations of accounting employers and educators regarding the competencies accounting graduates should acquire ('expectation gap');
(ii) constraints on the effectiveness of accounting education ('constraints gap') resulting from (a) institutional factors; and (b) accounting students' ability and aptitude;
(iii) differences in the competencies accounting educators can reasonably expect accounting graduates to acquire (given the constraints) and those employers perceive the graduates possess when they enter the workforce ('performance gap').

4. Exploring the Validity of the Hypothesised Structure

4.1. *Research Design*

In order to examine the validity of the hypothesised structure of accounting education's expectation-performance gap, a case study of the undergraduate accounting programme of a NZ university was conducted.[8] A document study of the formal outlines of each accounting course/module offered by the university was first undertaken in order to determine the learning objectives of each course and of the accounting degree programme as a whole. These provided insight into the competencies the accounting educators expect accounting students to acquire by the time they graduate.

Following the document study, semi-structured interviews were conducted with four key stakeholder groups, namely:

(a) partners and recruitment managers from accounting firms which had employed graduates from the case study programme in both 2004 and 2005;
(b) recent graduates from the case study programme;
(c) accounting lecturers who teach courses in the case study programme;
(d) final year students pursuing the case study programme who intend to join public accounting firms upon graduation.

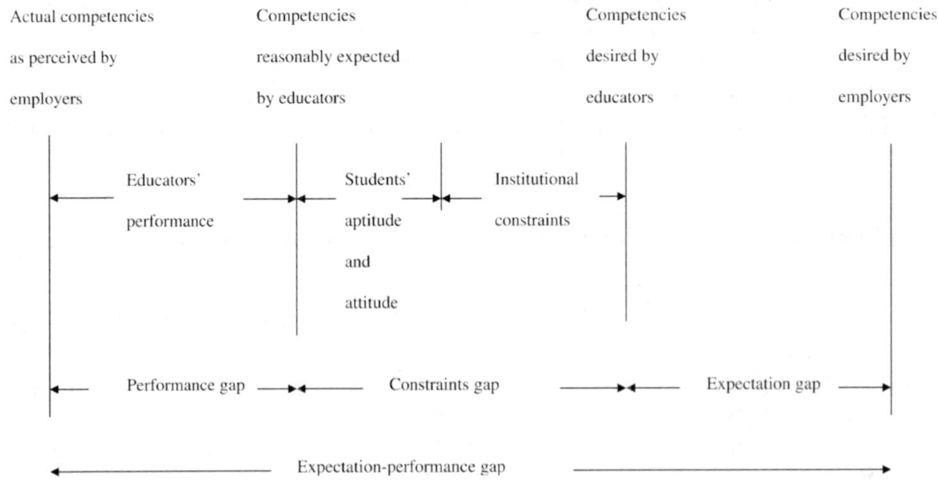

Figure 1. Hypothesised structure of accounting education's expectation-performance gap

Small and medium-sized accounting firms were randomly selected from the *Yellow Pages* (telephone directory) and a partner or the human resource manager was contacted to establish whether the firm had employed graduates from the case study programme in 2004 and 2005 and, if so, whether the firm was willing to participate in the study. The Big 4 firms were also contacted. Nine accounting firms agreed to participate in the study: each of the Big 4, and five small/medium sized firms. For one Big 4 and one medium-sized firm both a partner and manager agreed to be interviewed. Thus, a total of 11 'employers' of graduates from the case study programme were interviewed.

The same firms were requested to ask one or two recent graduates from the case study programme if they would be willing to participate in the study. Five graduates agreed to do so—two working in Big 4 firms and three in medium/small accounting firms. They had been with the relevant firm between six and 18 months.

Six academics who teach courses in the case study programme similarly agreed to participate in the study. Four of the six were formerly practitioners and, of these, two were former partners in Big 4 firms.

In order to identify final (third) year students to interview, two large final year accounting classes were given a short presentation on the project's aim and objectives, and volunteers who were intending to work in accounting firms were sought. Eighteen students volunteered: eight were selected (four from each class) on the basis of their availability for interview within a reasonable time frame.

The interviewees' opinions were sought on the following seven issues:

1. the competencies desired in accounting graduates;
2. the competencies graduates from the case study programme are perceived to possess;
3. the role of university accounting education;
4. the effectiveness of the case study programme in developing graduates' competencies;
5. students' expectations of the accounting profession and accounting education, and their academic ability and aptitude;
6. the major constraints on teaching effectiveness;
7. how teaching quality might be improved.

Some of the questions asked were common to all four stakeholder groups; others were specific to a particular group. The interviews lasted between one and two hours; each was tape-recorded and notes were also taken. The tapes were subsequently transcribed and coded to reflect their content.

Semi-structured interviews were selected as the research method as they provide flexibility in the order and manner in which questions are asked, and in the breadth and depth of interviewees' responses (Lillis, 1999). They also facilitate following up on interviewees' responses to explore, in greater detail, issues raised or observations made (Abernethy *et al.*, 1999). In order to ensure the seven issues noted above were addressed in each interview and also to provide some consistency in the questions posed to each stakeholder group, an interview guide, comprising open-ended, non-directive questions, was developed.[9]

4.2. *Analysis of the Interview Data*

Following Lillis (1999), the interview data were analysed using structural data displays.[10] In accordance with this approach, a thematic matrix was established with two parameters (a) the interview groups; and (b) the major issues addressed in the interviews. (The groups and issues are outlined above.)

The procedures followed to produce the structural data displays are similar to those adopted by Lillis (1999) and consistent with the analytical protocol recommended by Miles and Huberman (1994). These produce an 'auditable trail' from transcripts, though the steps of data reduction, summation, categorization to interpretation and reporting; they also help to minimize bias in the data analysis and increase the credibility of the findings (Lillis, 1999, p. 88). The procedures followed are outlined below:

1. The interview transcripts were coded by associating each sentence in a transcript with one of the seven major issues addressed (outlined above).
2. Each transcript was arranged in a spreadsheet with headings representing the seven major issues.
3. The spreadsheets were combined in a thematic matrix with columns representing the four stakeholder groups and the rows representing the major issues addressed.
4. The combined spreadsheet was analyzed to identify similarities and differences in the responses of each interview group on each major issue. Absolute numbers and percentages were calculated to reflect the level of agreement among the interviewees on each issue and 'extreme' comments, which highlight divergence from the general opinion of an interview group, were identified.

The results of the analysis are presented below along with illustrative quotations from the interviewees' responses. The results are reported in subsections which reflect the hypothesised structure of accounting education's expectation-performance gap depicted in Figure 1.

4.3. *Research Results*

(a) Competencies of accounting graduates desired by employers. The general level of competence required of accounting graduates seems to vary between firms of different size. Small and medium-sized firms expect accounting graduates to become competent and undertake complicated tasks more quickly than do large firms. In medium-sized firms, in particular, accounting graduates are often expected to do senior work within six to eight months of joining the firm. A partner in a medium-sized firm explained:

> Graduates get real work right after they join the firm. We cannot afford too much training but training is very necessary because we can't charge our clients high if our staff are not competent. There is no trial-and-error approach here. If you do it, you've got to do it right.

Similar variations in expectations are evident in the elements embraced by the term 'competencies' (i.e. knowledge, skills and personal attributes). All of the employer interviewees expressed the view that accounting graduates should have an understanding of accounting principles and concepts. However, while those from the medium and small firms considered that accounting graduates should possess a wide range of technical accounting knowledge, and skills such as bookkeeping are essential, those from the large firms indicated that graduates should acquire technical accounting knowledge and skills such as bookkeeping during their post-education training period within the firms rather than at university.

Employers from both large and medium-sized firms agreed that accounting graduates should possess business and general knowledge in addition to accounting knowledge. They signalled that university business courses are helpful in providing students with a conceptual understanding of business but they also observed that 'real' business knowledge can only be acquired through work experience. Along similar lines, these interviewees expressed a strong belief in a broadly-based education, and they intimated that this and, more particularly, liberal arts courses, provide students with a different world view and makes them 'more well-rounded'. Employers from small firms were less enthusiastic about liberal arts courses—with a partner from a small firm denying any benefit can be gained from studying such subjects.

Regarding the skills accounting graduates should possess, all of the employer interviewees considered communication skills (oral, written, and interpersonal) to be essential. To the Big 4 firms, oral (especially presentational) skills are particularly important as graduates are expected to present confidently and effectively to managers or directors of the firm's clients early in their careers. Similarly, writing skills are viewed as being essential by these firms. This was clearly conveyed by a partner from a Big 4 firm as follows:

> Excellent writing is a prerequisite. Staff always have to prepare reports for clients. Numbers don't self-explain. I often told my staff when they presented me with an account that 'please put it down in writing—give me a written explanation'.

For medium and small firms, interpersonal skills (i.e. the ability to interact with colleagues and the firm's small and medium clients) are more important than presentational skills; interpersonal skills determine graduates' ability to fit into the culture of the firm and to interact with the firm's clients in a relatively informal manner. Unlike the Big 4 firms, the medium and small firms also seem prepared to tolerate graduates' poor writing skills. As a partner from a medium-sized firm observed:

> They [accounting graduates] don't really have any skills in this [writing business reports]. This is something that university education cannot teach them. To be fair, they are very young. They have just left high school for a few years, studying at varsity and working at the same time. They are not prepared, and should not be expected, to be able to work effectively immediately in a professional firm.

All of the employer interviewees considered teamwork skills to be essential for accounting graduates and emphasised the importance of accounting students engaging in teamwork during their university education or through part-time jobs. They similarly agreed that computing skills are important but, in general, considered the required competence of accounting graduates is limited to (a) an ability to use computers; and (b) familiarity with basic office and accounting software. Nevertheless, a Big 4 firm partner thought their competence should extend beyond this. (S)he stated:

> Accountants need to be able to understand, utilise and analyse information for business purposes. IT skills are not just about spreadsheet and accounting software but, increasingly, about internal controls and understanding the purpose of information. Accounting programmes should teach students these skills.

Employer interviewees from the Big 4 firms conveyed that research skills (data collection, analyses and reporting) are further essential skills of accounting graduates. However, those from medium and small firms held the contrary view; they noted that such skills are irrelevant to entry-level accounting work. By contrast, interviewees from medium and small firms attached significantly greater importance to graduates possessing time management skills than did those from the Big 4 firms. Partners from the former observed that the ability to maintain a good work-life balance, and to switch readily between different tasks/assignments, is central to work productivity. A small firm partner explained:

> For our firm, because of our client base, staff need to have excellent organising skills. Since we have many clients at the same time, it is very easy to get confused. Therefore it is important to be able to switch between the jobs for different clients. As I say, not everyone has this capability. You need a breed to become a CA (Chartered Accountant).

Although the interviewees from the Big 4 firms did not consider time management skills to be a necessary competency for accounting graduates, two of them indicated that graduates with some life experience or personal interests outside accounting are more likely to fit into large accounting firms because they know how to engage with people and promote relationships. Relatedly, employer interviewees from the Big 4 firms considered it important for graduates to possess ‘client focus’ and cultural awareness. They explained that graduates joining their firms are able to engage in consulting work for large clients at a relatively early stage in their career and this requires a sound understanding of, and sensitivity to, the relevant client’s business. In this regard, they noted the value of graduates having travelled extensively and, thereby, having gained an understanding, and tolerance, of cultural differences. Employers from medium and small firms observed that their firms normally offer clients standard services, such as preparing accounts and tax returns and, therefore, client focus and cultural awareness are not considered to be important competencies of accounting graduates.

Regarding the personal attributes which accounting graduates are expected to possess, the employer interviewees identified intelligence, confidence, and a ‘learning to learn’ attitude as being important. They agreed that intelligent students attract recruiters and stand out from other applicants; they also agreed that intelligence is of particular importance for graduates wishing to specialise in tax. While interviewees from the medium-sized firms signalled that they, like the Big 4 firms, prefer to recruit bright graduates, they recognise that this is difficult because, compared with the large firms; they offer graduates lower salaries and fewer challenges and training opportunities. Perhaps for similar reasons, interviewees from the small firms indicated that they prefer students of average intelligence but who are hard-working, committed and tolerant of repetitive work assignments.

Another attribute considered important by interviewees from the Big 4 firms is that of confidence. According to these interviewees, confidence helps graduates to exercise professional scepticism and deal effectively with both prospective and current clients; it also enhances clients’ trust in the firm’s services. In contrast, interviewees from medium and small firms conveyed that they seek accounting graduates with limited confidence because, in their opinion, over-confidence hinders graduates from further learning and personal development.

Although most of the employer interviewees specified that accounting graduates should possess a sense of loyalty, they do not regard commitment as an important attribute because, in general, they do not expect graduates to remain with the firm longer than four or five years (two or three years after qualifying). They are, however, expected to remain with their initial firm for this period so as to enable the firm to recoup some of the internal and external training costs it has invested in them. An interesting observation by the employer interviewees is a perceived shift in graduates’ demands and needs over the last 10 or so years, stereotyped by the Generation X and Generation Y dichotomy. As expressed by a Big 4 firm manager:

> Generation Y are those who were born after 1980. They are more alert, more culturally aware, more confident and work with greater productivity than their Generation X counterparts. However, they also demand more rewards and career opportunities. They want everything now! They ask for ‘what they can get’ before asking themselves ‘what they can provide to the firm’. They have little loyalty to a firm unless it provides them with what they expect. In contrast, Generation X graduates tend to work for one firm throughout their career; they do not change and move between jobs.

Employers from the Big 4 firms indicated that they are able to accommodate Generation Y graduates by giving them challenges and responsibilities that match their capabilities. However, those from medium and small firms reported that they find it difficult to meet the career expectations of these graduates and that this results in high staff turnover. As a consequence, these firms recruit graduates regularly and limit their selection to those who have 'average' ambition and confidence.

According to the majority of the employer interviewees, a positive attitude to learning is essential for life-long learning and continuous professional development. However, although important, this competence is difficult to detect. Some of the interviewees suggested that it is partly reflected in a graduate's good academic record and apparent commitment to the accounting profession and desire to qualify as a Chartered Accountant.

The interviews were not intended to establish all of the competencies which employers expect accounting graduates to possess but to identify and examine those which the interviewees regard as being the most important. It is noticeable that, although the employers from the large, medium and small firms agreed on the key competencies they expect accounting graduates to possess, they accorded them different levels of importance. Differences were particularly evident in respect of graduates' technical accounting knowledge and skills, communication and research skills, and their level of intelligence and confidence.

(b) Competencies which graduates from the case study programme are perceived by employers to possess. The employer interviewees generally perceived graduates from the case study programme to have a solid base of accounting knowledge, especially of accounting concepts. The concepts were considered to provide a sound foundation upon which practical skills can be built. The interviewees observed that graduates' good accounting knowledge contributes to their firms' reputation and helps to justify the charge-out rate for services provided by those firms. The accounting programme was commended for providing graduates with a good conceptual understanding of accounting knowledge but was criticised for failing to equip graduates with adequate practical accounting knowledge and skills—a factor which more than half of the employer interviewees believe has worsened in recent years. A tax partner observed:

> Accounting graduates are not good at adapting knowledge or finding the answer to particular situations. As a tax consultant, you not only need to know the law, but you also need to apply that law to specific cases. This skill is obviously not trained at university.

The graduates were perceived to be particularly deficient in bookkeeping knowledge and skills. However, interviewees from the Big 4 firms observed that these can be taught cost-effectively within the firms, and a strong conceptual background enables graduates to pick up practical skills readily and also enables them to develop much further professionally. The graduates were also considered to be deficient in business knowledge and understanding. This was attributed to a lack of exposure to the business environment, and the lack of opportunity to interact with clients, within an accounting degree programme. However, as noted earlier, some interviewees expressed doubt about the ability of universities to teach students 'real' business knowledge and skills.

The interviewees intimated that graduates from the case study programme possess adequate face-to-face communication skills but their writing skills are poor. Of particular note is their inability to write well-structured and concise business reports or appropriately-expressed letters or emails to clients.

A further deficiency in graduates' competencies identified by the employers is their lack of preparedness for the work environment. A partner from a Big 4 firm observed:

> This is the biggest deficiency we find in accounting graduates. When they leave university, they think they know everything. When they join our firm, they realise that what they have

learnt at university is nothing compared to what they have to learn at work. The transition from being a student to being a professional can be very difficult and even painful. They have to get up early for work, dress and behave appropriately and, more especially, they have to learn to work productively and responsibly. They simply can't continue the way they lived during their varsity days. They have to learn to become disciplined. . . .

This partner explained why the 'reality shock' is particularly severe for accounting graduates:

These students enter university with the same attitude and background like any other students in other majors or disciplines. They study, work, and play like other students. They do not recognise that they are about to join a profession that is highly respected and whose members have to live up to such respect. Thus, they do not prepare themselves to behave like professionals and this makes the transition from university to the workplace particularly difficult.

Nevertheless, according to an employer from a medium-sized firm, the 'reality shock' is beneficial:

That (reality shock) acquaints them (accounting graduates) with change and uncertainty. Change and uncertainty are the characteristics that typify the accounting profession. This early challenge in their career is good preparation for the continuous learning and professional development that are integral elements of a career in accounting.

Reviewing the competencies that employers expect, and those which they perceive accounting graduates to possess, it is evident that there is a gap between the two. This provides some support (albeit limited in terms of the scope of the study) for the 'end points' of the hypothesised structure of accounting education's expectation-performance gap. The next sub-sections report the case study findings relating to the hypothesised causes of this gap.

(c) Expectation gap—gap between the competencies expected of accounting graduates by employers and accounting educators. The educator and employer interviewees conveyed different expectations with regard to accounting graduates possessing thinking skills (i.e. independent thinking and problem-solving skills). While five of the six educator interviewees expressed the view that employers of accounting graduates expect graduates to possess well-developed thinking skills, only one employer interviewee identified such skills as an expected competency. This difference may result from differences in their views on the role of university education. All of the accounting educator interviewees expressed a strong belief that the principal role of university education is to develop students' intellectual capabilities—a belief that is reflected in the formal written outlines of the case study accounting programme's 11 accounting courses/modules. Each emphasises the development of students' thinking and analytical skills as primary learning objectives. One lecturer saw this as a difference between universities and polytechnics. (S)he explained:

There are two ends to the role of accounting education. First, academic teaching is about expanding and encouraging thinking in different ways, about exploring different options, perspectives and paradigms to one particular issue or problem. [This university] focuses on this end. At the other end, practical training is about teaching how to do things. This is not seen much at [this university] but is the focus of polytechnics. . . .

Only three of the 11 employer interviewees (two from a large, and one from a medium, firm) shared this view of university education. These interviewees noted that universities are the only place where students can acquire a broad education and where they experience the best opportunity to develop intellectually. In their view, accounting students should incorporate as many liberal courses in their accounting degree programme as possible in order to develop their critical and creative thinking skills. However, one of these interviewees emphasised that such skills are not immediately applicable in accounting practice:

> I studied for my accounting degree when working full time as an accountant. University study and accounting practice require two very different mindsets. I remember always having to switch my mindset between work and study, which was very frustrating at times. I think, in the short- to medium-term, the academic thinking one gains from university education does not add direct value to his/her work as an accountant.

While only three employer interviewees believed that the role of university education is to develop students' intellectual capability, the majority expected an accounting degree to equip graduates with a solid base of accounting knowledge. However, these interviewees considered that this knowledge should have a theoretical, rather than practical, orientation. As a partner from a medium-sized firm explained:

> The complexity of practice makes it impossible to cover all in one programme. Teaching concepts and theory is a safer option.

The employer interviewees also observed that accounting concepts and principles are the core of all accounting practice. As one from a Big 4 firm explained:

> They [accounting concepts and principles] do not become obsolete no mater how far and high up you move within the accounting profession. They underpin everyday tasks and responsibilities attaching to all accounting positions—from junior to partner levels.

Notwithstanding their expectation that accounting graduates will possess accounting knowledge from a theoretical perspective, the interviewees (especially from smaller firms) were disapproving of the academic theories taught in the case study programme. In the words of a small firm partner:

> What education the student has is not important. At university they teach too many irrelevant subjects. I would like to recruit those who have not got a university degree but have good technical skills and none of those theoretical stuffs.

In contrast, the educator interviewees regard such theories as essential for developing students' intellectual capabilities and consider that the focus on concepts and theories is justified by the role of university education. As a lecturer expressed it:

> The debate of whether university should teach bookkeeping or not has been going on, and remained unresolved, for some 30 years. I personally think that students will find it easier to understand advanced and conceptual topics if they know the basic principles of accounting. But there is not enough time to teach both. Universities, as I understand, are supposed to teach concepts and theories, not technical skills.

As reported earlier, although most of the employer interviewees from medium and small firms conveyed that accounting graduates should possess practical accounting skills such as bookkeeping, and the ability to apply accounting knowledge to solve practical problems, those from the Big 4 firms believed that practical training is not the role of universities—it is better taught within the firms. In general, the educator interviewees strongly supported the latter view. They cited as reasons (i) the role of universities is to focus on concepts and theories, not practical skills; and (ii) the structured accounting programme combined with limited time prevents academics from covering everything that is desired by the profession. Nevertheless, two of the academics noted that bookkeeping is a fundamental skill of accountants and that it provides a sound foundation for more advanced university accounting study. In general, the educators considered that accounting firms are too demanding in their requirements of accounting graduates' competencies. One explained:

> The accounting firms want us to do everything for them, everything, from bookkeeping to business knowledge and general skills. A balance needs to be maintained between bookkeeping and other topics. We simply cannot satisfy all of their demands.

Three of the six academics expressed the view that universities also have a role in educating students to become 'good citizens' by encouraging and enabling them to develop holistically: more specifically, universities should enable students to think independently, adapt to changes in life, and become ethically aware. However, these academics also acknowledged that universities cannot achieve this goal on a 'mass' scale. No employer interviewee expressed an opinion in respect of accounting graduates possessing this competency.

Two other areas where the goals of accounting academics seem to be at variance with employers' expectations of accounting graduates are (i) students' ability to write business reports and letters to clients; and (ii) their possession of leadership and interpersonal skills. While the employees indicated that they expect graduates to able to communicate in 'business English', academics focus on teaching students 'academic English'. Nevertheless, five of the six academic interviewees noted that accounting graduates' inability to write 'business English' is a deficiency in their competencies and this needs to be rectified. In respect of leadership and interpersonal skills, the employers signalled that they expect graduates to possess these competencies but four of the six lecturer interviewees expressed the view that these skills are more necessary for senior, rather than entry-level, accounting positions and, therefore, it is not important for accounting programmes to equip graduates with these competencies.

From the opinions expressed by the educator and employer interviewees, it is evident that their expectations of the competencies accounting graduates should acquire through their university education differ quite markedly. The interview results, therefore, provide some support for the 'expectation gap' component of the hypothesised structure of the expectation-performance gap.

(d) Constraints gap: Institutional factors. The educator interviewees identified two key institutional factors as obstacles to their efforts to develop the competencies which they believe accounting graduates should possess (i) inadequate resources (funds, staff and facilities); and (ii) tenure and promotion criteria.

The case study programme, like all academic programmes in NZ universities, relies primarily on government funding (based on the number of full-time equivalent students) and student fees. The NZ Government has capped the fees which universities are able to charge domestic students and, as a result, all NZ universities seek to increase student numbers as a means of ensuring an adequate inflow of funds. Business programmes in general, and the accounting programme in particular, are exceptional within the case study university in that they are able to attract additional domestic and international students. Although the proportion of university funding allocated to business and accounting programmes falls far short of the proportion of the university's students enrolled in these programmes, increased student numbers in a programme results in some additional funding. One lecturer commented on the effect of the funding shortfall in the following terms:

> Accounting is the milk cow of universities. Accounting has always been a single major that attracts the most students of all the degrees offered at this university. The need for [university] revenues leads to big [accounting] classes, which in turn hinders teaching quality.

According to an employer interviewee from a Big 4 firm, funding is a primary reason for the case study programme failing to include a significant component of liberal courses. According to the interviewee:

> The Commerce Faculty has not been willing to let go of its students. It all comes down to funding interests. Commerce and accounting lecturers want their students to take as many commerce and accounting-related papers as possible so that they can retain the related fees within the Faculty. If accounting students want to become good accountants, they should choose subjects outside, and unrelated, to their major.

Some of the educator interviewees agreed with this view; they observed that they have an incentive to encourage students to take more accounting, and less non-accounting, courses. However, other educator interviewees noted that students prefer to take commerce papers as they perceive these to be directly relevant to their future career. A lecturer explained:

> We used to require students to take liberal papers to [final year] level as part of the BCA requirements. . . . . However, the students did not like this. They voted to get rid of this requirement. They wanted to learn only things that [they think] are directly relevant, or at least as close as possible to their major.

As a consequence of the university's funding policy, the accounting programme is not able to employ lecturing staff commensurate with student numbers; the programme has the highest student-lecturer ratio in the university. Added to this, as two of the educator interviewees noted, there is a shortage of large lecture theatres which results in limiting the number of students enrolled in courses for which there is a high demand.[11] This, in turn, gives rise to a demand by students for extra streams of the course to be offered—and pressure from the Faculty (with an eye on funding implications) to do so. If extra streams of courses are offered, this results in lecturers devoting more time to teaching and 'accepting' increased workloads. As a consequence of these factors, the case study programme is characterised by heavy work loads for lecturers and large class sizes for students. This applies especially to the 'core' introductory accounting course that is required for the commerce degree, and those second and third year courses that are required for entry to the accounting profession (i.e. the New Zealand Institute of Chartered Accountants, NZICA).[12]

Although the case study programme meets the requirements of, and is accredited by, NZICA, according to all of the educator interviewees, large classes and heavy work loads have a significant negative impact on teaching quality. More specifically, they noted that large class sizes are responsible for (i) eroding students' interest in the subject matter; (ii) making it impossible for lecturers to know, and address, all of the students' needs; (iii) making students feel intimidated and, therefore, reluctant to ask and answer questions; (iv) rendering each lecture session exhausting for the lecturer; and (v) making it difficult to make teaching engaging and interactive, and to implement innovative delivery modes such as student presentations and meaningful discussions. Along similar lines, they intimated that their heavy work loads make redesigning the content of courses/modules and adopting innovative delivery modes very difficult as they lack the necessary time and energy to devote to such developments.

The university's promotion and tenure policy also operates to hinder improvements in accounting education in the case study programme. As four of the educator interviewees observed, although academics have research, teaching and administration responsibilities, research productivity is the key factor in promotion and tenure decisions—and its supremacy has been heightened in recent years as a result of the introduction of performance based research funding (PBRF) by the NZ Government.[13] By contrast, teaching excellence attracts relatively little recognition. Two of the educator interviewees expressed concern about the differential reputational effect of excellence in teaching and research, with the possible effect of teaching becoming viewed by academics as a burden. Three other interviewees noted that they have a genuine interest in teaching but the combined effect of the university's reward system and the difficulty of simultaneously satisfying all of their academic responsibilities results in their according highest priority to research.

(e) Constraints gap: Student factors. Student factors, specifically students' ability and aptitude, like the institutional factors, constrain educators' efforts to develop the desired competencies of accounting graduates. Both student and educator interviewees were asked to comment on the intellectual ability of students in the case study programme. In general, the students were of the opinion that the ability of accounting students is similar to that of students pursuing other business degree programmes. However, they considered that accounting courses tend to be more challenging than other business degree courses and, possibly as a result of this, it is more difficult to gain high grades in accounting courses.

The educator interviewees intimated that there is something of a polarisation in the intellectual ability of students in the case study programme: about half of the accounting students are intelligent, hard-working and curious; however, the other half appears to have inadequate ability and to be indifferent to their studies. Clearly, this observation may reflect students' motivation as well as their intellectual ability. However, the educator interviewees also expressed concern about the university's entry criteria (which they perceive to be too liberal) and the recently introduced High School qualification—New Zealand Qualification of Achievement (NZQA). This qualification does not distinguish between excellent and average academic achievement and, to some extent, masks poor performance. These factors were seen as combining to lower the quality of the accounting degree programme and to limit the level of competence acquired by accounting graduates.

Acquiring desired competencies involves aptitude as well as ability. The student interviewees conveyed the belief that, to do well in an accounting programme, students must be interested in accounting subjects. In the words of one of theses interviewees:

> I define success at university study as not limited to getting good grades. Thus hard-work for me is not enough—there are other personal skills that need to be developed through university . . . such things as time management, motivation and genuine interest in the subjects and in learning are very important.

Interestingly, the student interviewees were critical of accounting students as a whole: in their view, the majority of the students are not interested in what they study. Three students asserted that the aim of most accounting students when joining the university is to get a 'quick and easy' degree, with as little effort as possible. The student interviewees identified five key reasons for what they see as a decline in accounting students' enthusiasm and interest in university study, namely (i) a greater proportion of the population entering universities; (ii) decreased availability of study-time resulting from the need to obtain part-time employment; (iii) reduced conduciveness to learning of the university environment; (iv) a flawed secondary education (and examination) system; and (v) student's selection of an accounting (rather than an alternative) programme for career-related reasons rather than interest in, and motivation to study, the discipline.

A student interviewee also indicated his/her belief that accounting students are not as creative and curious as students of other disciplines. Along similar lines, two educator interviewees observed that accounting students are not curious about the world around them and tend to prefer exact answers to questions rather than consider alternative solutions from different perspectives. These educators noted that they could adopt more challenging delivery modes if the students showed greater curiosity and creativity.

From comments expressed by the case study interviewees, it seems that, broadly speaking, accounting students' attitudes towards learning is not satisfactory. As an educator interviewee observed, lecturers and students both play important roles in the learning process and it is only with cooperation, and genuine effort, by both parties that the best results can be achieved.

(f) Performance gap—educators' performance. Most of the constraints discussed above are largely beyond the direct control of accounting educators. However, they have significant control over factors such as the amount of time and effort they invest in teaching, the design of the courses/modules they offer and delivery modes. If they fail to maximise the use of the resources under their control (including their personal attributes) to achieve the intended teaching objectives, it is likely to result in accounting graduates failing to develop at least some of the competencies which the educators expect them to acquire.

With few exceptions, the student interviewees were critical of accounting lecturers: most commented on lecturers' inability to explain subject matter clearly and, more particularly, their failure to present accounting material in a manner that is stimulating and motivating to students. The interviewees also observed that accounting courses include too few examples and case studies: in the students' view, these learning aids enable students to recognise the practical relevance of topics covered, enhance students' understanding, and heighten their interest in the subject matter. Three student interviewees also expressed disappointment that lecturers in the case study programme do not appear to be passionate and excited about the material they are teaching. One student pointed out:

> Lecturer attitude has a real impact on students' interest and motivation. Whether the students are willing to ask questions depends very much on the lecturer's patience to listen and answer. I think there is reciprocity here. Because the students are reluctant to answer questions, the lecturer is less willing to ask questions. . . .

Commenting on the same issue, two educator interviewees observed that lecturers have a role in motivating students and they can only fulfil this if they are enthusiastic about their teaching. These interviewees expressed the view that accounting lecturers should put more effort into teaching, to make it more stimulating, and thereby improve students' learning outcomes.

The use of *PowerPoint* slides as visual aids in lectures attracted negative comment from the students. They noted that slides facilitate note-taking and understanding but observed that, in their view, lecturers are increasingly relying on slides at the expense of interaction—asking questions and giving examples—features that make lectures interesting. The students also conveyed that, as a result of the deficiencies of lectures as means of learning, many students are de-motivated from attending. Three lecturer interviewees expressed views about *PowerPoint* slides that accord with those of the students. In the words of one of them:

> Using *PowerPoint* (slides) hinders interaction between lecturers and students, and reduces students' motivation. Students get the most value from what lecturers have got to say, not what they have on the slides. One can say that having slides helps students to grasp the main ideas and assists their learning. I personally think that students learn better when they take notes themselves. This helps them to develop a lot of skills such as writing, synthesis and note-taking. Lecturing needs to impress and motivate students. It is not purely about transferring knowledge; it also about how lecturers present themselves.

Commenting on the design of courses/modules in the case study programme, the majority of student interviewees reported that, when entering the university, they expected the programme to be practice-oriented. As two of them observed:

- I expected [the programme] to be narrowly focused and career-orientated.
- I expected to learn how to apply accounting knowledge to practice.

Contrary to their expectations, the students have found the courses comprise 'very theoretical knowledge with a strong academic focus' and they question the benefits of accounting theories for entry-level accounting work. One of the students noted:

> Accounting theories explain where accounting comes from and why people behave the way they do but, in the real world, you do simple technical tasks. Theory is only needed at senior levels. I don't think they [accounting theories] are directly relevant to being an accountant.

The student interviewees also conveyed that such an approach is 'only suited to those who intend to become academics'. They expressed concern about not being taught how to apply knowledge in practice and about much of the accounting programme material not being applicable in the real world. In the words of a student interviewee:

> I cannot say that what we study is not knowledge, but it is not the sort of knowledge that we can [readily] apply in practice ... I agree that university education should involve [critical] thinking and debate, but it still needs to be related to the requirements of the workplace.

Perhaps not surprisingly, given the students' views on the accounting programme, they consider most of the accounting courses/modules to be boring. The exceptions are the auditing and tax courses which require students to make presentations in selected topics. However, as the following quotations testify, while some students regard the presentations as being beneficial, others have the contrary opinion.

- The great thing about auditing presentations is that you have a second chance to improve. With the feedback from the lecturers/tutors, you know where you got it wrong, how to correct it, and observe that your efforts are recognised. It is very stimulating. I feel that I got a lot from the course.
- For seminar-style tutorials, presenters tend to focus on only one topic and ignore others. Other students in the same tutorials have to rely on the presenters for their knowledge. With traditional tutorials [discussion of a number of issues/problems with suggested answers provided] we are certain about what we get. With student-led presentations, it is much less certain what we learn. There is also insufficient feedback from the tutors about the quality of the presentations (i.e. what is covered and what has not been covered).

Three of the eight student interviewees complained about the overlap in topics taught in different courses and two others observed that some accounting courses are less interesting than is conveyed in their formal outlines. About half of the student interviewees signalled that 'lower' level accounting courses are more interesting than the advanced courses; the other half were of the contrary view. Further investigation revealed an almost perfect correlation with the background of the interviewees. Those who had studied accounting at secondary school found the introductory accounting course rather boring as it essentially repeated material already studied: these students found the more advanced level courses more interesting. In contrast, those who had not previously studied accounting found the interactive style adopted for the introductory accounting course[14] stimulating and motivating and the subject matter interesting. These interviewees found subsequent accounting courses to be less interesting.

It was noted earlier that the formal outlines of all the accounting courses in the case study programme emphasise the development of students' thinking and analytical skills as primary learning objectives. However, only four of the eight student interviewees believed that the programme has extended their intellectual abilities. These four interviewees also noted that the accounting programme seems to be carefully structured so that the increasing difficulty of courses matches the intellectual development of the students.

Considering the competencies which employers signalled that they expect accounting graduates to possess, only two of the student interviewees believe that their communication and, more particularly, their presentational skills have been enhanced by the case study programme. The same students indicated that they consider their research and teamwork skills have also been developed.[15] However, none of the interviewees perceived that their writing skills have been developed through the programme. This finding is surprising given that the formal outlines of most accounting courses indicate that writing assignments, research reports, critiques of articles or similar activities constitute a significant portion of the relevant course's assessment.

In summary, although the students considered the accounting programme provides sound knowledge of accounting concepts, some courses are too theoretical, irrelevant to the demands of the accounting profession and divorced from the real world. Possibly as a result of this assessment, the students stated that a number of courses are boring and some lecturers do not display good teaching skills. In the students' view, more courses should target developing the skills which employers expect accounting graduates to possess.[16]

5. Concluding Remarks

This research has examined the gap between the competencies (knowledge, skills and attitudes) which employers of accounting graduates expect, and perceive, the graduates to possess—the gap that has prompted calls for accounting education to change. Unlike prior studies, which focused on individual factors contributing to the gap, this research has adopted a holistic approach. A review of the literature indicated that the gap has three primary causes:

(i) differences in the expectations of accounting educators and employers regarding the competencies which accounting graduates should possess;
(ii) institutional and student factors that constrain accounting educators from developing the competencies which they expect/desire accounting graduates to acquire;
(iii) substandard performance by accounting educators resulting in accounting graduates not acquiring the competencies which educators can reasonably expect to develop, given the constraints.

Identification of these factors enabled the structure of the gap, termed accounting education's expectation-performance gap, to be hypothesised.

An exploratory study was conducted to examine the validity of the hypothesised structure. Using the accounting programme of a NZ university as a case study, small samples of key stakeholders were interviewed (i.e. eight final year students, five recent graduates, six educators, and 11 employers of the programme's graduates—from large, medium and small accounting firms) to ascertain their opinions about the competencies which accounting graduates should possess and the accounting programme's success in developing these competencies. The research findings provide broad support for the hypothesised structure.

The employers from all of the accounting firms expect accounting graduates to possess a sound knowledge of accounting principles and concepts, a basic understanding of business, and good communication, teamwork and interpersonal skills. They also conveyed that they place high value on a personality that accords with the firm's culture and a demonstrated potential for continuous learning. In other regards the expectations of employers from the different sized firms varied. Those from the Big 4 firms placed particular importance on well- developed analytical, critical and creative thinking skills, and oral presentational and writing skills. They attached relatively little importance to technical accounting skills. Employers from the medium and small firms emphasised the importance of graduates possessing good technical accounting skills, and good interpersonal (face-to-face communication) skills. While the Big 4 firms seek graduates with a high level of intelligence, medium and small firms, aware of their inability to compete with the big firms in terms of salary, challenge and training opportunities, tend to seek graduates with average intellectual ability.

As is evident from the literature review, the competencies expected of graduates by all of the employers have been identified by prior research. Similarly, the differences in the competencies expected by different sized firms support, to an extent, the finding of Humphrey *et al.* (2003). However, this research extends the findings of Humphrey *et al.* in that it has identified the specific competencies and attributes expected of graduates by firms of different sizes.

Differing from the employers (especially those from medium and small firms), the case study educators, like those in Watty's (2005) study, believe that the primary goal of accounting education is to extend students' intellectual capabilities. The educators highlighted the need to develop accounting students' thinking skills, and accorded secondary importance to technical accounting knowledge and bookkeeping skills—competencies expected of graduates by medium and small firms. These findings support the existence of a gap between the expectations of employers and educators regarding the competencies which accounting graduates should possesses; that is, the 'expectation gap' component of accounting education's expectation-performance gap.

Institutional factors identified by the study's interviewees as constraining educators from developing the competencies which they consider desirable for accounting graduates to possess include: inadequate resources (funds, staff and facilities); entry criteria (imposed by the University) that permit students with insufficient ability to enrol in the accounting programme; large class sizes; and the university's tenure and promotion policies which motivate educators to devote time and effort to research rather than teaching activities. Added to the institutional constraints are student-related constraints, specifically, students' ability and aptitude. The interview results suggest that students (at least in the case study programme) have little interest in acquiring accounting knowledge (especially through lectures) and they are not as creative or curious as students pursuing other degree programmes. These factors may reflect the paucity of interactive teaching in the accounting programme and students' apparent reluctance to take liberal arts courses. In general, the study's findings support those of earlier studies reported in the literature; they also provide support for the 'constraints gap' component of the expectation-performance gap.

A further factor contributing to the expectation-performance gap is that of substandard teaching by accounting educators. Although the 'institutional and student constraints' are largely beyond the direct control of the educators, this is not true of their performance. The two key shortcomings of educators identified by the interviewees are deficient teaching skills and a lack of passion for, and apparent interest in, the subject matter. These shortcomings result in students finding accounting lectures boring and not being motivated to study course material in a manner the educators expect (or desire). Thus, the educators' deficient teaching results in unsatisfactory educational outcomes for accounting students. Given this situation, it is not surprising that many, if not most, accounting graduates do not acquire the competencies which educators might reasonably expect to develop (after allowing for the 'constraints gap' factors). The main deficiencies in accounting graduates' competencies identified by the employers are their writing skills, applying knowledge to practical situations, and understanding the requirements of working as a member of the accounting profession. As for the 'expectation' and 'constraints' gaps, the case study provided support for the existence of the 'performance gap' component of the expectation-performance gap. Similarly, its findings in respect of educators' substandard performance, and the deficiencies which employers perceive in accounting graduates' competencies, accord with those of prior studies.

Understanding the structure of the expectation-performance gap enables efforts to narrow it to focus on its primary causes. It seems likely that the 'expectation gap' between employers and accounting educators results primarily from inadequate communication and understanding between the parties. It is, therefore, suggested that this component may be narrowed by greater interaction between 'town' and 'gown'. Part of the solution may lie in the accounting profession having greater input into accounting education; however, it may also lie, in part, in educators calling on the profession to amend its expectations of accounting graduates.

Reviewing the causes of the 'constraints gap', it seems that this gap can be narrowed only if the constraints are removed or alleviated. Suggestions from interviewees on ways in which the 'student factor constraints' may be reduced include (i) raising the academic entry level for accounting students; and (ii) increasing students' interest in accounting subjects. (The latter suggestion also clearly relates to narrowing the 'performance gap'.) The interviewees did not offer suggestions as to how the institutional constraints might be reduced or removed. Given their impact on teaching quality, this constitutes a fruitful avenue for future research.

The extent to which the 'performance gap' may be narrowed largely depends on accounting educators' own initiatives, combined with those of the faculty and the university. The case study interviewees recommended that:

(i) accounting lecturers (especially those who are inexperienced) be given increased training so as to improve their teaching skills; and
(ii) the profile of teaching, compared with research, be raised. This may be achieved by, for example, giving greater weight to teaching performance in promotion and tenure decisions and/or recognising and rewarding teaching excellence.

This study extends the extant literature by adopting a holistic approach to a problem which the accounting profession has lamented since the mid-1980s (that is, the perceived failure of accounting education to provide accounting graduates with the competencies which the profession expects them to possess). The study has identified the structure, and causal components, of accounting education's expectation-performance gap. By identifying its components, attempts to narrow the gap may focus on its causes, thereby increasing the likelihood of success.

Although the case study has provided support for the hypothesised structure of accounting education's expectation-performance gap, its findings are limited in their scope: only a small number of employers, students, graduates and educators were interviewed, and their comments relate only to the case study programme. The findings may have been different if the samples had been larger or if they related to accounting programmes in other universities in NZ or elsewhere. These limitations highlight opportunities for further research. Given the benefits to be derived from identifying the structure and components of the expectation-performance gap in terms of better aligning the expectations of accounting educators and employers with respect to the competencies which accounting graduates should possess, such research is potentially rewarding for the accounting profession, educators, graduates and students alike.

Notes

[1]'The profession' is used in this paper to mean professional accounting bodies, members of the profession in general, and public practice employers of accounting graduates.

[2]For example, the ICAA's 1998 study involved interviews with 28 Australian Chief Executive and Chief Financial Officers; in its 2001 study, it surveyed 46 Australian business people with a wide range of expertise and experience. This compares with Albrecht and Sack (2000) who surveyed 1,000 individuals, held discussions with 120 people in focus groups, and conducted interviews with 20 individuals from accounting academia, the profession, and university administrators from universities throughout the USA.

[3]It noted, in particular, the increased demand for assurance services as a result of the Sarbanes-Oxley Act of 2002.

[4]The Institute of Chartered Accountants in Australia (ICAA), the Australian Society of CPAs (now CPA Australia), and the New Zealand Society of Accountants (now the New Zealand Institute of Chartered Accountants) participated in this study.

[5]The QAA assesses and validates accounting degrees in the UK. Professional accreditation is undertaken by the relevant UK-based professional accounting bodies.

[6]The Carnegie classification divides accounting schools into three categories, namely: (i) doctoral-granting high research support school (Research I and II); (ii) doctoral granting low research support school (Doctorate I and II); and comprehensive schools (non-doctoral granting).

[7]As a consequence of this factor, the liberal component within the 'ideal' programme was significantly reduced.

[8]It is generally accepted that case studies are an appropriate method for research of an exploratory nature (Yin, 2009).

[9]The interview guide is available from the authors upon request.

[10]Structural data displays provide a summarised presentation of interview transcripts which facilitates an understanding of the full data set while enabling the research question to be addressed (Lillis, 1999).

[11]Under NZ's Health and Safety Regulations students are not permitted to sit or stand in aisles or on lecture theatre steps.

[12]The introductory accounting course has in excess of 1600 student enrolments each year, and courses required for entry to NZICA have in excess of 250 student enrolments each year.

[13]Since the introduction of PBRF in 2003, a portion of Government funding allocated to NZ universities is determined by the research productivity of academics in each university—as assessed by the Tertiary Education Commission (and the panels of research assessors it appoints).

[14]This course is taught by an exceptionally talented lecturer—but one who devotes virtually all of his/her efforts and time to teaching activities.

[15]At the time of the interviews, these two students were taking the final year auditing course that requires students to work in groups of three to four students to research a topic and present their findings to their tutorial group (of approximately 15 students).

[16]The final year auditing course was singled out as seeking to achieve this.

References

Abernethy, M. A., Chua, W., Luckett, P. F. and Selto, F. H. (1999) Research in managerial accounting: learning from others' experiences, *Accounting & Finance*, 39(1), pp. 1–27.

Accounting Education Change Commission (AECC) (1995) The need for change in accounting education: an educator survey, *Journal of Accounting Education*, 13(1), pp. 21–43.

Adams, S. J., Pryor, L. J. and Adams, S. L. (1994) Attraction and retention of high-aptitude students in accounting: an exploratory longitudinal study, *Issues in Accounting Education*, 9(1), pp. 45–58.

Ahadiat, N. and Smith, K. J. (1994) A factor-analytic investigation of employee selection factors of significance to recruiters of entry-level accountants, *Issues in Accounting Education*, 9(1), pp. 59–67.

Ahmed, K., Alam, K. F. and Alam, M. (1997) An empirical study of factors affecting accounting students' career choice in New Zealand, *Accounting Education: an international journal*, 6(4), pp. 325–335.

Albrecht, S. W. and Sack, R. J. (2000) Accounting education: charting a course through a perilous future, *Accounting Education Series, 16* (Sarasota, FL, American Accounting Association).

Ameen, E. C., Guffey, D. M. and Jackson, C. M. (2000) Silence is not golden: further evidence of oral communication apprehension in accounting majors, *Advances in Accounting Education*, 3, pp. 85–105.

American Accounting Association (AAA), Committee on the Future Structure and Content and Scope of Accounting Education (The Bedford Committee) (1986) Future accounting education: Preparing for the expanding profession, *Issues in Accounting Education*, 1(1), pp. 168–195.

American Institute of Certified Public Accountants (AICPA), CPA Vision Project: focus on the Horizon (1998) *Executive summary and CPA Vision Project Focus Groups: Public Practice, Industry and Government CPAs; Also Addendum: Student Focus Group.* (New York, NY, AICPA).

American Institute of Certified Public Accountants (AICPA) (1999) *Core competency framework for entry into the accounting profession* (New York: AICPA). Available at http://www.aicpa.org/edu/corecomp.htm (accessed 20 October 2005).

American Institute of Certified Public Accountants (AICPA) (2004) *The Supply of Accounting Graduates and the Demand for Public Accounting Recruits—2004 for Academic Year 2002–2003* (New York, NY, AICPA).

Armitage, J. L. (1991) Academics' and practitioners' views on the content and importance of the advanced financial accounting course, *Journal of Accounting Education*, 9(2), pp. 327–340.

Arquero, J., Anes, J. A. D., Hassall, T. and Joyce, J. (2001) Vocational skills in the accounting professional profile: The Chartered Institute of Management Accountants (CIMA) employers' opinion, *Accounting Education: an international journal*, 10(3), pp. 299–313.

Arthur Andersen & Co., Arthur Young, Coppers & Lybrand, Deloitte, Haskins & Sells, Ernst & Whinney, Peat Marwick Main & Co., Price Waterhouse and Touché Ross (1989) *Perspectives on Education for Success in the Accounting Profession (The White Paper)* (New York, NY: The Big Eight).

Australian Society of Certified Practicing Accountants (ASCPA) (1995) *Window to the Future: The Accountant's Role in an EDI Environment* (Melbourne: ASCPA).

Birkett, W. P. (1993) *Competency Based Standards for Professional Accountants in Australia and New Zealand* (Sydney: Institute of Chartered Accountants in Australia, Australian Society of CPAs, and the New Zealand Society of Accountants).

Brown, R. B. and McCartney, S. (1995) Competence is not enough: meta-competence and accounting education, *Accounting Education: an international journal*, 4(1), pp. 43–53.

Bullock, J. J., Ell, V., Inman, B. C., Jiambalvo, J. J., Krull Rf., G. W., Lathan, M. H., Mitchell, A. R., Schwartz, B. N., Scott, L. P., Williams, J. R. and Barefield, R. M. (1995) Accounting faculty/practitioners partnerships to address mutual education concern, *Issues in Accounting Education*, 10(1), pp. 197–206.

Camp, D. (1997) Universities' job is to challenge cult of marketability, *The Toronto Star*, , Sunday, 30 November.

Carr, S., Chua, F. and Perera, H. (2006) University accounting curricula: the perceptions of an alumni group, *Accounting Education: an international journal*, 15(4), pp. 359–376.

Cheng, R. H. and Saemann, G. (1997) Comparative evidence about the verbal and analytical aptitude of accounting students, *Journal of Accounting Education*, 15(4), pp. 485–501.

Craig, R. and Amernic, J. (2001) Accountability of accounting educators and the rhythm of the universities: resistance strategies for post-modern blues, *Accounting Education: an international journal*, 11(2), pp. 121–171.

De Lange, P., Jackling, B. and Gut, A. M. (2006) Accounting graduates' perceptions of skills emphasis in undergraduate courses: an investigation from two Victorian universities, *Accounting and Finance*, 46(3), pp. 365–386.

Dominelli, L. and Hoogvelt, A. (1996) Globalisation, the privatisation of welfare, and the changing role of professional academics in Britain, *Critical Perspectives in Accounting*, 7(1), pp. 191–212.

Duncan, J. and Schmutte, J. (2006) Change in accounting programs: the impact of influences and constraints, *The Accounting Educators' Journal*, 16, pp. 52–81.

Felton, S., Buhr, N. and Northey, M. (1994) Factors influencing the business student's choice of a career in chartered accountancy, *Issues in Accounting Education*, 9(1), pp. 131–141.

Fielding, R. (2005) War for talents hits audit salaries, *Accountancy Age*, 31 March, p. 1.

Francis, G. and Minchington, C. (1999) Quantitative skills: is there an expectation gap between the education and practice of management accountants? *Accounting Education: an international journal*, 8(4), pp. 301–319.

Gow, L., Kember, D. and Cooper, B. (1994) The teaching context and approaches to study of accounting students, *Issues in Accounting Education*, 9(1), pp. 118–130.

Haigh, N. (1994) *Promoting Intellectual Independence: A Legislative Catalyst* (Hamilton: University of Waikato).

Hassall, T., Joyce, J., Arquero Montaño, J. L. and Donoso Anes, J. A. (2005) Priorities for the development of vocational skills in management accountants: a European perspective, *Accounting Forum*, 29(4), pp. 379–394.

Howell, W. C. and Johnson, L. T. (1982) An evaluation of the compressed-course format for instruction in accounting, *The Accounting Review*, 57(2), pp. 403–413.

Hill, M. C. (1998) Class size and student performance in introductory accounting courses: further evidence, *Issues in Accounting Education*, 13(1), pp. 47–64.

Hill, W. Y. and Milner, M. M. (2007) The Placing of Skills in Accounting Degree Programmes in Higher Education: Some Contrasting Approaches in the UK, *BMAF Magazine*, 2, pp. 3–4.

Humphrey, C., Jones, J. and Khalifa, R. (2003) Business risk auditing and the auditing profession: status, identity and fragmentation. Paper presented at the Critical Management Studies Conference, Waikato University, 7–9 July 2003).

Inglis, R. and Dall'Alba, G. (1998) The redesign of a management accounting course upon principles for improving the quality of teaching and learning, *Accounting Education: an international journal*, 7(3), pp. 193–207.

Institute of Chartered Accountants in Australia (ICAA) (1994) *Chartered Accountants in the 21st Century: White Paper* (Melbourne: ICAA).

Institute of Chartered Accountants in Australia (ICAA) (1998a) *The Future for Business*, prepared by Chant Link and Associates (Sydney: ICAA).

Institute of Chartered Accountants in Australia (ICAA) (1998b) *The CFO of the Future*, prepared by M. Simister, P. Roest, and J. Sheldon of KPMG for the Chartered Accountants in Business Committee (Sydney: ICAA).

Institute of Chartered Accountants in Australia (ICAA) (2001) *The New CFO of the Future: Finance Functions in the Twenty-first Century*, prepared by M. Simister for KPMG Consulting for the ICAA (Sydney: ICAA).

International Federation of Accountants (IFAC) (2002) *International Education Standard on Professional Skills and General Education* (New York: IFAC).

Institute of Chartered Accountants of England and Wales (ICAEW), Education and Training Committee (1996) *Added Value Professionals: Chartered Accountants in 2005* (London: ICAEW).

Institute of Management Accountants (IMA) (1994) *What Corporate America Wants in Entry-Level Accountants. Executive Summary (with the Financial Executives Institute)* (Montvale, NJ, IMA).

Institute of Management Accountants (IMA) (1996) *The Practice Analysis of Management Accounting: Results of Research* (Montvale, NJ, IMA).

Institute of Management Accountants (IMA) (1999) *Counting More, Counting Less: Transformations in the Management Accounting Profession* (Montvale, NJ, IMA).

Kerr, S. (1975) On the folly of rewarding A, while hoping for B, *The Academy of Management Journal*, 18(4), pp. 769–783.

Kim, T. S., Ghosh, B. C. and Meng, L. A. (1993) Selection criteria: perception gap between employers and accounting graduates, *Singapore Accountant*, 9, pp. 32–33.

Kochanek, R. and Norgaard, C. (1985) Student perceptions of alternative accounting careers – Part II, *The CPA Journal*, 55(6), pp. 26–32.

Lillis, A. M. (1999) A framework for the analysis of interview data from multiple field research sites, *Accounting & Finance*, 39(1), pp. 79–105.

Lindsay, D. H. and Campbell, A. (1995) Accounting research as a determinant of teaching outcomes, *Accounting Perspectives*, 1(2), pp. 39–56.

Manakyan, W. and Tanner, J. R. (1994) Research productivity and teaching effectiveness: accounting faculty perspective, *The Accounting Educators' Journal*, 6, pp. 1–21.

Marriott, P. and Marriot, N. (2003) Are we turning them on? A longitudinal study of undergraduate accounting student's attitudes towards accounting as a profession, *Accounting Education: an international journal*, 12(2), pp. 113–133.

May, G. S., Windal, F. W. and Sylvestre, J. (1995) The need for change in accounting education: an educator survey, *Journal of Accounting Education*, 13(1), pp. 21–43.

Miles, M. B. and Huberman, A. M. (1994) *Qualitative Data Analysis: An Expanded Sourcebook* (Thousand Oaks: Sage).

Millard, P. (2003) Promoting the profession, *Chartered Accountant Journal of New Zealand*, 82(1), p. 13.

Murdoch, B. and Guy, P. W. (2002) Active learning in small and large classes, *Accounting Education: an international journal*, 11(3), pp. 271–282.

Novin, A. M., Fetyko, D. F. and Tucker, J. M. (1997) Perceptions of accounting educators and public accounting practitioners on the composition of 150-hour accounting programs: a comparison, *Issues in Accounting Education*, 2(2), pp. 331–352.

Polster, C. (2000) The future of the liberal university in the era of the global knowledge grab, *Higher Education*, 39(1), pp. 19–41.

Porter, B. A. and Carr, S. A. (1999) From strategic plan to practical realities: developing and implementing a zero-based accounting curriculum, *Issues in Accounting Education*, 14(4), pp. 565–588.

Quality Assurance Agency for Higher Education (QAA) (2000) *Accounting Benchmarks* (Gloucester, QAA).

Riodan, M. P., Pierre, E. K. and Matoney, J. (1996) Some initial empirical evidence regarding the impact of introductory accounting sequence on the selection of accounting as a major, *Accounting Education: A Journal of Theory, Practice and Research*, 1(2), pp. 127–136.

Robert Half International (RHI) (2001) *Next generation accountants*. Available at http://www.nextgenaccountant.com (accessed).

Saemann, G. P. and Crooker, K. J. (1999) Student perceptions of the profession and its effect on decisions to major in accounting, *Journal of Accounting Education*, 17(1), pp. 1–22.

Sander, J. F. and Reding, K. F. (1993) An empirical investigation of entry-level accountants' cognitive abilities, *The Accounting Educators' Journal*, 5(1), pp. 42–54.

Schultz, J. J., Meade, J. A. and Khurana, I. (1989) The changing roles of teaching, research, and service in the promotion and tenure decisions for accounting faculty, *Issues in Accounting Education*, 4(1), pp. 109–119.

Sharma, D. S. (1997) Accounting students' learning conceptions approaches to learning and the influence of the learning-teaching context on approaches to learning, *Accounting Education: an international journal*, 6(2), pp. 125–146.

Shivaswamy, M. K. and Hanks, G. F. (1985a) Accounting education: how students view a career in management accounting, *Management Accounting*, 68(5), pp. 32–34.

Shivaswamy, M. K. and Hanks, G. F. (1985b) Attitudes towards governmental accounting: are students turned off? *The Government Accountants Journal*, 34(3), pp. 58–61.

Simons, K. and Higgins, M. (1993) An examination of practitioners and academics' views on the content of the accounting curriculum, *Accounting Educators' Journal*, 5(1), pp. 24–34.

Simons, K., Higgins, M. and Lowe, D. (1995) A profile of communication apprehension in accounting majors: implication for teaching and curriculum revision, *Journal of Accounting Education*, 13(2), pp. 159–176.

Stice, J. D. and Stocks, K. D. (2000) Effective teaching techniques: perceptions of accounting faculty, *Advances in Accounting Education*, 2, pp. 179–191.

Stout, D. E. and Schweikart, J. A. (1989) The relevance of international accounting to the accounting curriculum: a comparison of practitioner and educator opinions, *Issues in Accounting Education*, 4(1), pp. 126–143.

Street, D. L., Baril, C. P., Benke, R. L. Jr (1993) Research, teaching, and service in promotion and tenure decisions of accounting faculty, *Journal of Accounting Education*, 11(1), pp. 43–60.

Swain, M. R. and Stout, D. E. (2000) Survey evidence of teacher development based on AECC recommendations, *Journal of Accounting Education*, 18(2), pp. 99–113.

Tang, T. L.-P. and Chamberlain, M. (1997) Attitudes toward research and teaching: differences between administrators and faculty members, *Journal of Higher Education*, 68(2), pp. 212–227.

Theuri, P. M. and Gunn, R. (1998) Accounting information systems course structure and employer systems skills expectations, *Journal of Accounting Education*, 16(1), pp. 101–121.

Thompson, P. J. (1995) Competence-based learning and qualifications in the UK, *Accounting Education: an international journal*, 4(1), pp. 5–15.

Watty, K (2005) Quality in accounting education: what say academics? *Quality Assurance in Education*, 13(2), pp. 120–132.

Wolk, C., Schmidt, T. and Sweeney, J. (1997) Accounting educators' problem-solving style and their pedagogical perceptions and preferences, *Journal of Accounting Education*, 15(4), pp. 469–484.

Wooten, T. C. (1998) Factors influencing student learning in introductory accounting classes: a comparison of traditional and non-traditional students, *Issues in Accounting Education*, 13(2), pp. 357–373.

Yin, R. K. (2009) *Case Study Research: Design and Methods*. 4th ed. (Thousand Oaks: Sage Publications Inc).

Accounting Students' Expectations and Transition Experiences of Supervised Work Experience

LOUISE GRACIA

University of Warwick, Coventry, UK

ABSTRACT *Political and economic discourses position employability as a responsibility of higher education, which utilise mechanisms such as supervised work experience (SWE) to embed employability into the undergraduate curriculum. However, sparse investigation of students' contextualised experiences of SWE results in little being known about the mechanisms through which students derive employability benefits from SWE. The aim of this study is to examine the impact of students' expectation and conception of workplace learning on their transition into SWE. Analysis of accounting students' experiences reveal two broad conceptions of workplace learning, the differing impacts of which on transition experience are explored using existing learning transfer perspectives. Students displaying the more common 'technical' conception construct SWE as an opportunity to develop technical, knowledge-based expertise and abilities that prioritize product-based or cognitive learning transfer. Students with an 'experiential' conception were found to construct SWE primarily as an experience through which the development of personal skills and abilities beyond technical expertise are prioritized using process-based or socio-cultural learning transfer. Further data analysis suggests that these two learning transfer approaches have differing impacts on students' employability development which may indicate a need for universities to consider how to develop appropriate student expectations of and approaches to SWE and meaningful support for students' SWE transition.*

Introduction

Enhancing employability has, since the Dearing Report (1997), become a significant aim of undergraduate programmes within UK higher education institutions (HEIs). Increasingly, political and economic agendas link the global competitive strength of

UK industry and commerce to UK HEIs ability to produce skilled and employable graduates. Hence employability, despite having 'an elusive quality ... [with] no precise definition' (Cranmer 2006, p. 169), lies at the centre of contemporary UK higher education.

Supervised work experience (SWE) is one widespread attempt by HEIs to address employability and embed workplace learning into the curriculum. Widely recognized within the UK, much of Europe, and internationally, including the USA (Dykxhoorn and Sinning, 1999), Canada (Ryder and Wilson, 1987), New Zealand (Ahmed *et al.*, 1997), and Australia (Gillen, 1993) as being a desirable component of higher education courses, it usually takes the form of a one-year placement between the second and final years of academic study (typical in the UK, New Zealand and Australia), or shorter periods of three to six months (common in the USA) spread throughout a degree programme.

In contemporary higher education, SWE figures prominently—especially within 'new' (post 1992) universities in the UK, which have a stronger vocational tradition and, particularly, but not confined to, professional courses such as medicine, pharmacy, civil engineering and accountancy. Proponents argue that SWE lends a practical and vocational dimension to study, providing a wider contextual relevance and understanding to classroom-based learning. However, beyond this generalised view, there is little understanding of the mechanisms through which students derive benefit from SWE or how their preconceptions of it impact on their transition into it. Beck and Halim (2008, p. 3) identify a 'paucity of research' into the impact of workplace learning on students and Schaafsma (1996, p. 5) too is critical of the failure to include students' experiences of SWE into understandings of it, such that SWE is 'seldom critically examined—particularly by those who espouse their achievements'. This is problematic since universities, through SWE, routinely despatch large numbers of students into the workplace, yet relatively little is known about the impact of students' conceptions of workplace learning on their transition or subsequent experience of it, nor of its ability to enhance students' employability skills. Moreover, sector massification and the knowledge economy further increase the pressures which higher education (HE) is under to deliver adequate employability development opportunities to students. In this light the need to develop a fuller understanding of the factors that influence SWEs ability to deliver employability development is heightened. This study aims to respond to this by examining students' expectations and transition experiences of SWE within the wider context of developing employability. The key question of this research paper is therefore: How do students' conceptions of SWE influence their transition into and early experiences of SWE as an employability development mechanism within higher education? It follows that the contribution of this study lies in developing a fuller understanding of the ability of SWE to develop students' employability skills, specifically through identifying how students' prior construction of SWE can be more or less effective in enhancing students' employability by influencing their approaches to and subsequent experiences of SWE. The paper therefore addresses academic staff who have responsibility for preparing students for SWE; and students themselves who play an active role in the success or otherwise of SWE.

This paper firstly examines the existing literature on SWE to reveal some of the tensions inherent in understanding its nature and role in developing employability. Student data relating to their expectations, transition and experience of placement learning are subsequently collected via interviews. Two broad student constructions of SWE emerge from the data analysis, the impact of which on students' transition and experiences of SWE are explored.

Literature Review

Within HE, the practice of SWE is widespread (Wallace and Murray, 1999). Furthermore, a National Centre for Work Experience discussion document suggests that, in periods of change (typical of the current knowledge economy which prioritizes softer, transferable skills, over technical knowledge), work experience becomes an essential ingredient of undergraduate programmes assisting students to 'take responsibility for their own learning and thus improve their performance in the market place' (Wallace and Murray, 1999, p. 2). Employability is increasingly viewed as a fundamental graduate characteristic (Quality Assurance Agency, QAA, 2001) which, together with the dynamic demands placed on employees by the knowledge economy and increasing numbers of students entering higher education, intensifies competition within the graduate employment market. Therefore graduates, more than ever, need to develop employability skills as a means of deriving a competitive employment edge, causing the demands placed on SWE in delivering employability within HE to be heightened (Harvey *et al.*, 1997, p. 3).

Most research in the area attempts to identify the personal and professional skills developed through work experience (National Centre for Work Experience, 1999, p. 2). The employability benefits of SWE, including the application of knowledge, self-development, an understanding of the language and culture of organisations and increased self-confidence (Hawkins *et al.*, 1999, p. 4) are well-documented within the literature. Other studies include the views of SWE employers who identify 'the ability to seek out information; problem-solving ability; and ability to work on one's own without supervision ... numeracy; written communication skills; formal presentation skills [and] team-working skills' (Mason *et al.*, 2003, p. 2) as being key employability features.

Despite having some understanding of the characteristics of employability Harvey (2001) identifies a number of difficulties concerning the measurement of such outcomes centring on the evaluation criteria used. Auburn (2007, p. 118) also questions the findings of such studies in that 'one of the main difficulties for evaluating SWE has been the lack of an accepted model of it as part of the undergraduate curriculum'.

In this work Auburn is critical of existing models—the 'magic ingredient model' (where SWE is the magic input ingredient for the output of employable graduates) and the 'role transition model' (where SWE is viewed as one input element of a developmental process the output of which is employable graduates). The former is criticised for its simplistic view of the role of SWE, what Auburn (2007, p. 118) describes as its inability to address 'how supervised work experience engages with other components of the student's programme of study ... [and] tends towards a rhetoric of unalloyed goodness relating to supervised work experience'.

Similarly, criticisms of the role transition model centre around its failure to consider the management of students' role transitions from learning to work leading to a 'mechanistic understanding of placement learning' (Auburn 2007, p. 120). As such neither model focuses on how students construct their understanding of the experiential process of SWE in a meaning-making process. Indeed, within the literature there are numerous gaps in our understanding of SWE of which Zemblyas (2006, p. 291) provides an extensive list including: 'knowledge production in action, the interrelation of contexts and knowledge, the dynamics of continual change, politics and power relations, subjectivity and ethics and knowledge processes in work and organizations'. It is perhaps unsurprising therefore that there are no reported studies of the impact of students' prior construction of SWE on their subsequent experiences of it *per se*. A few studies do consider issues of transition into employment, but from the perspective of school-leavers or graduates. Moreover, such studies ignore personal or experiential factors, and focus instead on a range of issues including the reporting of first destination employment statistics, the influence of work patterns on employment transition (Try, 2004), the impact of demographic factors on employment choices and employability (Tomlinson, 2007), and the development of efficient employer induction programmes (Pare and Le Maistre, 2006). Furthermore, such studies have been criticised for considering SWE after the event (Knight, 2001) and therefore ignoring transition, or for ignoring students within discussions of employment and employability linked to SWE (Morley, 2001).

Brown (2002) argues that the lack of consideration of young people's experiences of transition into employment results in a positive skew within the reporting of studies of SWE, where weak evidence is used to support it with considerable downplay of the negative experiences of it (Duignan, 2003). This problematic position has resulted in calls for a meaningful consideration of students' experiences of SWE (Auburn, 2007) that creates a 'richer conceptualisation of young people's transition into work' (Vaughan and Roberts, 2007, p. 91).

Therefore a need for studies that include the influence of students' conceptions of work place learning on subsequent transition experiences of SWE is identified within the literature. This research responds to this need by exploring students' construction of SWE and examining how these different constructions frame and influence their transition into and early experiences of SWE. This approach therefore offers a broader understanding of students' SWE transition and experience beyond simplistic outcome-based and static based models. This is considered important since, in common with any change experience, the transition phase is identified as key to expediting successful learning transfer (Mann, 2001). This initial transition into SWE is therefore likely to be pivotal in stimulating the potentially positive outcomes of SWE thereby influencing the access to opportunities for students to integrate theoretical learning from the academic environment to the practical experience of workplace learning. The effectiveness of this transition will depend upon the students themselves as well as upon institutions and their representatives responsible for facilitating students' transfer, hence the transition phase of students' placement learning, although under-researched, may be important in contributing to our understanding of employability development.

Methodology

This research takes place within a UK Business School and is based on second year students ($n = 30$) enrolled on the BA (Hons) degree in Accounting and Finance who undertook an optional 48 week period of SWE between their second and final (third) years of study.

This study is concerned with understanding the impact of students' prior expectations and learning conceptions on their SWE transition and subsequent employability development. Students' SWE experiences do not take place within a workplace vacuum but are influenced by pre-existing dispositions and attitudes including their learning conceptions, and data is required that facilitates deep insights into students' experiences from within their own frame of reference. Through the analysis of such data, I seek to offer explanations or accounts of students' workplace learning that focuses on the meaning within, rather than the measurement of, their SWE experiences. This lends itself to a qualitative or phenomenological research approach in order to capture the complexity and intricacy of the subjective and personal meanings within students' experiences, and draws on the techniques of grounded theory (Glaser and Strauss, 1967) where theory emerges from the data analysis.

Student data concerning their expectations of and transition into SWE were collected via semi-structured interviews, which Easterby-Smith, Thorpe and Lowe (1991) suggest are useful in revealing interviewees' subjective reality or perceptions of a social phenomenon. Exponents of semi-structured interviewing place emphasis on their exploratory ability through open discovery (Hussey and Hussey, 1997) that facilitates the exploration of human experiences, feelings and attitudes at a deep level (Easterby-Smith *et al.*, 1991). Within the interviews, respondents were encouraged to tell their story (Reinharz, 1992) creating oral, personal narratives or accounts of their learning conception and SWE experiences. Gubrium and Holstein (1997) find personal narratives effective in eliciting personal experiences and, for this reason, questions to participants were specifically designed to elicit narratives of their personal experience and encourage reflection on those experiences, using the semi-structured nature of the encounter to provide a loose framework. The intention was to pursue 'thick descriptions' (Patton, 1987) of how participants saw the issues around SWE. Open-ended questions were used to probe aspects of the students' narratives to maximise discovery and description and allow the participants to shape the flow and structure of their account. Infrequently used within accounting research, Haynes (2008) argues for the use of narratives within accounting research with participants who are frequently voiceless—such as SWE students (see Brown, 2002).

Mason *et al.* (2003) suggest that measuring the transfer of employability skills should focus on students' early experience of SWE to avoid the impact of the workplace itself on the transition experience. To allow for this, students were interviewed immediately prior to the commencement of their period of SWE (to collect expectations data) and again six weeks into placement (to collect transition data). Interviews varied in length from approximately 45 to 90 min.

An interview schedule was drawn up, designed to explore the issues of expectations, transition and experience. Each interview was recorded and transcribed verbatim, the transcripts being read through several times to gain initial familiarity with the data. The data was subsequently analysed using a series of coding steps beginning with open coding where the data was broken down and initial categories ascribed to the data. Links between categories were then explored through axial coding allowing the identification of the conditions under which categories occur and the impact of these to be recorded. Finally, selective coding was used where key or main categories emerged to capture the meaning from the data analysis.

The analytical process uses an inductive 'method of difference' approach—where, other things being equal, different effects (transition into and experiences of SWE) are considered to arise from different causes (different student learning constructions). This has some significant limitations, not least of which being that human behaviour is so complex it undermines simplistic cause and effect relationships. However, this study is not concerned with testing particular hypotheses but rather sets out to explore how patterns of expectation and construction influence students' transition experiences and how these experiences subsequently impact issues of employability. Therefore, this approach is useful in exploring the potential existence and implications of any linkages between students' prior learning construction and SWE transition experiences rather than seek to prove that one event is the cause of another.

Data were collected from a sample of 30 students within one institution whose main subject of study was accounting. These characteristics potentially limit the general applicability of the findings of this study. However, as noted above, this study is based in grounded theory as opposed to a positivist framework and aims to explore and interpret the personal employment experiences of students. Accordingly, participants were selected to exemplify different facets of student conception and subsequent experience rather than to form a representative group or sample of a specific population. The selection of participants was therefore made on the basis of theoretical interest rather than random sampling. As a consequence, limitations surrounding students being drawn from a single cohort within one program of study from one Business School are mitigated. Notwithstanding this, the phenomenological approach does not preclude generalisations being made from the data. Norman (1970) supports the possibility of generalizing from very few, or even a single case, to other settings, if the analysis captures the interactions and characteristics of the phenomena under study. As a result it may be possible to generalise the results of this study to SWE students across other HEIs or to inform understanding generally of the issues surrounding students' SWE transition and subsequent employability skills development.

The data analysis that follows initially explores students' expectations of placement learning and conception of workplace learning. It progresses to consider how differing conceptions impact upon students' SWE transition experiences and employability development.

Results and Discussion of Findings

Approximately 85% of the student group were aged 20 years, commencing their degree studies directly after 'A' levels (or equivalent university entry qualifications) with no prior work experience. Students' SWE took place in a variety of business organisations, ranging from small accounting practices to public sector organisations and large accounting firms, thus data are drawn from students with a wide exposure of accounting SWE that itself offers a first introduction to the world of work, but more importantly presents what may be the only opportunity which many students have to develop work-based skills prior to graduating and seeking full-time employment.

The age, gender and prior work experience profiles of the students interviewed are given in Table 1. In addition the grade point average (GPA scale of 0 to 6) for students within the sample for their second year of studies ranged from 3.6 to 5.2 with an average GPA of 4.4. This compared to an average of 4.3 for the remainder of the cohort.

Expectations and Construction of SWE

To assist the understanding of the reader, the number of students identifying each of the key themes discussed below is indicated as a rating out of a maximum of 30 ($\times/30$). In addition, the frequency of each key theme across all and within individual students' accounts is summarised in Appendix 1.

The analysis of students' expectations of SWE reveals a number of commonalities, the most frequent being that of 'making myself more employable' (27/30), followed by an opportunity to 'help me decide if I want a full time career in accounting' (22/30) as a

Table 1. Student profiles

Age Groups (Years)	Number	Number with prior work experience
18–20	25	0
21–23	2	1
24 to 26	2	1
Over 26	1	1

$n = 30$, nationality = British, gender: 21 male, 9 female.

means of testing out career choices. That students had enrolled on a vocationally-based degree may imply the intention to pursue an accountancy career. However, research evidence suggests that students decide on a course of study for a variety of reasons many of which use 'vague or negatively focused reasoning' (Gracia and Jenkins 2002, p. 104) including pressure from family and friends, a failure to achieve the grades for other programmes of study or merely drifting into courses. It is evident that the subject of undergraduate study and career interests do not necessarily coincide. Findings here support this and provide some insight into the career uncertainty which students experience even within vocationally-based subject areas.

A further common theme within students' expectations is the lack of certainty about the experience (28/30): 'I don't really know what to expect'; 'I've never had a job before, so the whole thing feels like a step into the unknown'. Analysis reveals that these uncertainties give rise to a number of anxieties: 'I feel very nervous about it . . . I'm not sure I'll fit in (17/30) or be able to cope (13/30)'. Students are also concerned about being accepted into this new environment: 'I don't want to feel on the outside of things' (16/30), or not enjoying the experience: 'I'm worried I won't like it' (11/30), or of failing to be successful within it: 'I'm anxious that I won't be any good at the job, be useless and just feel like a failure' (24/30). Richardson and Blakeney (1998) conclude that SWE is frequently a 'painful' experience for students. The identification of students' anxieties within this study supports and supplements this finding, providing an indication of the nature of the 'pain' experienced in relation to fitting in, being able to cope, unfamiliarity with employers' expectations, feeling accepted, not enjoying the experience and of feeling a failure.

Students' accounts of their expectations of SWE are littered with emotional language, descriptions of feelings and anxieties concerning their transition into SWE, indicating a strong affective or emotional dimension to SWE transition. Frequently, HEIs SWE support for students focuses on the provision of factual information and guidance which treats SWE transition as a cognitive or intellectual process. However, students' accounts are inconsistent with this, demonstrating that it is a much broader, whole person experience including the affective as well as cognitive realms. If HEIs are concerned about providing meaningful SWE support to students (in terms of preparing them for it and undertaking it) it may be helpful to recognize the nature and extent of their uncertainty, concerns and anxieties in order to better understand the type of support that is required.

Beyond these commonalities, exploring students' accounts of their expectations reveal some prominent differences in terms of workplace learning conception—the students' views or construction of their learning. Dahlgren and Marton (1978) identified two broad categories of learning conception, each having a different orientation, which were developed by others, most notably Marton *et al.* (1993). The polarisation of students into two types of learning approach, conception or mode is a well-established practice within the education literature, mirrored in the work of amongst others, Fromm (1982) who identified two modes of learning termed 'having' and 'being'; Ramsden (1987) who identified two main approaches to learning (namely deep and surface); and Mann (2001) who formulated two alternative approaches to learning (namely alienated and engaged).

Within this study, the classification of students into two categories of learning conception (termed 'technical' and 'experiential'), followed the principles suggested by Saljo (1979) that students should be categorised on the basis of their own personal descriptions of their learning, by identifying dominant strands of description. Moreover, students' positioning within a particular category (at least in the short- to medium-term) is relatively, though not entirely, fixed (Flood and Wilson, 2002). The potential for movement does exist, but requires a degree of personal change and self-development occurring over time.

Technical Conception ($n = 21$)

Analysis of students' accounts reveal that most (21/30) fall within this category, typified by the following characteristics:

- Prioritize practical skills: 'I think it's important to focus on developing my technical expertise ... to get some practice of doing accounting' (15/21).
- View SWE as providing knowledge—a product to be received: 'I'm hoping to learn things that I can take away and use at other times when I might need them' (16/21).
- Describe their contribution to the experience of SWE as restricted to an ability to 'remember and apply what I already know so that I can be useful' (17/21).
- Consider SWE in terms of its potential to 'increase my technical accountancy knowledge', and 'improve my degree results' (19/21).
- Hold a relatively simplistic understanding of the role of work experience in developing employability: 'I don't think employers are that bothered about what skills you have ... what they are looking for is that you have worked and you can work' (12/21).

Experiential Conception ($n = 9$)

Fewer students fell within this category (9/30), characterised by:

- Prioritize the process of learning: 'I think the whole experience is more important than the day-to-day things I'll be doing' (8/9).
- Recognize SWE as an experience: 'I want to learn about the whole experience of work, not just focus on the technical stuff' (7/9).
- Position employment as fluid and dynamic: 'Work these days is changing all the time so it's important to be able to adapt and change quickly, to respond to what is going on around you' (5/9).
- View themselves as active participants in their SWE: 'I want to show my employer how useful I am ... make a difference within the organization, really make a contribution' (8/9).
- Demonstrate awareness of the workplace context: 'It's important to be aware of the nature of the business you work in, and what the organisation is trying to achieve ..., otherwise you won't be as effective as you should be' (5/9).
- Understand the importance of soft or transferable skills development: 'Working should help me to become better organized ... maybe get better at time management' (6/9).
- Recognize SWE as an opportunity to engage in self-development beyond technical skills: 'It may transform me and the way I think ... not just about accounting but also about myself' (8/9).

The next stage of the analysis explores the impact that the two identified conceptions of workplace learning have on students' SWE transition experiences.

Transition Experiences

For all students, regardless of their learning conception, the expectation that SWE has the potential to be a 'painful' experience is evident within their transition experiences: 'Everything is very new and strange ... I don't know how everything works, or what I'm supposed to be doing a lot of the time' (26/30). Some describe the impact of this on their self-confidence; 'I'm normally quite a confident person, but I feel a bit out of my depth and I tend to keep myself to myself' (19/30). Students understood that some of these early difficulties stem from their lack of understanding of what is expected of them within SWE: 'I don't really feel like I know what is going on or what I should be doing': 'It's a bit like being dumped in a foreign land and not being able to speak the language or understand what is going on around you' (23/30). This suggests that HEIs and employers may need to be more explicit and inclusive about the expectations of SWE they hold for students. A more collaborative, partnership approach based on shared objectives may enhance students' understanding of what is required of them, reducing transition 'pain' and promoting more effective skills development.

Students' isolation is further exacerbated by the poor levels of support they report from their HEI supervisors: 'I haven't seen my supervisor yet . . . I feel a bit abandoned here . . . like the university have just forgotten about me'; 'I had a meeting with my supervisor yesterday, but he wasn't very helpful . . . I'm finding it hard to settle in here but he just ignored what I was saying . . . he wasn't interested in talking about how I was feeling' (20/30). HEIs need to support students more effectively during their SWE perhaps in terms of moving away from individual learning transfer towards a more integrated approach between students, employers and universities. Such a shift would create different knowledge and practices based on shared objectives—what Konkola *et al.* (2007, p. 2) describe as 'a collective conceptualisation of transfer', prioritizing integration of theory and practice across sector boundaries thereby supporting students' transfer into SWE.

Turning the analysis to the comparison of the transition experiences of students with differing experiential and technical conceptions of SWE reveals a number of differences, explored through current understandings of learning transfer within education theory. Learning transfer is essentially concerned with the application and development of knowledge, skills, ability and practice across sector boundaries such as exist between higher education and the workplace.

Findings suggest that students with a technical construction lean towards a cognitive learning transfer approach. Here learning transfer occurs through the application or adaptation of relevant and known relational patterns from prior academic learning (either theoretical or practical) in order to solve current problems or issues: 'At work I try to remember what I have learnt and look at how I could apply that to the current situation'; 'I tend to rely on what I already know and draw on it to help me' (17/21). Students within this conception are reluctant to use more creative, flexible or intuitive approaches to workplace learning: 'I don't think it is appropriate for me to think too much for myself here . . . it's more about using what I know to be useful' (12/21). 'Technical' students thus favour cognitive learning transfer that relies on the recognition and recall of pre-existing patterns of understanding or knowledge (mental schemas) and their modification.

Criticisms or limitations of such cognitive learning transfer centre around its static quality, 'taking a given item and applying it somewhere else' Konkola *et al.* (2007, p. 212) largely in isolation from the socio-cultural context of the situation (Hatano and Greeno, 1999). Students with a technical conception may not recognize the value which the socio-cultural context of their SWE presents, in terms of developing valuable employability skills such as communication and personal skills: 'I don't think it matters where you do your placement . . . you can learn accountancy skills wherever you are': 'Accountancy is really about being good with numbers and understanding the rules so I don't focus so much on the people around me or the organisation too much'. This approach has implications for employability development which the literature suggests is not focused on technical knowledge but encompasses wider softer or transferable skills, highly regarded by employers (HEFCE, 2003). Consequently, students with a technical conception may not be positioned to exploit fully SWEs usefulness in developing employability skills.

In contrast 'experiential' students who recognize the importance of soft skills may be better placed to use SWE to develop employability skills.

The majority of students (21/30) within this study are categorised with a technical conception of SWE, which is perhaps unsurprising given the finding of Konkola *et al.* (2007) that higher education itself prioritizes cognitive transfer as its dominant learning approach, placing emphasis on individuals' acquisition of knowledge rather than situated learning. This may warrant consideration by HEIs of the impact of its learning transfer approach on employability development indirectly, through its engagement with and shaping of students' learning approaches. The impact of higher education's dominant approach to learning on students' learning conceptions is an area requiring further research.

In contrast, learning transfer for experiential students is more consistent with a socio-cultural approach. Here learning results from the movement across the boundaries of different activity contexts, such as higher education and the workplace; 'The best thing about being here is that I am learning about how the nature of a particular business type impacts on the way accountancy is done'; 'The way we learn things in class is totally different to how things are really done in practice ... it's good to be able to experience new ways of doing things' (7/9).

Students with an experiential construct recognize that learning transfer is an active and engaged phenomenon; 'You have to just get stuck in and not worry too much about not knowing enough' (5/9). Students here understand learning transfer as including personal development: 'I'm learning more about myself and how I need to be to be successful as I am about accounting' (8/9). Such comments are characteristic of a socio-cultural approach to learning transfer which Konkola *et al* (2007, p. 214) describe as being 'multi-dimensional and reciprocal ... [where] it is not only the knowledge that moves, but the entire human being, including his or her identity and social participation, changes as well'. Such an approach positions SWE beyond knowledge transfer to include engaged personal development which may enable such students to more readily develop employability skills.

Drawing on the work of Mann (2001) provides a further opportunity to consider the impact of different students' conceptions on SWE transition. Mann (2001) identifies two arguably rational responses by students to their transition into higher education—namely alienated and engaged: 'Most students entering the new world of the academy are in an equivalent position to those crossing the borders of a new country .. they may have limited knowledge of the local language, and are alone ... the experience of alienation arises from being in a place where those in power have the potential to impose their particular ways of perceiving and understanding the world' (2001, p. 11). Extending this, it is arguable that students' transition into SWE—where they have to negotiate a 'new world' of employment with limited knowledge of the language, procedures, and rules that exist, finding themselves in a strange place surrounded by employers and workmates whose power relations and cultural understandings impose unspoken ways of being on them—may be just as engaging or alienating, the latter having the capacity to compromise the value of SWE to students. Moreover, findings of this study suggest that students with different conceptions of SWE display differing general patterns of SWE transition experience. This is significant since Mann (2001, p. 11) suggests that students who respond positively to transition, engaging with it, are better able to derive benefit from the experience than those who do not assimilate their new environment as readily and become alienated from it.

Within this study, students with an experiential construction of SWE demonstrate greater flexibility and creativity during their transition; 'I have adapted really quickly to the way they do things here ... you have to be responsive'; 'I learned really quickly that I had to think on my feet and be able to be flexible to what was going on around me'; 'The best bit has been being able to think outside of what I know . . . use my initiative to make decisions' (8/9). An experiential disposition may enable students to respond more readily to their workplace environments, rapidly adapting to the new experience. They also indicate a general openness to change: 'I've realized that what I have learnt in university so far is not the whole picture . . . things are different in the real world and you have to be able to accept that difference and work with it not against it'(6/9). Students with an experiential conception also tend to express transition as being a more engaged experience: 'I'm really enjoying it'; 'Working here gives me a good feeling . . . I feel like I'm really coming into my own now' (7/9).

By contrast, students with a technical conception are more likely to describe their workplace transition using language that indicates an alienated experience. They express more resistance (in comparison to their experiential peers) to the changes that placement learning brings, with a tendency to oppose this change and struggle with assimilating the new environment or activities that contradict or challenge their existing understanding: 'Its difficult to get used to things here. They do things differently to what we have learned and I find that confusing'; 'I struggle with reconciling what I have learnt with how things are really done in practice. It would be a lot easier if they had just taught us how things really are in the first place' (14/21). Students' response to change is less positive and indicates some resistance to it: 'I don't like the way they do things here . . . I wish they did things the way I know how to . . . I don't want to have to relearn what I already know!' (10/21). This may suggest inadequate consideration of the context of their SWE and its impact on practices, creating difficulty in negotiating the boundary between higher education and workplace learning for these students.

It is evident that a technical construction may encourage a level of dissatisfaction with SWE that leads to a more alienated experience and compromises students' ability to maximise the potential to be drawn from SWE: 'I'm not very happy with the whole thing really . . . it's difficult to fit in and I'm not sure it's the best use of my time' (13/21).

Conclusion

Findings of this study suggest that students commonly anticipate SWE with some degree of uncertainty of what is expected of them together with a range of emotional anxieties (e.g. a fear of failure) which contribute towards the 'pain' of transition. This suggests that SWE transition is as much an emotional process as it is an intellectual one, which has implications for the type of support (including affective as well as cognitive dimensions) and timing of it, that is required of HEIs, particularly given that many students identify current HEI support during their early SWE as being inadequate.

Using existing patterns of students' learning conceptions, student data was analysed to classify students into two distinct categories—'technical' and 'experiential'. Students with an experiential conception were found to frame SWE as a dynamic, context-specific experience with which they actively engage, to prioritize the development of soft, transferable skills in a process of personal development. In contrast, findings indicate that students with a technical conception frame SWE as a practical, knowledge-producing event within which they are largely passive recipients of packages of knowledge.

Analysis indicates that students with a technical conception favour a cognitive approach to learning transfer. In contrast, students with an experiential conception tend towards a socio-cultural learning transfer that recognizes the relationship between the individual and the context of the workplace learning, and identifies situated learning as an active and engaged process. The cognitive approach to learning transfer is linked, within the literature, to restricted levels of creativity and flexibility and this is supported by the findings of this study which also indicate that such 'technical' students experience a more alienated SWE transition experience in comparison to 'experiential' students, which may subsequently distance 'technical' students from SWEs employability-enhancing potential.

In addition, this study finds that students with a technical disposition are not as explorative as their experiential counterparts. It seems likely that, drawing on the work of Barnett (2004), technically-focussed students arguably engage with SWE on an epistemological basis that prioritizes knowledge acquisition, whereas experiential narratives suggest an affinity with SWE that uses an ontological basis that priorities self-development. This is significant, since although research evidence suggests that work experience develops both hard and soft skills, the current knowledge economy (and employers) prioritize the latter, as knowledge becomes rapidly outdated. Therefore, 'technical' students who view and engage with work experience to improve their (hard) practical and technical accountancy skills may miss the opportunity to improve desirable soft skills and hence fail to maximise the 'value-added' potential of SWE in terms of developing employability skills. Unlike their experiential peers, they may find it more difficult to 'make sense' of SWE in a way that enhances personal development and hence employability. Given this finding, HEIs may need to consider how best to collaboratively engage with their students to encourage an experiential, process-based conception of workplace learning amongst those students, where the technical and personal components of learning are integrated. This would support students in being responsive to the current diverse and rapidly changing employment market.

References

Ahmed, K., Alam, K. F. and Alam, M. (1997) An empirical study of factors affecting accounting students' career choice in New Zealand, *Accounting Education: an international Journal*, 6(4), pp. 325–339.

Auburn, T. (2007) Identity and placement learning: student accounts of the transition back to university following a placement year, *Studies in Higher Education*, 32(1), pp. 117–133.

Barnett, R. (2004) Learning for an unknown future, *Higher Education Research and Development*, 23(3), pp. 247–260.

Beck, J. E. and Halim, H. (2008) Undergraduate internships in accounting: what and how do Singapore interns learn from experience? *Accounting Education: an international Journal*, 17(2), pp. 151–172.

Brown, M. (2002) Feeling like a fully fledged psychologist, *The Psychologist*, 15(12), pp. 629–630.

Cranmer, S. (2006) Enhancing graduate employability: best intentions and mixed outcomes, *Studies In Higher Education*, 31(2), pp. 169–184.

Dahlgren, L. and Marton, F. (1978) Students' conceptions of subject matter: an aspect of learning and teaching in higher education, *Studies in Higher Education*, 3(1), pp. 25–35.

Dearing Report (1997) *Higher Education in the Learning Society—report of the National Committee of Inquiry into Higher Education* (London: National Committee of Inquiry into Higher Education).

Dykxhoorn, H. J. and Sinning, K. E. (1999) Perceptions of master of accountancy graduates concerning their job search and employment experiences with public accounting firms, *Journal of Accounting Education*, 14(4), pp. 415–434.

Duignan, J. (2003) Placement and adding value to the academic performance of undergraduates; reconfiguring the architecture—an empirical investigation, *Journal of Vocational Education and Training*, 55(3), pp. 335–350.

Easterby-Smith, M., Thorpe, R. and Lowe, A. (1991) *Management Research: An Introduction* (London: Sage).

Flood, B. and Wilson, R. M. S. (2002) *Conceptions of Learning of Prospective Professional Accountants*, Paper presented at the British Accounting Association Annual Conference, April, 2002, Jersey.

Fromm, F. (1982) *To Have Or To Be?—A New Blueprint for Mankind* (London: Abacus).

Gillen, M. (1993) New models of co-operative education in Australia. Proceedings of the 8th World Conference on Co-operative Education, Dublin City University, pp. 43–44 .

Glaser, B. J. and Strauss, A. (1967) *The Discovery of Grounded Theory* (Chicago: Aldine).

Gracia, L. and Jenkins, E. (2002) An exploration of students' failure on an undergraduate accounting programme of study, *Accounting Education: an international Journal*, 11(1), pp. 93–107.

Gubrium, J. F. and Holstein, J. A. (1997) *The New Language of Qualitative Method* (Oxford: Oxford University Press).

Harvey, L. (2001) Defining and measuring employability, *Quality in Higher Education*, 7, pp. 99–109.

Harvey, L., Moon, S. and Gaell, V. (1997) *Graduates Work: Organisational Change and Students Attribute*, (Centre for Research & Quality) (Birmingham: University of Central England).

Hatano, G. and Greeno, J. G. (1999) Commentary: Alternative perspectives on transfer studies, *International Journal of Educational Research*, 31, pp. 645–654.

Hawkins, P., Butcher, V. and Jackson, P. (1999) *Making the most of Work Experience* (London: The National Centre for Work Experience).

Haynes, K. (2008) Transforming identities: accounting professionals and the transition to motherhood, *Critical Perspectives on Accounting*, 19(5), pp. 620–642.

HEFCE (2003) *Widening Participation Initiative 2000–02. The Graduate Employability Project: enhancing employability of non-traditional students.* Available at http://www.londonmet.as.uk/gem (accessed 15 October 2006).

Hussey, J. and Hussey, R. (1997) *Business Research: A Practical Guide for Undergraduate and Postgraduate Students* (Basingstoke: Macmillan).

Konkola, R., Tuomi-Grohn, T., Lambert, P. and Ludvigsen, S. (2007) Promoting learning and transfer between school and workplace, *Journal of Education and Work*, 20(3), pp. 211–228.

Knight, P. T. (2001) Employability and quality, *Quality in Higher Education*, 7(2), pp. 93–95.

Mann, S. (2001) Alternative perspectives on the student experience: alienation and engagement, *Studies in Higher Education*, 26(1), pp. 7–19.

Marton, F., Dall'alba, G. and Beaty, E. (1993) Conceptions of learning, *International Journal of Educational Research*, 19, pp. 277–300.

Mason, G., Williams, G., Cranmer, S. and Guile, D. (2003) *How Much Does Higher Education Enhance the Employability of Graduates?* (London: Higher Education Funding Council for England).

Morley, L. (2001) Producing new workers: quality, equality and employability in higher education, *Quality in Higher Education*, 7(2), pp. 131–138.

National Centre for Work Experience (1999) *The Value of Work Experience for Undergraduates—A Discussion Paper for Higher Education Institutions* (London: The National Centre for Work Experience).

Norman, D. A. (1970) *Models of Human Memory* (New York: Academic Press).

Pare, A. and Le Maistre, C. (2006) Active learning in the workplace: transforming individual and institutions, *Journal of Education and Work*, 19(4), pp. 363–381.

Patton, M. Q. (1987) *How to Use Qualitative Methods in Evaluation* (Newbury Park, California: Sage).

Quality Assurance Agency (2001) *The Framework for Higher Education in England, Wales and Northern Ireland.* Available at http://qaa.ac.uk/crnwork/nqf/ewni2001.html (accessed 2 February 2008).

Ramsden, P. (1987) Improving teaching and learning in higher education: the case for a relational perspective, *Studies in Higher Education*, 12(3), pp. 275–286.

Reinharz, S. (1992) *Feminist Methods in Social Research* (Oxford: Oxford University Press).

Richardson, S. and Blakeney, C. (1998) The Undergraduate Placement System: an empirical study, *Accounting Education: an international Journal*, 7(2), pp. 101–121.

Ryder, K. G. and Wilson, J. W. (1987) *Cooperative Education in a New Era. Understanding and Strengthening the Links between College and the Workplace* (San Francisco: Jossey Bass).

Saljo, D. (1979) Learning in the learner's perspective, *Reports from the Department of Education* (Sweden: Goteborg University, No. 76).

Schaafsma, H. (1996) Back to the real world: work placements revisited, *Education and Training*, 38(1), pp. 5–13.

Tomlinson, M. (2007) Graduate employability and student attributes and orientations to the labour market, *Journal of Education and Work*, 20(4), pp. 285–304.

Try, S. (2004) The role of flexible work in the transition from higher education into the labour market, *Journal of Education and Work*, 17(1), pp. 27–43.

Vaughan, K. and Roberts, J. (2007) Developing a 'productive' account of young people's transition perspectives, *Journal of Education and Work*, 20(2), pp. 91–105.

Wallace, R. and Murray, B. (1999) *Good Practice in Industrial Work Placement* (Nottingham: Nottingham Trent University), Available at http://science.ntu.ac.uk/chph/improve/gpiwp.html (accessed 14 February 2007).

Zemblyas, M. (2006) Work-based learning, power and subjectivity; creating space for a Foucaudian research ethic, *Journal of Education and Work*, 19(3), pp. 291–303.

Appendix 1

Analysis of Key Themes

Table A1.

Key theme	Number of students identifying theme	Total number of times theme identified within all accounts
Expectation		
Enhance employability	27	127
Test out career choice	22	121
Fitting in	17	109
Ability to cope	13	88
Being accepted	16	119
Enjoying SWE	11	57
Uncertain of employer expectations	21	129
Failure	24	113
Transition		
Feelings of 'newness'	26	131
Self-confidence	19	114
Lack of understanding of role	23	128
Inadequate mentor support	20	116
SWE as a process	8	66
SWE as an experience	7	69
Need to adapt and be responsive	5	71
Active participation	8	94
Awareness of context	5	53
Soft/transferable skills	6	72
Flexibility and creativity	8	86
Openness to change	7	77
Technical expertise	19	109
Practice of accounting	16	101
SWE as knowledge	16	94
Application/adaptation of existing knowledge	17	122
Experience new ways of learning/doing	7	85
Engaged process	5	49
SWE as self-development	8	92
Struggling with change	14	102
Resisting change	10	81

A Whole-of-program Approach to the Development of Generic and Professional Skills in a University Accounting Program

LESLEY WILLCOXSON, MONTE WYNDER and GREGORY K. LAING

University of the Sunshine Coast, Queensland, Australia

ABSTRACT *This paper describes a strategy for conducting a whole-of-program review of the teaching of generic skills in a university Accounting program. Importantly, the strategy also builds the longer-term capacity of accounting staff to maintain the relevance and coherence of their program. In a systematic process, Accounting staff first map the courses they teach, ensuring alignment between generic skills and objectives, and objectives and teaching and assessment activities. On the basis of the individual course maps, an Accounting program map is then developed. The information contained in the program map is subsequently analysed to provide data about the depth to which generic skills are being taught. This analysis underpins a review of the teaching of generic skills by all academic staff teaching on the Accounting program and, as discussed, can lead to changes in objectives, teaching activities and teaching methods. The strategy thus builds in academic staff an awareness of and the capacity to apply effective course design principles while at the same time improving generic skill learning outcomes for students.*

Introduction

Universities around the world continue to face pressure from governments and the professions to demonstrate accountability for outcomes, particularly with regard to competency-based education in the vocational training sector (Curry & Wergin, 1993; Daigle *et al.*, 2007). Over the past decade most universities in Australia have responded by embarking upon the task of defining the attributes or generic skills that their graduates will develop as a consequence of their studies. Paralleling this movement within the education sector generally, over the past decade or so the Accounting profession throughout the world has been engaged in defining the competencies required for successful workplace performance by accountants. This has inevitably led to a focus upon the adequacy of university accounting education as preparation for employment in the accounting profession and, in turn, has led to a discussion of what may be done within universities to assure accounting graduate outcomes.

This paper describes an educationally sound process for:

1. linking the requirements of the accounting profession to the graduate attributes defined by a university;
2. systematically ensuring that all courses[1] in a university Accounting program contribute to the development of required professional competencies and graduate attributes; and
3. addressing 'assurance of learning' requirements (of accrediting bodies such as AACSB[2]) by directly relating course and program objectives to teaching and assessment[3] activities.

It begins by providing a brief overview of the diverse educational contexts within which 'competencies' and 'graduate attributes' are implemented, and of some of the difficulties associated with implementation. Following this, professional competencies in Accounting are discussed, with reference to the impact of these upon accounting programs in universities and to the strategies advanced to incorporate them into the curriculum. Finally, the paper presents a detailed description of a strategy that has enabled a university Accounting program to engage in a collegial review of its curriculum and identify changes deriving from professional body, institutional and educational notions of 'best practice'.

The Muddied Waters of Competencies and Attributes

Before commencing a discussion of 'competencies' and 'graduate attributes', it is necessary to acknowledge that the meaning of these terms is contested. Depending upon the context of their use – professional, vocational training or higher education—they may be construed positively or negatively, as atomistic or holistic, and used variously as synonyms for 'generic skills', 'professional skills', 'employability skills', 'graduate outcomes', 'graduate capabilities', 'transferable skills', or 'core skills' (Clanchy and Ballard, 1995; De La Harpe *et al.*, 2000; van Schalkwyk, 2002; James *et al.*, 2004). Broadly speaking, however, 'competencies' have generally been associated with the requirements of vocational training and professional bodies while 'graduate attributes' (or outcomes or capabilities) have been associated with university education (Barrie, 2005; Cranmer, 2006), especially in Australia where, since 1998, the national government has required every university to produce a statement of 'graduate attributes'. Accompanying this sectoral differentiation in terminology has been a focus on atomistic definitions of required behaviours versus more holistic definitions expressing capacity in a general area. For example, Birkett's detailed 1993 specification of competency-based standards for professional accountants in Australia and New Zealand is in contrast to broad outcomes such as 'an interested and enquiring mind capable of critical judgement' and 'graduates will be effective problem solvers' (capacities developed within Sydney University and the University of New England, respectively).

Fundamentally, as Boritz and Carnaghan (2003) point out, the two approaches reflect, respectively, an output-based analysis of functional behaviours required in the workplace and an input-based analysis of the capabilities underlying competence in the workplace.

This differentiation in the scope and definition of competencies and attributes has been attended by different pathways to and problems in implementation. Although the antecedents of competency-based education in the USA date from the early twentieth century, in the USA, the UK, Australia, New Zealand, South Africa and Canada, competency-based education really took hold only in the last two decades of that century (Brown and McCartney 1995; Johns, 1995; Langley, 1995; Thompson, 1995; van Schalkwyk, 2002; Boritz and Carnaghan, 2003). Within the vocational training sector, competencies were initially associated with specification of detailed, often micro-level, performance behaviours which were necessarily developed and measured, *in situ*, in the workplace. Critics of competency-based education argue that 'the methodology for arriving at a set of national standards of competence is time-consuming and costly and is probably over complex' (Purcell, 2001, p. 33), and the behavioural patterns developed in the workplace do not build capacity to examine the rationale for, or create alternatives to, those patterns. For many in the higher education sector, the perceived focus on skills at the expense of thought was an anathema (Sin and Reid, 2005). The apparent need for direct engagement with the workplace as the site for skill development posed an additional barrier to the integration of competency-based education within this sector (Purcell, 2001).

Nevertheless, concurrent with moves towards competency-based vocational training, professional bodies in several discipline areas, including Accounting, began to question the effectiveness of a university education for developing competent professionals. In the 1990s in Australia, New Zealand, the UK, and South Africa such questions were also raised by governments determined to increase national productivity and the employability of graduates and simultaneously open higher education to a much larger number of participants (Purcell, 2001; van Schalkwyk, 2002; *Bath et al.*, 2004). Thus universities were challenged or required to specify the outcomes of a graduate's education.

To define these at a level of generality which would appropriately span the needs of employers in all professional areas, university graduate outcome or attribute statements were necessarily expressed broadly. Even when terms such as 'communication skills', 'problem- solving skills' or 'teamwork skills' were used, the components of each 'skill' were rarely listed. It was almost always left up to each university teacher to establish a relationship between a specific teaching or assessment activity and a specified graduate attribute. The development of 'skills' mostly occurred in contexts that served as proxies for workplace experience (e.g. group work to construct an assessable 'consultant's report').

In contrast with the very targeted specification of and teaching and assessment for competencies in the vocational training sector, claims to have developed a specific graduate attribute within the university sector have variously been made with reference to teaching activities imputed to develop the attribute. Assessment activities have been imputed to test possession of the attribute, or with both teaching and assessment activities (see, for example, De La Harpe *et al.*, 2000; Medlin *et al.*, 2003; Bath *et al.*, 2004). Reports of strategies designed to develop attributes have generally focussed on attribute development in the context of one course or unit, rather than in a whole degree program. Identification of the attributes that are developed in any given course or unit has generally been left up to the teacher of that course or unit, despite the inherent unreliability in this attributable to 'differences in staff interpretations of the descriptors ... provided for each generic skill or quality' (Sumison and Goodfellow 2004, p. 337).

The tensions found in the higher education and training sectors generally about the nature and purpose of education and the locus of curriculum control are also reflected in Accounting education, as the literature referred to in the following section makes apparent.

Competencies in Accounting—Professional and Educational Practice

Within the USA, the landmark 1986 study of Accounting education commissioned by the American Accounting Association (AAA) identified a growing gap between what was needed by Accounting professionals and what was being taught by Accounting educators (Williams, 1993; Dyer, 1999). Subsequently, the 1989 *White Paper* commissioned by the 'Big 8' Accounting firms—*Perspectives on Education: Capabilities for Success in the Accounting Profession*—highlighted the importance for Accounting professionals of communication skills, intellectual skills, general knowledge, organisational and business knowledge, and Accounting and auditing knowledge. In 1999 the American Institute of Certified Public Accountants (AICPA) delivered its *Core Competency Framework for Entry into the Accounting Profession* (Dyer, 1999; Foster and Bolt-Lee, 2002).

Despite this lengthy history of reflection upon the requirements and efficacy of Accounting education in the USA, in 2000 Albecht and Sack (p. 1) still reported that 'Accounting leaders and practicing accountants are telling us that Accounting education, as currently structured, is outdated, broken, and needs to be modified significantly'. While researchers continued to probe practitioners' academics' and students' perceptions of required competencies (e.g. Doucet *et al.*, 1998; Lee and Blaszczynski, 1999; Burnett, 2003), accounting practitioners continued to identify gaps in the preparation of Accounting graduates (e.g. Simmons and Williams, 1996; Siegel and Sorensen, 1999; Taylor and Rudnick, 2005). It appeared that professional body accreditation of the accounting curriculum did not guarantee professional readiness, and nor did the requirement for graduates to sit for a professional qualifying examination (Bierstaker *et al.*, 2004) despite the impact this requirement could be expected to have on university Accounting curricula.

In Australia, the move towards specification of professional competencies commenced with Birkett's (1993) study (commissioned by the Australian and New Zealand Accounting professional bodies) which produced a list of required cognitive skills and behavioural skills, supported by a very detailed list of indicators of competency in each field of Accounting. In 1995 the Joint Accreditation Review Task Force, established by the Institute for Chartered Accountants in Australia (ICAA) and the Certified Practising Accountants Australia (CPAA) listed seven generic skills 'valued by the Accounting profession and which the Accounting bodies expect to see developed in Accounting graduates' (ASCPA and ICAA, 1995, p. 16). A 2005 review of accreditation guidelines confirmed the CPAA's and ICAA's continuing requirement that university education develop generic skills (CPAA and ICAA, 2005, p. 12) and resulted in the distillation of Birkett's competencies into a revised list of generic skills valued by employers and the professional bodies. Table A1 lists the generic skills highlighted by the CPAA and ICAA in 1995 and 2005 as necessary for accounting graduates, and relates this to the generic skills identified as being essential for graduates by Graduate Careers Australia and the graduate attributes that the University of the Sunshine Coast seeks to develop. As might be anticipated, because professional bodies can more readily identify the range of activities in which a graduate is likely to engage, the level of detail specified in a professional body's lists of generic skills is necessarily much greater than that associated with a list of generic skills designed to meet the needs of all discipline areas.

Professional accreditation of Australian university Accounting degrees has acted as an attractor for students and therefore as a driver for the integration of professional and generic skills into the Accounting curriculum. Nevertheless, as in the USA, some studies still highlight graduates' lack of preparedness for the Accounting workplace (De Lange *et al.*, 2006; Jackling and Sullivan, 2006; Richardson and Desriyani, 2006). Despite the visible nexus between the Accounting profession's requirements and university curricula, integration of professional and generic skills[4] often follows the patterns described in relation to the implementation of graduate attributes in universities and is attended by a similar set of problems. From the perspective of university teaching staff required to develop professional or generic skills within the curriculum 'these accreditation requirements were imposed on Accounting academics, often without due regard to the space in the curriculum to accommodate these additions, and the capacity of academics to develop students' generic skills. Skill expectations related to the ability to 'listen effectively', 'present, discuss and defend views', and 'negotiate with people from different backgrounds and with different value systems' (Tindale *et al.*, 2005, p. 11).

Perhaps in consequence, a significant amount of the literature relating to the development of professional skills or generic skills focuses on accounts of the attempts of an individual or small group to grapple with these tensions when teaching a specific course or unit or on providing an overview of how to teach a specific skill. This occurs despite the CPAA and ICAA (2005, p. 13) guidelines recommending that 'generic skills should be developed in an integrated fashion throughout the various subject areas taught rather than be treated separately'. Sin and Reid (2005), for example, outline teaching innovations designed to develop professional skills in several Australian accounting courses, Weil *et al.* (2004) describe the use of case studies to teach Accounting competencies in New Zealand, while in the USA Doney and Lephardt (1993) describe general strategies for teaching critical thinking, and Boyd *et al.* (2000) describe a methodology for teaching critical thinking skills in an introductory Accounting course.

In recent years, however, several educators have also explored Accounting education from the assurance of learning perspective, focussing not primarily on how or what to teach, but on how to ensure that what is taught is actually learnt or that, *prima facie*, what is taught is likely to lead to the required learning. Thus, Herring and Williams (2000) emphasise the need for program goals and for course objectives and the need also for evaluation (i.e. assurance of learning measures) to occur at the course level. Ammons and Mills (2005) emphasise the importance of evaluating learning outcomes at course-level, and provide a detailed account of systematic assurance of learning in the context of a single Accounting course. Stivers *et al.* (2000), responding to the need for evaluation of outcomes identified by Apostolou (1999), sketch relationships between specified generic skill outcomes and strategies for assuring learning across a whole undergraduate Accounting program – strategies which encompass students' performance on tests as well as student, employer and faculty surveys. The ASHE-ERIC Higher Education Report (2002) into curriculum reforms in the professions similarly provides case studies of program-wide implementation of generic skills for accounting students, with the focus on discussion of the teaching and assessment activities designed to develop specified generic skills.

Whole-of-program Development of Generic and Professional Skills in Accounting—a Case Study

As indicated previously, despite the professional bodies' recommendation that 'generic skills should be developed in an integrated fashion throughout the various subject areas taught rather than be treated separately' (CPAA and ICAA, 2005, p. 13), most accounts of the implementation of generic skills relate to implementation within a specific course. Only two articles describe in significant detail the practicalities associated with transforming curricula across a whole program to ensure development of generic and professional skills: one of these relates to accounting, and one to education.

Stivers *et al.* (2000) present a list of six skills needed in Accounting (e.g. communication, Accounting knowledge) together with a list of standardised tests associated with the skills and a detailed list of other methods for evaluating how effectively the skills were taught (e.g. student or employer surveys, syllabi review, teacher/course evaluations, etc.). Sumison and Goodfellow's (2004) discussion of whole-of-program development of generic skills relates to a Bachelor of Education (early childhood) program, but their experience sheds light on the difficulties faced in such a whole-of-program approach. They asked staff to place ticks on a matrix that listed a set of generic skills (e.g. literacy, numeracy, communication, interpersonal) and strategies associated with development of the skills, i.e.

- Assumed (students are assumed to have acquired this skill prior to the unit);
- Encouraged (students are encouraged to gain/practice/refine this skill in this unit);
- Modelled (for students in this unit);
- Explicitly taught (to students in this unit);
- Required (students are required to demonstrate this skill in this unit); and
- Evaluated (students are evaluated on this skill in this unit).

They observe, however, that it soon became apparent that the placement of the ticks was 'not a reliable indicator of whether and/or how generic skills and qualities were promoted within each of the 35 units included in the mapping exercise' (Sumison and Goodfellow, 2004, p. 337). Staff had interpreted the generic skills as encompassing different sets of capabilities and had adopted different stances about the inherent teachability of a particular skill or what type of teaching was needed before a tick could be given.

The Accounting program in the USC Faculty of Business began a review and modification of its existing program (and the courses therein). This review had the aim of ensuring that: (1) the program objectives were aligned with both the Accounting profession's required generic skills and the university's desired graduate attributes; and (2) the objectives, teaching activities and assessment activities within courses were aligned. Based on Sumison and Goodfellow's (2004) experience it was clear that care was necessary to avoid a perfunctory and ineffective mapping process. Guidance was also taken from the experience of Stivers *et al.* (2000) and Sumison and Goodfellow (2004), and from models of curriculum which stress the need for alignment between objectives, teaching activities and assessment activities (e.g. Ramsden, 1992; Cannon and Newble, 2000; De La Harpe *et al.*, 2000; Bath *et al.*, 2004).

At the time the review commenced the program had gained professional body accreditation. It had a set of program objectives which related well to the profession's required generic skills and it had detailed course outlines which specified course objectives and assessment activities. There was, however, no clear mechanism for ensuring that program and course objectives were linked to university graduate attributes. Nor was there any way of being sure that what was actually being taught in each course related well to its specified objectives and assessment activities, or that each course appropriately built on other courses to provide students overall with a comprehensive set of opportunities for developing Accounting generic skills and university graduate attributes. It was these gaps that the review and modification process sought to address.

Mapping Accounting Courses

As courses in the program had already been accepted by the professional body and academic staff felt ownership of the courses which they taught, they were asked to map these courses to a grid containing the full set of university graduate attributes on one axis, and objectives, teaching activities and assessment activities on the other. The mapping process contrasted with that described by Sumison and Goodfellow (2004) in that it involved the provision of comparatively detailed information rather than ticks. It was guided by the Learning and Teaching Coordinator who has extensive experience working one-to-one and in workshops with academic staff from various disciplines to develop teaching capacity and understanding of students' learning processes.

The course mapping process took the following form:

- During discussion between the course coordinator and the Learning and Teaching Coordinator existing objectives were allocated to what were considered to be appropriate graduate attributes, and then each objective was examined from two perspectives.
- First, objectives were examined for their language. Did the objective express something that the student would be able to *do* by the end of the course? Was the objective expressed in language that gave students clear messages about what, and at what level, they were required to perform (e.g. if they were required to 'understand' something, would adequate understanding be demonstrated by description, application or evaluation of the thing)?
- Second, objectives were examined for alignment. Was there a teaching and an assessment activity directly related to the outcome specified in the objective? A critical issue in consideration of alignment was the directness of the relationship between teaching, assessment and the objective (e.g. if students were required to undertake an oral presentation on a specific topic, an objective relating to the development of presentation skills was considered appropriate only if there was a teaching activity specifically directed to the development of presentation skills *and* if there were also marks dedicated to the assessment of students' effectiveness as presenters). Where presentation was a by-product of a different activity focus—i.e. where marks were allocated for presentation of appropriate content, but not for demonstrated skill in the delivery of the presentation—an objective relating to the development of presentation skills was not considered appropriate.

Examination of objectives in these terms produced diverse outcomes for courses:

1. in several courses objectives were removed as it was realised that the objective was either not specifically addressed in the curriculum, or the assessment, or, in some cases neither the curriculum nor the assessment;
2. in some courses, feedback from students had suggested the need for a new objective and related teaching and assessment activities. In these cases the new objective, teaching and assessment activities were developed;
3. in several courses, discussion about the relationship between an objective, teaching and assessment activities led to that objective being re-allocated to a different attribute as it was realised that what was being taught and assessed was not what had at first been perceived;
4. in many courses, objectives were rewritten to indicate more clearly to students what they were required to be able to *do* by the end of the course. This in turn better reflected what students would be required to demonstrate they could do in the assessment task.

As a consequence of this process, although the course mapped was essentially the course being taught at that time, the map produced did not necessarily reflect the same range of objectives and assessment activities as appeared in the existing course outline. Furthermore, the raising of course coordinators' awareness of the principles of effective course design—including the need for alignment of objectives with teaching *and* assessment activities—led not only to changes in specified objectives and assessment activities, but also to changes in teaching activities. Table A2 provides an example of mapping, presenting the current Management Accounting course.

Mapping the Accounting Program to the Required Graduate Attributes

Once all *courses* in the Accounting program had been mapped they were compiled into a detailed *program* map structured around the university graduate attributes. On this program map were listed all the university graduate attributes—to think, to communicate, etc.—which, in their totality, correspond well to the generic skills identified as being necessary for Accounting graduates by the CPAA and ICAA (2005). Under each attribute was listed the name of each course in which the attribute was taught, together with the relevant course objectives, teaching and assessment activities. A cover sheet presented a tabular summary of the information regarding the attributes taught, and this table also contained a column listing the Accounting program's objectives, mapped against the university graduate attributes by senior members of the Accounting discipline and the Learning and Teaching Coordinator. Table A3 exemplifies this mapping of courses using the university graduate attribute 'to communicate', which mirrors some of the 'routine skills' and 'interpersonal skills' competencies listed by the CPAA and ICAA (2005). Table A4 presents the summary cover sheet (including program objectives) as it appeared after all courses had been mapped.

As can be seen in Table A4, the initial mapping process yielded the surprising information that in no course were interpersonal competencies related to interaction with others actually taught and assessed (even though interaction is recognised by the professional body as being an important generic skill area for accountants). This is not to say that the issue of interpersonal competency was not raised in the classroom – indeed some courses had objectives relating to interpersonal competencies—but in no courses did these appear to be systematically taught *and* assessed. A similar situation pertained in respect of the attribute 'to initiate', which relates to competencies listed by the professional bodies under 'personal skills' and 'analytic/design skills' (CPAA and ICAA, 2005).

The next step in the program review and modification process was to pose the problem for course coordinators teaching on the program: what should we do about this? The initial intention of the Learning and Teaching Coordinator was to use the program map as the basis for facilitated discussion with Accounting course coordinators of gaps in what was being taught and/or assessed or instances of 'over-teaching' in a specific skill area. However, in preliminary consultations with senior members of the Accounting discipline it soon became apparent that it was untenable to use a twelve page document—the program map—as the basis for reviewing the skills taught, for the level of detail in the program map made it impossible to gain the broad overview of the program needed to facilitate discussion. The Learning and Teaching Coordinator thus developed a provisional one page tabular analysis of attribute/generic skills development in the program.

As discussed previously, during the creation of course maps alignment between university graduate attributes, objectives, teaching and assessment activities had been established. For the purposes of the analysis it could therefore be assumed that the generic skills (graduate attributes) to which objectives related were actually being taught and assessed, but what had not been drawn out was information about the depth of generic skill development. To ascertain this, course maps were analysed and each generic skill taught in a given course was categorised in terms of one of the following teaching strategies:

1. teaching activities which involved modelling or discussion prior to assessment of capacity in that area (described as 'discussion' in the analysis); or
2. teaching activities which involved modelling or discussion, then application or practice on which feedback was given, then assessment (described as 'skills' in the analysis). For example, if the features of a good oral presentation were discussed with students before they gave oral presentations which were assessed, this was categorised as

skill development at the 'discussion' level. However, if the features of a good oral presentation were discussed with students, and they then did a 'trial' presentation on which they were given feedback, and subsequently gave their oral presentations which were assessed, this was categorised as skill development at the 'skills' level. The use of a case study to elicit students' responses and give feedback on these (for example, in areas related to ethical reasoning) was characterised under 'skills', although it is clear that in such cases the skills being developed are cognitive rather than practical. Table A5 presents this provisional tabular analysis, which formed the basis for discussion during the meeting of course coordinators teaching on the Accounting program.

Meeting to Review the Accounting Program Map

Prior to the meeting, both the full Accounting program map and the provisional tabular analysis of the program map were distributed electronically to all Accounting course coordinators. The meeting of the Accounting program course coordinators commenced with brainstorming a list of skills that coordinators perceived employers to be seeking—a strategy designed to focus attention on the generic skills that might thus be expected to be developed throughout the accounting program. Not surprisingly, identified skills clustered around communication, problem-solving and interpersonal capacities, and related well to the list of generic skills identified in Birkett's (1993) study, which was then distributed.

Course coordinators were next asked to use the tabular analysis to examine the sequencing of skill development. The aim was to ensure that the teaching of each generic skill moved from the development of basic principles or performance capability to engagement in tasks of increasing complexity or performance at higher levels. Coordinators were also asked to review the correlation between the stated program objectives (which reflected professional body requirements) and the range of generic skills taught, and comment on any obvious gaps or redundancies in the skills developed.

No redundancies were identified, but course coordinators were surprised to discover deficiencies in the overall program. In particular, teamwork and interpersonal skills and initiative and creativity were not currently being taught. An additional gap commented upon was that relating to the attribute 'to learn'. Several course coordinators noted that they do actually teach and assess information literacy skills associated with their Accounting specialisation, but had neglected to develop an objective to signal to students that they considered learning in this area to be an important part of the curriculum. As in most universities, teaching has tended to be 'an activity undertaken in private, behind closed doors' and consequently, unless meetings such as this are convened, at least some staff will inevitably be unaware of what colleagues are teaching and many staff will not know how their colleagues teach specific content.

Once gaps in the program's development of required generic skills had been identified, the question became how and where to address these and, to this end, course coordinators were asked to examine the analysis of their own courses. In doing this they were to consider whether:

- the provisional analysis had accurately captured the discussion/skill distinction (for a couple of courses, the information provided about teaching was not clear enough for the Learning and Teaching Coordinator to be sure that this was the case);
- there were any skills they actually taught or examined but for which they did not have objectives;
- the content in their courses lent itself to development of a type of skill that was not currently being taught, but which should be taught.

This consideration led to a number of specific outcomes. For example, objectives were added to reflect skills which were being taught and assessed but not recognised. Similarly, in one case, what had been characterised as skill development at the level of 'discussion' proved to be development at a depth which was more accurately described as 'skills'. Once these needed modifications had been dealt with, discussion turned to how to address the gaps in the generic skills developed in the program. The benefits of intra-disciplinary stimulation generated by this process was evidenced in a lively exchange between course coordinators in which they identified the potential for additional skill development in their own and in others' courses.

Ultimately, it was decided that modifications should be made to all but one course in the program. This integrated, program-based curriculum development approach reflected the recommendation of the CPAA and ICAA (2005) and has made it possible for each course coordinator to highlight to students not only what they are expected to be able to do by the end of each course but also by the end of the program as a whole.

Subsequent to the meeting of all Accounting program course coordinators, coordinators modified their course maps to reflect the changes agreed upon in the meeting. In some cases this modification was effected alone and, in some cases, it was achieved with assistance from the Learning and Teaching Coordinator. In some cases this modification involved the addition of an objective, with no requirement for change in teaching and assessment, but in several other cases (especially associated with the attribute 'to interact') the addition of a new objective led inevitably to the need to construct new teaching and assessment activities. The revised program map analysis, which provides an overview of the changes made to courses and to the program as a whole as a result of the meeting of accounting program course coordinators, is presented in Table A6.

Planning for Future Development of Generic Skills for Accounting

Overall, the course and program mapping process described above achieves several beneficial outcomes:

- first, for Business Schools seeking accreditation through international accrediting bodies such as AACSB, it provides 'assurance of learning' at a program level. It does this by directly linking graduate attributes and program goals (which are, in turn, linked to professional body requirements) to the well-aligned objectives and teaching and assessment activities of the courses that make up the program;
- second, it provides each accounting program course coordinator with an opportunity to see and discuss in detail what colleagues in the program are teaching and assessing and how and why they are doing this;
- third, it provides staff with information that enables them to draw links for students between the courses they are teaching and other courses in the program. In the absence of program mapping, many students experience programs as a set of disconnected courses and, in consequence, often do not transfer learning from one course to another; and
- fourth, it addresses the CPAA and ICAA (2005, p. 13) recommendation that 'generic skills should be developed in an integrated fashion throughout the various subject areas taught rather than be treated separately'.

The process described above provides a model that potentially overcomes the objections about lack of academic staff involvement raised by Tindale *et al.* (2005) and it addresses the problems inherent in Sumison and Goodfellow's (2004) approach to mapping, which was characterised by different interpretations of what type of teaching was needed before it could be said that a generic skill was being developed. Further, it responds to Herring and Williams' (2000) and Ammons and Mills' (2005) emphasis upon assurance of learning at the course level, and Stivers *et al.'s* (2000) emphasis upon assurance of learning at program level.

As a case study, the benefits of an in-depth description of our experience are balanced against the limitations on generalisability inherent in such an approach. It is hoped, however, that the successful outcomes we have documented assure those contemplating a whole-of-program review that the strategy described herein is a viable and effective way to proceed. The following possible notes of caution are offered.

The limitations of the process are primarily related to the skills of the process facilitator and to time. For the process to be effective, the facilitator requires a sound understanding of how to achieve alignment of objectives, teaching and assessment activities, and familiarity with a wide range of potential teaching and assessment strategies. Good working relationships with academic staff and the ability to manage group dynamics are also important, particularly in cases where interpersonal tensions exist or arise between those teaching on a program. Significant time is required to assist course coordinators in the initial mapping of courses, and in the compilation and analysis of the program map, although it is anticipated that electronic data management systems may in the future reduce some of the time taken to compile a program map. Nevertheless, in this case study organisation the time expended on the process has been repaid by the demonstrable development of academic staff capacity to design effective courses and reflect in an ongoing way on the efficacy of their teaching-related activities. This capacity over the longer term has led to continuing improvements in course design at course and program level and an increased interest in and discussion of teaching amongst course coordinators.

The review and modification process—mapping of courses, of the program, and resultant change designed to enable the program to better address needs related to generic skill development—is planned to occur every two years. The interactive nature of the review process, facilitated by the skill set of the Learning and Teaching Coordinator, permits the generic skills to be developed in an integrated fashion. It is anticipated that a two year cycle will ensure that the Accounting program is appropriately positioned in relation to the needs of the profession. The two year period will also allow staff to gain sufficient feedback on the success of new teaching and assessment activities—which at the end of two years will generally have been trialled twice—before being asked to consider whether changes are warranted.

Acknowledgements

The authors would like to express their gratitude to Associate Professor Chris Lambert who suggested development of this article and provided feedback on its first draft.

Notes

[1]The term 'course' refers to a subject or unit that forms part of a degree program.

[2]The Association to Advance Collegiate Schools of Business.

[3]Throughout this paper the term 'assessment' will be used to refer to strategies for evaluating students' performance or achievement; 'evaluation' will be used to refer to strategies related to assurance of learning or feedback on course or program efficacy in terms of specified learning outcomes.

[4]As indicated in the second section of this paper, the terms 'professional skills' and 'generic skills' are often used synonymously. Here, they essentially both refer to generic skills, but the term 'professional skills' is used to denote the generic skills specifically related to professional body or workplace requirements.

References

Albecht, W. S. and Sack, R. (2000) *Accounting Education: Charting the Course through a Perilous Future* (Florida: American Accounting Association).

Ammons, J. and Mills, S. (2005) Course-embedded assessments for evaluating cross-functional integration and improving the teaching-learning process, *Issues in Accounting Education*, 20(1), pp. 1–19.

Apostolou, B. (1999) Outcomes assessment, *Issues in Accounting Education*, 14(1), pp. 177–197.

ASHE-ERIC Higher Education Report (2002) *Curriculum Reforms in the Professions: Responding to Calls for Change*, 29(3), pp. 17–63, AN10297246.

Australian Society of Certified Practising Accountants and the Institute of Chartered Accountants in Australia (1995) *Exposure Draft. Guidelines for Joint Administration of Accreditation of Tertiary Courses by the Professional Accounting Bodies* (Sydney: Australian Society of Certified Practising Accountants and the Institute of Chartered Accountants in Australia).

Barrie, S. (2005) Rethinking Generic Graduate Attributes, *HERDSA News* (Online). Available at http://www.itl.usyd.edu.au/GraduateAttributes/barriepaper3.pdf (accessed 16 February 2007).

Bath, D., Smith, C., Stein, S. and Swann, R. (2004) Beyond mapping and embedding graduate attributes: bringing together quality assurance and action learning to create a validated and living curriculum, *Higher Education Research and Development*, 23(3), pp. 313–328.

Bierstaker, J., Howe, M. and Seol, I. (2004) Accounting majors' perceptions regarding the 150-hour rule, *Issues in Accounting Education*, 19(2), pp. 211–227.

Birkett, W. (1993) *Competency Based Standards for Professional Accountants in Australia and New Zealand* (Sydney: Australian Society of Certified Practising Accountants, The Institute of Chartered Accountants in Australia and the new Zealand Society of Accountants).

Boritz, J. E. and Carnaghan, C. (2003) Competency-based education and assessment for the accounting profession: a critical review, *Canadian Accounting Perspectives*, 2(1), pp. 7–42.

Boyd, D., Boyd, S. and Boyd, W. (2000) Changes in accounting education: improving principles content for better understanding, *Journal of Education for Business*, 76(1), pp. 36–42.

Brown, R. B. and McCartney, S. (1995) Competence is not enough: meta-competence and accounting education, *Accounting Education: an international journal*, 4(1), pp. 43–53.

Burnett, S. (2003) The future of accounting education: a regional perspective, *Journal of Education for Business*, 78(3), pp. 129–134.

Cannon, R. and Newble, D. (2000) *A Handbook for Teachers in Universities and Colleges. A Guide to Improving Teaching Methods* (London: Kogan Page).

Certified Practising Accountants Australia (CPAA) and the Institute of Chartered Accountants in Australia (ICAA) (2005) Accreditation Guidelines for Universities (Online). Available at http://www.cpacareers.com.au/uploads/pdfs/accreditation_guidelines.pdf (accessed 5 December 2006).

Clanchy, J. and Ballard, B. (1995) Generic skills in the context of higher education, *Higher Education Research and Development*, 14(2), pp. 155–166.

Cranmer, S. (2006) Enhancing graduate employability: best intentions and mixed outcomes, *Studies in Higher Education*, 31(2), pp. 169–184.

Curry, L. and Wergin, J. Educating professionals: Responding to new expectations for competence and accountability. Available at http://proquest.umi.com/pqdweb?did=7690848€sid=1€Fmt=2€clientId=20906€RQT=309€VName=PQD (accessed 15 October 2008).

Daigle, R., Hayes, D. and Hughes II, K. (2007) Assessing student Learning outcomes in the introductory accounting information systems course using the AICPA's core competency framework, *Journal of Information Systems*, 21(1), pp. 149–169.

De la Harpe, B., Radloff, A. and Wyber, J. (2000) Quality and generic (professional) skills, *Quality in Higher Education*, 6(3), pp. 231–243.

De Lange, P., Jackling, B. and Gut, A. (2006) Accounting graduates' perceptions of skills emphasis in undergraduate courses: an investigation from two Victorian universities, *Accounting and Finance*, 46(3), pp. 365–386.

DEST (n.d.) Graduate Attributes in Australian Universities (Online). Available at http://www.dest.gov.au/NR/rdonlyres/887C29CE-77FF-4998-9B62-705AADAB0BF2/1326/appendix_grad_attributes.pdf (accessed 16 February 2007).

Doney, L. and Lephardt, N. (1993) Developing critical thinking skills in accounting students, *Journal of Education for Business*, 68(5), pp. 297–300.

Doucet, M., Doucet, T. and Essex, P. (1998) Competencies for the introductory accounting sequence, *Journal of Accounting Education*, 16(3–4), pp. 473–495.

Dyer, J. (1999) Accounting education on the threshold of a new century, *The Government Accountant's Journal*, 48(4), pp. 40–48.

Foster, S. and Bolt-Lee, C. (2002) New competencies for accounting students, *The CPA Journal*, 72(1), pp. 68–71.

Graduate Careers Australia (n.d.) Course Experience Questionnaire (Online). Available at http://www.studentservices.utas.edu.au/careers/forms_files/CourseExperienceandGraduateDestinationSurveyOct07.pdf (accessed 10 June 2008).

Herring, H. and Williams, J. (2000) The role of objectives in curriculum development, *Journal of Accounting Education*, 18(1), pp. 1–14.

James, B., Lefoe, G. and Hadi, M. (2004) Working 'through' graduate attributes: a bottom up approach, in: F. Sheehy and B. Stauble (Eds) *Transforming Knowledge into Wisdom: Holistic Approaches to Teaching and Learning. Proceedings of Higher Education Research and Development Society*, 27, pp. 174–184.

Jackling, B. and Sullivan, C. (2006) Financial planners in Australia—a critical evaluation of gaps in behavioural skills and competencies. Paper presented at the Annual Conference of the Accounting and Finance Association of Australia and New Zealand, Wellington, New Zealand, 2–4 July.

Johns, A. (1995) Competency standards for professional accountants in Australia and New Zealand, *Accounting Education: an international journal*, 4(1), pp. 37–42.

Langley, F. (1995) The application of competences to an accounting qualification (the experience of the UK Association of Accounting Technicians (AAT)), *Accounting Education: an international journal*, 4(1), pp. 29–36.

Lee, D.-W. and Blaszczynski, C. (1999) Perspective of 'Fortune 500' executives on the competency requirements for accounting graduates, *Journal of Education for Business*, 75(2), pp. 104–107.

Medlin, J., Graves, C. and McGowan, S. (2003) Using diverse professional teams and a graduate qualities framework to develop generic skills within a commerce degree, *Innovations in Education and Teaching International*, 40(1), pp. 61–77.

Purcell, J. (2001) National vocational qualifications and competence-based assessment for technicians—from sound principles to dogma, *Education and Training*, 43(1), pp. 30–39.

Ramsden, P. (1992) *Learning to Teach in Higher Education* (London: Routledge).

Richardson, B. and Desriyani, L. (2006) Curriculum requirements for entry-level management Accounting in Australian business organisations. Paper presented at the Annual Conference of the Accounting and Finance Association of Australia and New Zealand, Wellington, New Zealand, 2–4 July.

Siegel, G. and Sorensen, J. (1999) Counting more, counting less. Transformations in the management accounting profession, *The 1999 Practice Analysis of Management Accounting* (USA: Institute of Management Accountants).

Simmons, S. and Williams, A. (1996) What do accounting practitioners want? How do entry-level accountants measure up? *Arkansas Business and Economic Review*, 29(1), pp. 1–10.

Sin, S. and Reid, A. (2005) Developing Generic Skills in Accounting: Resourcing and Reflecting on Trans-Disciplinary Research and Insights. Australian Association for Research in Education (AARE) Conference, Sydney, 28 November–1 December.

Stivers, B., Campbell, J and Hermanson, H. (2000) An assessment program for accounting: design, implementation, and reflection, *Issues in Accounting Education*, 15(4), pp. 553–581.

Sumison, J. and Goodfellow, J. (2004) Identifying generic skills through curriculum mapping: a critical evaluation, *Higher Education Research and Development*, 14(2), pp. 329–346.

Taylor, V. and Rudnick, M. (2005) Accounting education: designing a curriculum for the 21st century, *Journal of American Academy of Business*, 6(2), pp. 321–323.

Thompson, P. (1995) Competence-based learning and qualifications in the UK, *Accounting Education: an international journal*, 4(1), pp. 5–15.

Tindale, J., Evans, E., Mead, S. and Cable, D. (2005) Are our accounting programs preparing graduates for professional accounting work? AARE Conference, Sydney, Australia, 27 November–1 December.

van Schalkwyk, S. (2002) Issues of quality when integrating generic learning outcomes in study programmes geared at career-oriented education. Unrefereed paper presented at the 2002 Annual International Conference of the Higher Education Research and Development Society of Australasia (HERDSA), Perth, Western Australia, 7–10 July.

Weil, S., Oyelere, P. and Rainsbury, E. (2004) The usefulness of case studies in developing core competencies in a professional accounting programme: a New Zealand study, *Accounting Education: an international journal*, 13(2), pp. 139–169.

Williams, D. (1993) Reforming accounting education, *Journal of Accountancy*, 176(2), pp. 76–82.

Appendix

Table A1. Generic skills required by CPAA and ICAA, Graduate Careers Australia, and University of the Sunshine Coast

ASCPA/ICAA required generic skills, 1995	CPAA/ICAA required generic skills, 2005	Generic skills - Course Experience Questionnaire (GCA)	Graduate attributes – University of the Sunshine Coast
Adaptation skills – apply accounting knowledge to solve real – world problems – receive, evaluate & react to new ideas – adapt to new situations – act strategically **Communication skills** – transfer & receive knowledge – present, discuss & defend views – read & write effectively – negotiate with people from different backgrounds and with different value systems **Intellectual skills** – identify, find, evaluate, organise & manage information & evidence – analyse, reason logically, conceptualise issues, construct & solve problems & construct arguments – think critically – engage in ethical reasoning **Interpersonal skills** – work in diverse groups – listen effectively – understand group dynamics	**COGNITIVE SKILLS** **Routine skills** – report writing – computer literacy **Analytic/design skills** – identify, find, evaluate, organise & manage information & evidence – initiate & conduct research – analyse, reason logically, conceptualise issues – solve problems & construct arguments – interpret data & reports – engage in ethical reasoning **Appreciative skills** – receive, evaluate & react to new ideas – adapt & respond positively to challenges – make judgements derived from one's own value framework – think & act critically – know what questions to ask – engage in lifelong learning – recognise own strengths & limitations – appreciate ethical dimensions of situations – apply disciplinary & multi-disciplinary perspectives – appreciate processes of professional adaptation & behaviour	– problem-solving skills. – analytical skills. – ability to work as a team member – confident about tackling unfamiliar problems. – skills in written communication. – ability to plan work.	**To understand** – To have relevant, discipline-based knowledge, skills and values – To be able to apply and evaluate knowledge **To think** – To value and respect reason – To be able to reason competently – To be self-aware, independent learners **To learn** – To be able to collect, organise, analyse, evaluate and use information in a range of contexts **To interact** – To be able to interrelate and collaborate – To value and respect difference and diversity **To communicate** – To speak, listen and write competently – To be competent users of information and communication technologies **To initiate** – To be constructive and creative – To be enterprising

Personal skills – think creatively – exercise judgement based on complete or incomplete sets of information **Professional skills** – a sense of professionalism in relation to work performed – a personal commitment to lifelong education – a commitment to think and behave ethically	BEHAVIOURAL SKILLS **Personal skills** – be flexible in new/different situations – act strategically – think & act independently – be focused on outcomes – tolerate ambiguity – think creatively **Interpersonal skills** – listen effectively – present, discuss & defend views – transfer & receive knowledge – negotiate with people from different backgrounds & with different value systems – understand group dynamics – collaborate with colleagues		**To value** – To have self-respect and a sense of personal agency – To have a sense of personal and social responsibility – To understand and apply ethical professional practices

Table A2. Course map for ACC310 management accounting.

USC graduate attribute	***Learning objectives*** *On completion of this course students should be able to:*	***Teaching activities***	***Assessment tasks***
To understand • To have relevant, discipline-based knowledge, skills and values • To be able to apply and evaluate knowledge	1. Identify and describe management Accounting concepts.	1. Lectures and tutorials begin with a description of management Accounting concepts.	1. Spreadsheet assignment; group presentation; individual research assignment; final exam
	2. Discuss the role and ethical responsibilities of management accountants.	2. Tutorial discussion based on ethical issue vignettes	2. Spreadsheet assignment, group presentation, final exam - sound ethical practice a requirement for solutions provided
	3. Apply appropriate management Accounting techniques and statistical methods for costing, decision-making, planning and control.	3. Demonstrations in lectures, and application in tutorials, of management Accounting techniques. Computer-based simulations in which students apply specific methods, and receive immediate, context-specific feedback.	3. Spreadsheet assignment – modelling of cost functions for decision-making, planning and control purposes. Group presentation - focuses on a specific management Accounting method or technology.Final exam -calculative questions.
	4. Compare and justify the use of traditional and more recently developed practices, techniques and methods of management Accounting.	4. Comparisons made in lectures between traditional and contemporary management Accounting practices	4. Individual research assignment - explores contemporary issues in management Accounting, comparisons to traditional practices
	5. Identify and explain the various theoretical concepts as they apply to management Accounting practices and research.	5. Theoretical underpinnings discussed in lectures and tutorials	5. Final exam - discursive questions requiring the exposition of contemporary theory
To think	6. Develop and justify solutions based on appropriate theories and information.	6. Lectures and tutorial discussions emphasise the application of theory to solving specific problems in organisations.	6. Individual research assignment, spreadsheet assignment, and group presentation require application of theory.

• To value and respect reason • To be able to reason competently	7. Determine the most appropriate management accounting response based on the strategic goals of organisations.	7. Lectures and tutorial discussion emphasise the importance of strategic goals in the choice of an appropriate problem-solving technology or philosophy	7. Final exam - calculative and discursive questions require choice and justification of appropriate management Accounting method to address specific organisational problem.
To interact • To be able to interrelate and collaborate • To value and respect difference and diversity	8. Understand the role of management accountants in cross functional teams. 9. Utilise appropriate techniques to manage individuals' contribution to team projects	8. Discussion of theory and practice of cross functional teams 9. Practice using GANTT charts for team management	8. Final exam – theory of cross functional teams 9. Group presentation (incl presentation of GANTT chart)
To communicate • To speak, listen and write competently • To be competent users of information and communication technologies	10. Demonstrate skills in oral presentation and report writing. 11. Apply a spreadsheet package to solve Accounting problems.	10. A lecture modelling effective presentations and discussion of report writing skills. 11. Computer workshop exercises that use spreadsheet models to solve Accounting problems	10. Group presentation - marks for oral presentation skills; Individual research assignment – marks for report writing skills 11. Spreadsheet assignment - development of a spreadsheet model as a decision-making tool for a business scenario

Table A3. Mapping of courses to form a program map.

To communicate			
• To speak, listen and write competently • To be competent users of information and communication technologies			
Courses	***Learning objectives*** *On completion of this course students should be able to:*	***Teaching activities***	***Assessment tasks***
BUS106 Introductory Accounting	11. Apply the use of computer technology in the solution of Accounting problems. 12. Demonstrate skills in writing business reports.	11. Computer workshops learning how to use spreadsheets. 12. Lectures and tutorials demonstrating how to write business reports.	11. Assignment 1 (business report on financial Accounting process) & Assignment 2 (business report on cost Accounting process) 12. Assignments 1 & 2
ACC220 Law of Business Associations	9. Demonstrate skills of communication relevant to critical thinking and legal analysis.	9. Students given guidance on topic and present on topic in following tutorial; guidelines on how to work through, structure, and present a legal argument, orally and in writing	9. Assignment – individual written essay; Tutorial Participation; Final Exam (problem-based)
ACC221 Company Accounting	8. Read and communicate the appropriate regulatory framework effectively	8. Lectures modelling reading process of Corporate Law, Tutorials practicing reading process, Case Studies (problem identification, facts development)	8. Tutorial Questions (in mini tutes); Case Studies
ACC310 Management Accounting	10. Demonstrate skills in oral presentation and report writing. 11. Apply a spreadsheet package to solve Accounting problems.	10. A lecture modelling effective presentations and discussion of report writing skills. 11. Computer workshop exercises that use spreadsheet models to solve Accounting problems	10. Group presentation - marks for oral presentation skills; Individual research assignment – marks for report writing skills 11. Spreadsheet assignment - development of a spreadsheet model as a decision-making tool for a business scenario

ACC311 Taxation Law and Practice	10. Read and communicate tax law to others in a written and oral form	10. Lectures modelling reading process, Tutorials practicing reading process, Case Study (problem identification, facts development, debate for and against in light of tax law, I-form explanation and completion)	10. Tutorial Questions (in mini tutes); Case Study based on scenarios
ACC320 Contemporary Accounting Issues	8. Demonstrate skills in written and oral communication.	8. Guidelines for presentation and participation.Discussion of quality of answers to tutorial questions.	8. Workshop presentation assessed using presentation criteria.Workshop participation assessed using participation criteria.
ACC321 Auditing and Professional Practice	9. Write an effective report 10. Orally present a logical, structured argument	9. Discussion in tutorials about structuring of a report 10. Discussion in tutorials about oral presentation and structuring of a logical argument	9. Written report on an auditing topic 10. Oral presentation in tutorials

Table A4. Program map cover sheet summarising relationship between program objectives and attributes, and attributes developed in each course

Program Map: Accounting										
USC graduate attribute	*Program Objectives*	**BUS106**	**ACC210**	**ACC211**	**ACC220**	**ACC221**	**ACC310**	**ACC311**	**ACC320**	*ACC321*
To understand • To have relevant, discipline-based knowledge, skills and values • To be able to apply and evaluate knowledge	• Understand the operation of the financial, legal and ethical environment of business related to professional Accounting practice • Understand the basis for Accounting in accordance with Australian Accounting Standards and the Australian Accounting Conceptual Framework. • Understand and apply Accounting principles related to corporate activities. • Apply management Accounting tools for decision making, planning and control.	X	X	X	X	X	X	X	X	X
To think • To value and respect reason • To be able to reason competently	• Analyse and employ finance techniques applicable to business.	X	X	X	X	X	X	X	X	X
To learn • To be self-aware, independent learners	• Understand the impact that Accounting theory and issues have on professional Accounting practice.									

• To be able to collect, organise, analyse, evaluate and use information in a range of contexts		X								
To interact • To be able to interrelate and collaborate • To value and respect difference and diversity	• Demonstrate personal and interpersonal competencies. • Appreciate the value of human diversity and equity in organisations and apply these principles.									
To communicate • To speak, listen and write competently • To be competent users of information and communication technologies	• Effectively communicate their Accounting knowledge.	X			X	X	X	X	X	X
To initiate • To be constructive and creative • To be enterprising	• Exercise initiative in identifying issues and applying relevant skills to their resolution.									
To value • To have self-respect and a sense of personal agency • To have a sense of personal and social responsibility • To understand and apply ethical professional practices	• Demonstrate responsible ethical decision making approach to resolving issues.		X	X		X				X

Table A5. Preliminary analysis of attribute/skill development Accounting program: Overview of generic skill development

Accounting Program: Overview of generic skill development										
USC graduate attribute	*Program Objectives*	**BUS106**	**ACC210**	**ACC211**	**ACC220**	**ACC221**	**ACC310**	**ACC311**	**ACC320**	*ACC321*
To understand • To have relevant, discipline-based knowledge, skills and values • To be able to apply and evaluate knowledge	• Understand the operation of the financial, legal and ethical environment of business related to professional Accounting practice • Understand the basis for Accounting in accordance with Australian Accounting Standards and the Australian Accounting Conceptual Framework. • Understand and apply Accounting principles related to corporate activities. • Apply management Accounting tools for decision making, planning and control.	X	X	X	X	X	X	X	X	X
To think • To value and respect reason • To be able to reason competently	• Analyse and employ finance techniques applicable to business.	Accounting analysis - skills	Accounting analysis frameworks - skills	Financial calculation – skills Capital finance - skills	Legal analysis - skills	Analysis - discussion	Problem solving - discussion	Analysis - skills	Analysis - skills	Analysis - discussion

To learn • To be self-aware, independent learners • To be able to collect, organise, analyse, evaluate and use information in a range of contexts	• Understand the impact that Accounting theory and issues have on professional Accounting practice.	Accounting info literacy - skills			Legal reading - skills					
To interact • To be able to interrelate and collaborate • To value and respect difference and diversity	• Demonstrate personal and interpersonal competencies. • Appreciate the value of human diversity and equity in organisations and apply these principles.									
To communicate • To speak, listen and write competently • To be competent users of information and communication technologies	• Effectively communicate their Accounting knowledge.	Spreadsheet – skills Report writing - discussion			Oral and written presentation - skills	Legal reading - skills	Presentation – discussion Report writing – discussion Spreadsheet - skills	Legal reading – discussion Problem solving - skills	Presentation/ participation - discussion	
To initiate • To be constructive and creative • To be enterprising	• Exercise initiative in identifying issues and applying relevant skills to their resolution.									

(*Continued*)

Table A5. Continued

Accounting Program: Overview of generic skill development										
USC graduate attribute	***Program Objectives***	**BUS106**	**ACC210**	**ACC211**	**ACC220**	**ACC221**	**ACC310**	**ACC311**	**ACC320**	***ACC321***
To value • To have self-respect and a sense of personal agency • To have a sense of personal and social responsibility • To understand and apply ethical professional practices	• Demonstrate responsible ethical decision making approach to resolving issues.	Ethics - skills Corporate social responsibility - skills	Ethics - skills	Corporate responsibility - discussion						Ethics - skills

Table A6. Revised analysis of attribute/skill development Accounting program: Overview of generic skill development

Accounting Program: Overview of generic skill development										
USC graduate attribute	***Program Objectives***	**BUS106**	**ACC210**	**ACC211**	**ACC220**	**ACC221**	**ACC310**	**ACC311**	**ACC320**	***ACC321***
To understand • To have relevant, discipline-based knowledge, skills and values • To be able to apply and evaluate knowledge	• Understand the operation of the financial, legal and ethical environment of business related to professional Accounting practice (including financial Accounting, tax and audit). • Understand the basis for Accounting in accordance with Australian Accounting Standards and the Australian Accounting Conceptual Framework. • Understand and apply Accounting principles related to corporate activities. • Apply management Accounting tools for decision making, planning and control. • Satisfy the academic requirements for membership of CPAA and ICAA	X	X	X	X	X	X	X	X	X
To think • To value and respect reason • To be able to reason competently	• Analyse and employ finance techniques applicable to business.	Accounting analysis - skills	Accounting analysis frameworks - skills	Financial calculation – skills Capital finance - skills	Legal analysis - skills	Analysis - discussion	Problem solving - discussion	Analysis - skills‘	Analysis - skills	Auditing analysis - skills

(Continued)

Table A6. Continued

Accounting Program: Overview of generic skill development										
USC graduate attribute	***Program Objectives***	**BUS106**	**ACC210**	**ACC211**	**ACC220**	**ACC221**	**ACC310**	**ACC311**	**ACC320**	***ACC321***
• **To learn** • To be self-aware, independent learners • To be able to collect, organise, analyse, evaluate and use information in a range of contexts	• Understand the impact that Accounting theory and issues have on professional Accounting practice.	Accounting info literacy - skills	Accounting standard info literacy - skills		Legal reading - skills			Taxation info literacy - skills		Auditing info literacy - skills
• **To interact** • To be able to interrelate and collaborate • To value and respect difference and diversity	• Demonstrate personal and interpersonal competencies. • Appreciate the value of human diversity and equity in organisations and apply these principles.	Organisation behaviour - discussion					Team management (GANTT chart) - skills	Client interaction – skiills		
• **To communicate** • To speak, listen and write competently • To be competent users of information and communication technologies	• Effectively communicate their Accounting knowledge.	Spreadsheet – skills Report writing - discussion			Oral and written presentation - skills	Legal reading - skills	Presentation – discussion Report writing – discussion Spreadsheet - skills	Legal reading – discussion Problem solving - skills	Presentation/ participation - discussion	Oral and written presentation - discussion
• **To initiate** • To be constructive and creative • To be enterprising	• Exercise initiative in identifying issues and applying relevant skills to their resolution						Process analysis - skills			

• **To value** • To have self-respect and a sense of personal agency • To have a sense of personal and social responsibility • To understand and apply ethical professional practices	• Demonstrate responsible ethical decision making approach to resolving issues.	Ethics - skills Corporate social responsibility - skills	Ethics - skills		Corporate responsibility - discussion			Sustainable business practices - skills		Ethics - skills

Development of Generic Competencies: Impact of a Mixed Teaching Approach on Students' Perceptions

ANNE FORTIN* and MICHÈLE LEGAULT**

**Université du Québec à Montréal, Montréal, Canada, ***Université du Québec à Trois-Rivières, Trois-Rivières, Canada*

ABSTRACT *Accounting education in recent years has emphasized the need for developing generic competencies and, to this end, has advocated various pedagogies other than the traditional lecture format. The Université du Québec à Trois-Rivières (Canada) started an award-winning program, Vire, Tuelle & Associates (VTA), which uses a mixed teaching approach to develop students' generic competencies in preparation for the Chartered Accountant designation. This questionnaire-based study asked students to rate this approach at the end of their training in the mock firm (VTA) and while they were trainees in an accounting firm. It also asked the office supervisors to assess their trainees' competency levels during the training period. It was found that the mixed approach program significantly enhanced the development/improvement of all 32 generic competencies investigated. After a few months' work as CA trainees, students had not substantially changed their views of the usefulness of VTA activities for the development of their competencies. Students' perceptions of some benefits of the mixed approach differed significantly according to accounting work experience and prior academic performance. The office supervisors generally viewed the UQTR trainees as being highly competent or excellent. This study provides educators, schools and professional accounting bodies with feedback on the mixed approach to help them develop similar programs.*

From the mid-1980s, academics (Accounting Education Change Commission, AECC, 1990; Albrecht and Sack, 2000; American Accounting Association, AAA, 1986; Deppe *et al.*, 1991) and professionals (Arthur Andersen & Co., *et al.*, 1989) started lobbying for the reform of accounting education as a way to meet industry needs for candidates with a strong command of accounting and business principles and more generic skills in areas such as decision-making, communication and interpersonal relations.

Accounting bodies accordingly began qualifying candidates for the profession through a competency-based approach (e.g. the American Institute of Certified Public Accountants, AICPA, 1999 and the Canadian Institute of Chartered Accountants, CICA, 2001) that assesses qualities and skills (Boritz and Carnaghan, 2003). The International Federation of Accountants also adopted this new focus in its International Education Standard for Professional Skills (IES 3), which took effect on 1 January 2005 (International Federation of Accountants, IFAC, 2003).

In Canada, the Conférence des recteurs et des principaux des universités du Québec (CREPUQ) and the Ordre des comptables agréés du Québec (OCAQ) developed a graduate program in 1994 to prepare candidates for the chartered accounting profession, recognising that curriculum reform was necessary in the face of increasingly complex market conditions and accounting procedures (CREPUQ/OCAQ, 1994). Heralding a shift to knowledge integration and development of professional attitudes and competencies, particularly intellectual, interpersonal, communication, and cognitive skills (Comité consultatif et d'orientation du programme de formation professionnelle, COCOPFP, 1994; OCAQ, 1995), the program prescribed solving complex, practical accounting problems through knowledge acquisition and competency development (COCOPFP, 1994). Case studies were the educational method of choice, requiring students to simulate the delivery of professional services. The OCAQ subsidized teams of academics and practitioners to develop complex cases about topics such as assurance, acquisitions, financially-troubled businesses, business opportunities, and personal financial planning.[1]

Accordingly, Quebec's universities developed the requisite graduate programs and, by 1998, each institution was offering its own version of the graduate accountancy program, using different course content distribution, sequencing and teaching methods.

The Université du Québec à Trois-Rivières (UQTR) established an innovative program that includes a 10-week training period at the mock accounting firm of Vire, Tuelle & Associates (VTA) (Gosselin, 1998), exposing students to a wide variety of tasks and a combination of educational methods aimed at fostering generic skills for professional competency. In 2000, the VTA project received the Alan Blizzard Award of the Society for Teaching and Learning in Higher Education, an honour granted to '... collaborative projects that increase the effectiveness of learning' (Society for Teaching and Learning in Higher Education, 2000, p. 1).

The objective of this paper is to describe the mixed teaching approach used in VTA and review students' and employers' perceptions of its success in developing professional competencies (generic skills). In the words of Watson *et al.* (2007, p. 44), 'for those educators who use a classroom case or undertake a new technique, [...], an accompanying study of its effectiveness is an appropriate contribution to the literature'. The contribution of the mixed teaching approach to the development of students' competencies was investigated for 32 skills drawn from the *CA Candidates' Competency Map* (CICA, 2005) and the literature. The validity of the first survey's results was challenged by administering the questionnaire once again to the same students after they had started working in an accounting firm. Students' field supervisors were also asked about their competency levels and their performance relative to trainees from other universities. The results will help accounting educators and institutions develop competency-based programs or evaluate their current programs.

The remainder of the paper is organized as follows. First, the relevant literature on educational methods is reviewed and is followed by a description of the *Canadian CA Candidates' Competency Map*, the graduate program at UQTR and the activities of VTA. After the methodology is explained, the results of the study are reported and discussed, followed by a summary and conclusion.

1. Literature Review

This section reviews the literature on accounting education methods, with a particular focus on how they contribute to the development of generic skills/competencies. This review is followed by a description of the competencies in the *Canadian CA Candidates' Competency Map* (2005) that were adapted to the OCAQ's professional program, the graduate programs and the VTA module.

1.1. Accounting Education Methods

Bonner (1999) advocates gearing teaching methods to learning objectives, whether they are accounting knowledge, communications or teamwork skills, and advocates a more active pedagogy: 'Further, learning objectives involving complex cognitive skills require teaching methods that promote active student learning' (Bonner, 1999, p. 12). Active learning can be achieved through case studies, problem-based learning (PBL), individual and group projects, student presentations, role play, simulations, discussions, and cooperative learning. Passive methods include lectures, videos, and guest speakers. Some studies have examined the impact of these teaching methods on student performance in examinations, while others have measured the effectiveness of the case method, PBL, role play, simulations, and cooperative learning in developing generic skills. The following sections present an overview of the results of research on case studies and problem-based, cooperative and experiential learning methods.

1.1.1. Case studies. The case method is conducive to deep, elaborative learning and the development of generic skills (Arquero Montano *et al.*, 2004; Boyce *et al.*, 2001). It motivates students by using real-world scenarios and unstructured problems, helping them interact through group work, discussion and self-expression. The case method requires students to be actively involved in the learning process and draws on their analytical skills, forcing them to consider complex problems with multiple acceptable solutions from several perspectives and apply judgment to uncertain situations (Boyce *et al.*, 2001; Easton, 1992; Libby, 1991). The case method's effectiveness has been proven to help students acquire and apply professional knowledge, particularly when accounting procedures relate to a variety of hypothetical settings as well as to real-world business situations.

By engaging and motivating students, the case method improves content assimilation through developing problem-solving, communication and teamwork skills, as demonstrated by Arquero Montano *et al.* (2004), who found a strong relationship among the variables of motivation, improvement in content learning and non-technical skills.

Furthermore, case-based education has proven more effective than the lecture and example format in helping students assimilate the taxation curriculum (Anderson *et al.*, 1990). In a strategic management course, Banning (2003), demonstrated that case studies improve students' tolerance for ambiguity, which is positively associated with performance. Students tend to do better on elaborative questions with a case study curriculum than they do with a lecture format (Stewart and Dougherty, 1993). Although improvement in performance was not significant overall when more complex cases were used, Arquero Montano *et al.* (2004) noted that students who work on complex cases tend to make and justify recommendations, and can identify and discuss a problem's core issues.

In studies investigating different skills, students noted that the case method enhanced their intellectual, interpersonal and communication skills (Arquero Montano *et al.*, 2004; Ballantine and McCourt Larres, 2004; Hassall *et al.*, 1998; Sawyer *et al.*, 2000;

Stout, 1996; Weil *et al.*, 2001; Weil *et al.*, 2004). The three to six skills the respondents most commonly mentioned in each of these studies are discussed below.

In Stout (1996), US students in a cost accounting class ranked ability to organize time effectively, awareness of group dynamic issues and improvement in oral and written communication skills highest among the seven most enhanced skills. Hassall *et al.*'s (1998) UK students improved their negotiation and presentation skills, ability to work in groups, ability to apply and integrate subject skills and knowledge, and ability to question assumptions. Sawyer *et al.* (2000) found that advanced taxation students benefited most from a case study about working as a professional tax adviser, which developed their professionalism as well as their writing and problem-solving skills.

A group of New Zealand honours accounting students in Weil *et al.* (2001) ranked engaging in real-world business decision-making, arriving at several solutions to business problems, applying theory to the real world, distinguishing facts from opinions, and applying and integrating knowledge highest among 31 skills. Students in a New Zealand chartered accounting program reported that among the 15 competencies about which they were asked, cases were most effective in helping them evaluate a situation from several perspectives, consider alternative solutions and apply judgment, analyse and solve problems, identify the information relevant to the issues they were analysing, and integrate knowledge (Weil *et al.*, 2004). Students in a financial statement analysis course in Spain rated cases as the method most likely to improve participation in debates, writing skills, ability to evaluate and debate opinions, analysis and synthesis skills, and critical and unstructured problem-solving (Arquero Montano *et al.*, 2004).

In a study by Ballantine and McCourt Larres (2004), UK honours accounting students who were asked to rate the influence of case studies on 28 intellectual or other skills frequently mentioned awareness of multiple solutions, insight into complex real-world situations, consideration of multiple perspectives, questioning, interpretation and data organisation skills, as well as verbal and written communication skills. Moreover, students viewed the case method as benefiting them cognitively and contributing to their skills development, whether or not they had accounting work experience (Ballantine and McCourt Larres, 2004).

Only two studies investigated differences in students' perceptions based on gender, age or prior academic performance (Weil *et al.*, 2001; Weil *et al.*, 2004). Overall, few differences were noted as a function of these characteristics.

In Weil *et al.* (2001), men found case studies more useful than did women for the following four categories: developing critical thinking ability, asking pertinent questions, developing interpretation skills, and learning to deal with uncertainty and ambiguity. In Weil *et al.* (2004), men found case studies more useful in developing their ability to present and justify a viewpoint, influence others' thinking, and learn appropriate questioning skills.

The respondents' age influenced their perceptions with respect to only four skills: students over 30 found the case method more useful in distinguishing cause and effect in unstructured business situations, integrating knowledge, presenting a viewpoint, and evaluating situations from more than one perspective (Weil *et al.*, 2004).

Prior performance in an undergraduate advanced finance class influenced three perceptions: below-average students found cases more useful than above-average students for relating theory to real-life practice, applying knowledge to new situations, and enhancing their ability to summarize information (Weil *et al.*, 2001).

In summary, according to the literature review, students find case studies most beneficial for developing their analytical and problem-solving skills; improving their oral and written communication skills; integrating knowledge; developing their abilities to work in groups, face real-world problems and consider multiple perspectives; as well as for developing or improving their awareness of multiple solutions.

1.1.2. Problem-based learning. While case studies provide opportunities to apply knowledge acquired in previous subject-based courses, PBL helps students acquire knowledge (Milne and McConnell, 2001) by prompting their analytical skills through the challenge of problem-solving, conducting in-depth investigations and disseminating knowledge to other group members. PBL emphasizes self-directed learning, thereby promoting life-long cognitive abilities (Johnstone and Biggs, 1998; Milne and McConnell, 2001).

To ensure that students do not develop inappropriately organized knowledge structures, Johnstone and Biggs (1998) have suggested implementing PBL only after basic technical accounting knowledge has been acquired. PBL is therefore most appropriate for the last year of a 150-h program. Its benefits include the development of self-directed learning skills, problem-solving and interpersonal skills, and increased comprehension, learning, and student motivation (Milne and McConnell, 2001). Most research on PBL has been conducted in the medical field, where it has been widely studied and applied.

Few accounting studies, however, have documented the benefits of using PBL. Edmonds *et al.* (2003) used PBL in an introductory accounting course and provide anecdotal evidence that it helped develop critical and creative thinking, decision-making, communication, and leadership skills. Comparing the performance of graduate and undergraduate students in a PBL accounting information systems course with that of students in a traditional lecture/activities format, Heagy and Lehman (2005) found that both groups scored similarly in basic knowledge examinations. However, in an accounting theory course, Breton's (1999) PBL group outperformed the lecture group on a theoretical question and on a case, but not on a technical question.

After using PBL in a management accounting class, Adler and Milne (1997) asked the students about the method's contribution to the development of their generic skills. Among the 18 skills, 12 attitudes, and 12 knowledge attributes investigated, students found ability to work as a team member, need for flexibility and adaptability, understanding how different firms require different subject outcomes, finding and assessing information, desire for self-improvement, and oral communication skills to be particularly enhanced with work on and presentation of a PBL case study.

Combining cases and PBL with role play, class discussions, student presentations, and cooperative learning is very effective in developing generic skills such as oral communication, analytical skills, critical thinking, and listening skills (Arquero Montano *et al.*, 2004; Boyce *et al.*, 2001). Proponents of accounting education reform have urged a move to these active pedagogies (AAA, 1986; AECC, 1990; Arthur Andersen & Co. *et al.*, 1989; IFAC, 1996). Experiential methods, such as simulations, videos and guest speakers, are also useful. The following paragraphs outline the results of studies on these educational methods, grouped under cooperative learning and experiential learning methods.

1.1.3. Cooperative learning. Ravenscroft *et al.* (1999, p. 163) describe cooperative learning as 'those learning approaches in which peer interaction plays a significant role, but where content and construction of knowledge are still primarily determined and driven by the faculty member'. It contributes to deeper learning because students play an active role, from summarising reading assignments to completing problem assignments and giving class presentations. Students in cooperative learning programs outperform their peers in examinations (Ciccotello *et al.*, 1997; Dillard-Eggers and Wooten, 2003; Etter *et al.*, 2000; Hite, 1996; Hwang *et al.*, 2005 and 2008; Ravenscroft *et al.*, 1995), particularly when incentives are offered (Grudnitski, 2000). However, in assessing the impact of cooperative study groups, Parry (1990) and Ravenscroft *et al.* (1997) found no differential effect on performance; nor did Clinton and Kohlmeyer (2005) on group quizzes or Lancaster and Strand (2001) on team learning. These results may be attributable to the effect of prior academic achievement and group formation on performance (Van der Laan Smith and Spindle, 2007).

Cooperative instruction not only enhances students' learning, but also improves communication and group process skills. Berry (1993) found that students who work on case studies in groups and are required to write reports and give oral presentations improve their group process skills. Similarly, cooperative learning develops critical thinking skills, as Kern (2000) demonstrates in her description of a financial statement analysis project. Students who facilitated a seminar (as a group) improved their teamwork ability, flexibility and adaptability, ability to interact with others, oral communication skills, ability to find and assess information, and self-confidence (Adler and Milne, 1997).

1.1.4. Experiential learning methods. Experiential learning (i.e. experiencing real work tasks through course activities) can take many forms—simulations, videos, guest speakers, and role play. Reality-based cases are also a form of experiential learning. As Green and Calderon (2005, p. 2) pointed out, '... cases and simulations require students to assimilate unstructured information and use multiple sources of data to define, analyse, and solve business problems ... [and they] prepare them for professional practice'. These teaching methods can improve performance and skills alike. Furthermore, 'action-oriented learning tasks do impact on the extent to which lifelong learning attributes are developed' (Adler and Milne, 1997, p. 210).

Students who simulated business planning in an introductory management accounting course said the experience improved their critical thinking and oral communication skills (Barsky and Catanach, 2005). Others who simulated fraud risk assessment in an auditing class found that their learning, confidence and judgment skills were enhanced (Green and Calderon, 2005). Female students who simulated a preliminary audit of a sales and accounts receivables system performed better in an examination. The experience also changed the students' perceptions of the importance of interpersonal relationships (Fortin and Legault, 2006).

In addition, videos about a first audit mandate (Groomer *et al.*, 1992; Siegel *et al.*, 1997) and audit planning and risk assessment concepts (Mohrweis, 1993) helped students internalize auditing concepts. Using interactive educational multimedia as a supplemental resource for learning about accounting information system cycles, students improved their understanding of the relationship between theory and practice and key concepts, and saw how these concepts applied to real life (Stanley and Edwards, 2005).

Guest speakers can also 'provide a very effective real-life learning experience for students' (Metrejean *et al.*, 2002, p. 347). Metrejean *et al.* (2002) found that guest speakers improve the learning experience because they inspire students to pay closer attention to class topics and increase students' awareness of accounting career opportunities.

Role play is useful in enhancing students' communication and interpersonal skills and in stimulating their creativity (Crumbley *et al.*, 1998), ranking first for contribution to education among the alternative teaching methods evaluated by senior-level accounting students at a US university (Crumbley *et al.*, 1998). Craig and Amernic (1994) and Blanchette and Brouard (1994) used role play to demonstrate the usefulness of accounting information in the contexts of union contract negotiations and bankers' loan decisions. Craig and Amernic's (1994) students benefited from the experiential nature of the activity and felt that it improved their understanding of the topics covered in the course. However, no difference was noted in the performance in an accounting methods examination between Blanchette and Brouard's (1994) introductory accounting students who participated in role play and that of a control group.

While there is mixed evidence concerning the impact of these techniques on examination performance, case studies, PBL, and cooperative and experiential learning have been shown to significantly impact on the development/improvement of generic skills/competencies.

The following section explains the Quebec program for CA students and shows how it helps develop their generic competencies.

1.2. The Canadian CA Candidates' Competency Map

Although chartered accountancy is a national profession in Canada, the educational requirements for admission to the profession are determined locally by the provincial institutes/ordre. As mentioned previously, the OCAQ and CREPUQ worked together on a joint initiative to establish a Professional Education Program (PEP) in Quebec to help meet the increasingly complex needs of the business world. The focus of this program is to teach the development of competencies through the application of knowledge to practical situations (CREPUQ/OCAQ, 1994). The OCAQ divided these competencies into three categories—knowledge, skills and attitudes (COCOPFP, 1994), with knowledge referring to the body of knowledge required by chartered accountants, skills to their intellectual, communication and interpersonal abilities, and attitudes to the professional and personal conduct expected of a member of the profession. Approved by the OCAQ in 1995 (OCAQ, 1995), the program has been offered by every university in Quebec since 1998 as part of their OCAQ-accredited graduate programs.

At the national level, an Inter-Institute Vision Task Force was established in late 1994 to articulate the mission, vision and future direction of the profession. The Task Force developed a new mission and vision that required changes to be made to the training of future chartered accountants (CICA, 1996). An Education Reengineering Task Force was created in 1997 to design a blueprint to ensure the success of the education reform. In 1998, on the basis of the preliminary report of the Education Reengineering Task Force, the CICA Board of Directors approved a new competency-based approach for CA training (CICA, 1999).

A prototype competency map that integrated findings in the literature and the approaches of accounting organisations in other countries was then elaborated and submitted to CAs and provincial institutes/ordre for consultation. The *CA Competency Map* was published in September 2001 (CICA, 2001). The first Canadian national examination focusing exclusively on competencies,[2] called the Uniform Evaluation, was not introduced until 2003, after Quebec had become the first province to offer competency-based CA education. While the initial PEP may have differed from the national CA competency map in its presentation and the wording of individual competencies, the components of the individual competencies were similar in nature. After the *Canadian CA Competency Map* received nationwide approval, it was adopted in its entirety in the Quebec PEP.

The *CA Competency Map* explains in great detail the basic knowledge and skills which experienced CAs must have to meet the expectations of the public, businesses and government. A simplified version, called the *CA Candidates' Competency Map*, was developed specifically for CA candidates (CICA, 2005)[3] to establish the level of competence new CAs should possess. This map is divided into two main competency categories: Pervasive Qualities and Skills, and Specific Competencies. Table 1 presents

Table 1. Pervasive attributes and skills selected from the *CA Candidates' Competency Map* (CICA, 2005)

Type of attributes/skills	Specific attributes/skills (competencies) The candidate ...	Competency aspects[a]	Question number
Ethical behaviour and professionalism (EB)	1. Protects the public interest		21
	2. Acts with honesty and integrity		
	3. Exercises due care		
	4. Maintains objectivity and independence		
	5. Protects the confidentiality of information		
	6. Adheres to the rules of professional conduct		
Personal attributes (PA)	1. Is self managing		18
	2. Demonstrates initiative		16
	3. Applies strategic thinking		17
	4. Develops innovative ideas/is creative		15
	5. Adapts to change		19
	6. Treats others in a professional manner		20
Professional skills (PS)	1. Obtains information	Identifies the needs of internal and external clients	22
	2. Examines and interprets information and ideas critically	Critically analyses information or ideas (verifies and evaluates)	2–4–14
		Synthesises and/or integrates ideas and information	6
		Draws conclusions/forms opinions	10
	3. Solves problems and makes decisions	Identifies and diagnoses problems	1–7
		Develops solutions	3
		Decides/recommends	23
	4. Communicates effectively and efficiently	Shares information and opinions through discussions and presentations	5–8–9 11–12
		Communicates in written form	13
	5. Manages and supervises	Plans and manages projects	24
		Provides leadership	25
		Facilitates group processes	30–31–32
		Negotiates	26
	6. Uses technology efficiently		27
	7. Provides professional services	Plans to meet clients' expectations in each assignment	29
		Analyses own development needs	28

[a]Aspects related to the competencies in the *CA Candidates' Competency Map* are detailed only for professional skills.

the main subcategories of pervasive qualities and skills and the competencies that will be examined in this study.

The pervasive qualities and skills break down into the following three subcategories: ethical behaviour and professionalism, personal attributes, and professional skills. Ethical behaviour and professionalism encompass protecting the public, honesty and integrity, exercising due care, objectivity and independence, confidentiality of information, and compliance with the rules of professional conduct. Personal attributes are the qualities that guide the CA's professional conduct: maintaining independence, demonstrating initiative, applying strategic thinking, being creative, adapting to change, and treating others in a professional manner.

The third category, professional skills, has eight components: obtaining information, examining and interpreting information and ideas critically, solving problems and making decisions, communicating effectively and efficiently, managing and supervising, using technology efficiently and effectively, providing professional services, and considering basic legal concepts. This last component is the only concept that will not be examined in this study since the mock firm does not focus on developing this competency. Furthermore, the professional services component will be dealt with only briefly because it pertains specifically to the operations of a real-life accounting firm.

The second major category in the competency map, called specific competencies, is content based and is divided into six categories of CA skills: organisation effectiveness, control and risk management, finance, taxation, assurance, performance measurement, and information and information technology. This study does not examine the development of specific competencies since the mock firm focuses mainly on the development of the pervasive qualities and skills.

2. The UQTR Graduate Program in Accounting and VTA

The graduate program at UQTR includes a training period in a mock accounting firm called VTA. This section describes UQTR's graduate program before taking a closer look at VTA and its activities.

2.1. UQTR graduate program in accounting

In Canada, CAs must complete a post-undergraduate degree, the details of which vary from one province to another. In Quebec, CA programs are offered only at universities, either as a graduate diploma or a Master's degree. At UQTR, the program offering the PEP and leading to the CA designation is a Master's in business administration (MBA) (see Figure 1). As a 45-credit graduate program, it is comprised of 15 more credits than the graduate diploma required by the profession.

The program is taken over a 15-month period (early May to mid-August of the following year). During the first nine weeks, students take three core courses and then spend the next 10 weeks working for VTA, a mock firm that simulates the environment of a CA firm where the educators play the role of the partners and the students are the young professionals. This experience is intended to prepare students to become chartered accountants and develop their generic and professional skills by emphasising the integration of knowledge rather than its acquisition. At the end of this experience, students leave the university for a seven-month training period in a CA firm. After this training period, they return to UQTR to complete the MBA courses that prepare them for the national CA examination, held in September of each year.[4] Once students have written the examination, they return to the CA firm to complete the 17 months remaining in the mandatory 24-month training period.

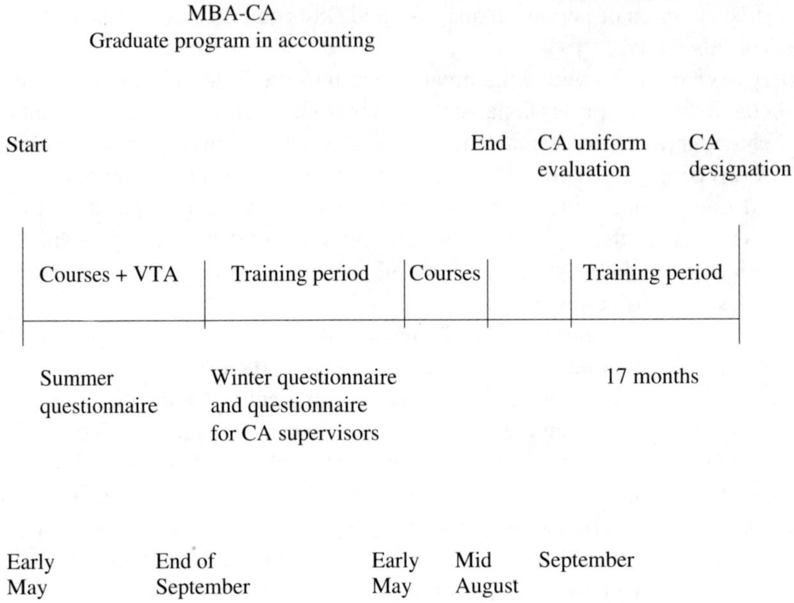

Figure 1. Time line of the graduate program in accounting

2.2. VTA

VTA is an innovative concept that enables students to experience the professional life of a public accountant. During this part of their studies, they forego regular lectures for active participation in the firm's operations by taking on the role of trainees, while the educators simulate the role of partners, consultants, specialists, or managers. Early in the program, the students are given a handbook describing the firm's mission, values, market, organisation chart, operational rules, and statement of compliance, as well as its policies on ethical conduct, independence and objectivity, prohibited investments, conflicts of interest, confidentiality, and restricted professional activities (Gosselin, 1998). As these policies illustrate the key points of the *Code of Ethics of Chartered Accountants of Quebec* (OCAQ, 2005), this handbook ensures students are familiar with the ethical aspects of the profession from the outset. As a new employee in the firm, the student must return the signed statement of compliance to the appropriate instructor to confirm his or her commitment. This requirement helps drive home the principle that values are just as important as knowledge.

The students in the VTA program work 45 h a week (i.e. nine hours a day, Monday to Friday). The facilities are located in two multimedia rooms. Each student has a laptop on loan from the practitioner firms that will be hosting the CA students after their 10-week experience in the mock firm. The required use of a computer encourages students to learn to use information technology effectively and efficiently. The software most frequently used is Word, Excel, PowerPoint, and Taxprep. In addition, a CD-Rom version of the *CICA Handbook* (CICA, 2007) is available, along with numerous Internet sources.

Students are exposed to a wide variety of learning experiences in the mock firm. To promote the acquisition of the principles of ethical conduct, professionalism and professional skills, the instructors use case studies, group discussions, in-class student presentations, individual and group research projects, role plays, and problem-solving via problem-based learning. Formal lectures and individual reading assignments are given as knowledge acquisition tools, as are presentations by guest speakers, which also help students relate to real-life practice. Formal lectures, however, are kept to a minimum and are used mainly to teach new concepts for writing case studies.

The different pedagogical methods are subject to a formal evaluation, which in turn increases students' motivation and participation in the various activities of the mock firm. To motivate the students to develop their writing skills, they are also assessed on the quality of language used in their written work. The students do most of their work in teams of four, which are determined either by the instructor or the students themselves. Teamwork helps develop oral[5] and interpersonal skills.

As mentioned previously, the case studies were developed by experienced practitioners and university professors. They are mainly real-life, multidisciplinary situations of varying degrees of complexity. Some cases clearly explain the work to be performed, while others require students to identify the problems. Depending on the case, the students may be expected to take on the different roles of auditor, advisor, expert witness, or controller for instance. The cases focus on different areas of practice such as financial and tax planning, business opportunities, settlement of legal disputes, business combinations, organisational environment, organisational performance, consulting, and ethical conduct. The pedagogical methods used in the VTA program are presented by topic in Table 2.

To solve the case studies, students have to apply relevant theories, identify problems, analyse possible solutions, and forward their recommendations to the client either verbally or in writing. Some instructors encourage the students to solve cases through role play. For example, to role-play the opening of a firm, students in the team are assigned to simulate either the role of non-CA tax specialists and partners or the role of CA partners. Together they must establish the future firm's legal structure, marketing plan, and organisational structure (tasks, responsibilities and compensation methods). This assignment requires them to refer to the relevant sections of the *Code of Ethics of Chartered Accountants of Quebec* (OCAQ, 2005) and then use their powers of persuasion and negotiation skills to promote their viewpoints as accountants or tax specialists, taking care to remain within the provisions of the Code. They quickly learn that both groups have diverging interests and identify potential conflicts. At the end of the discussions and negotiations, and keeping in mind the different rules of conduct, each team is required to prepare a report setting out its conclusions on how all the partners can benefit.

One instructor uses a PBL approach to teach the concepts of comprehensive audits. After the group is divided into seven or eight teams, the team members meet on two separate occasions, and spend one period in personal study. At the first meeting, the students learn about the problem through individual reading and then hold a brainstorming session to define and circumscribe the problem, listing additional questions about the issue. Using this list, they then identify the questions requiring further study to complete or enhance their knowledge. At the end of the first meeting, they divide and assign individual projects to work on during their personal study period. For their research, they can use the library or the Internet, or conduct interviews with resource persons for example.

At their second meeting, the students share the results of their research and briefly comment on and critique the references they consulted. They then proceed to the analysis phase, and begin by summarising the problem. The second meeting ends with each member giving his or her individual evaluation of the level of learning achieved, the effectiveness of the steps involved in problem-based learning, and their degree of motivation. Each student is expected to identify the individual work that remains to be done on comprehensive audits.

Table 2. Pedagogical methods used for VTA topic areas

VTA topic areas	Pedagogical methods									
	Lectures[a]	Program of readings	Problem-based learning (PBL)	Role playing	Cases	Guest speakers	Group discussions	Individual research project	Group research project	Class presentations
Financial and tax planning	X	X			X	X	X			X
Business opportunities	X			X	X	X	X			
Conflict resolution and forensic accounting	X				X	X				
Business combinations	X			X	X				X	X
Organizational environment	X	X			X		X			X
Organizational performance	X	X	X	X	X		X		X	
Consultation and ethical behaviour	X	X		X	X	X	X	X	X	X

[a]Lectures are solely intended to cover specific new concepts which students need to learn to solve cases.

A typical day at VTA might go like this: at 8 a.m., a partner announces that he has just received a call from a client asking for advice on a business acquisition. Since the situation is urgent, the client wants an answer before the end of the day. The partner tells the CA students that he will need their help to meet the deadline and asks them to e-mail him a report by 6 p.m. with the information he needs to properly advise the client. He also tells them that he will be in his office all day and available for consultation if they need additional information or advice on any aspects of the work.

Each team, composed of four students, is expected to produce a report. The team members work together to divide the tasks and determine the contents of the report (i.e. find the information, conduct the research and the quantitative and qualitative analysis, and present conclusions and recommendations). The students base their work on the information they are given in the case and complete the data as needed. Once they have assessed the situation, they divide the work among themselves. When the work is completed, they meet again to ensure that all their work forms a coherent whole that meets the partner's expectations. The day ends at 6 p.m. when they e-mail the report to the partner. On some days, the students have two cases to prepare. All the work must be done during VTA office hours, including individual reading for the acquisition of new knowledge, reviewing the concepts that must be understood to solve the case, drafting individual and group work, preparing in-class presentations, and all other previously mentioned activities.

3. Method

After permission to conduct the study was obtained from the University's Ethics Committee, a questionnaire was used to investigate the contribution of VTA activities to the development/improvement of students' generic competencies. The instrument design, data collection procedures and characteristics of the sample are presented in the following sections.

3.1. Instrument Design and Data Collection

The preliminary version of the questionnaire contained 34 preliminary questions on competencies listed in the *CA Candidates' Competency Map* that were considered likely to benefit from VTA activities, including the 15 questions in Weil *et al.*'s (2004) study on students' perceptions of case studies in New Zealand's Professional Accounting School. The questionnaire was pre-tested with two groups of students (48 in total) from the same population who were in the second summer of their Master's program.[6] The final version of the questionnaire contained 32 questions on the contribution of VTA activities to the development/improvement of generic skills and attributes, followed by a question asking which competency had most benefited from VTA activities. The questions on the competencies are listed in Table 4. Column four of Table 1 indicates the related components in the *CA Candidates' Competency Map*.

The questionnaire also contained eight questions on students' satisfaction with their teamwork experience at VTA. The first part of the questionnaire requested demographic information on gender, age, previous programs, undergraduate cumulative average, grade in the undergraduate comprehensive case analysis course, and accounting work experience, including duration in months. A covering letter explained the purpose of the study, its voluntary and anonymous nature, and the fact that data would be analysed only in aggregate form. Students were asked to sign a separate consent letter.

The students were given the questionnaire towards the end of VTA activities in early September of 2006 (summer questionnaire); 33 out of 34 students (97%) responded and also completed the same questionnaire the following winter midway through their training period (winter questionnaire) (see Figure 1). The questionnaire was administered twice to determine whether students' perceptions of the contribution of VTA activities to the development/improvement of their competencies had changed (Stout, 1996). In addition, because students had to use their competencies during their apprenticeship, responding to the questionnaire after entering the field improved their ability to assess the effect of VTA activities on their development.

When the students were asked to complete the questionnaire a second time, their office supervisors were also asked to answer separate questions about the competency of their trainees and how they compared to their peers from other universities. This external validation supported claims about the contribution of VTA activities to the development of competencies and enhanced the validity of the results obtained about students' perceptions of this contribution. The students' own academic supervisors administered the questionnaire during the mid-apprenticeship visit, pairing each questionnaire with the appropriate office supervisor's questionnaire to facilitate analysis by student demographics. Finally, using the demographic information, the two questionnaires each student had answered were paired in order to analyse changes in students' perceptions.

The questionnaire for the CA supervisors included a covering letter explaining the study's objective and the voluntary and anonymous nature of their participation. The supervisors were asked to rate the UQTR novices' competency level on a four-point Likert scale (unsatisfactory, good, very good, and excellent) and compare their abilities to those of their fellow trainees from other universities, using a five-point Likert scale ranging from considerably below average to considerably above average, or else indicate that they were unable to perform this comparison (accounting offices that hosted only UQTR trainees). Furthermore, they were asked to choose among the following responses to describe the size of the accounting office: 50 professionals or less, between 51 and 100, between 101 and 200, and more than 200. To allow for validation of the novices' relative rankings, the supervisors were also asked to indicate the number of trainees at their office and how many came from UQTR.

Another external validation of VTA's impact on the development/improvement of skills was obtained using the global pass rate of students who sat the CA uniform evaluation in the year following their participation in VTA, i.e. 2007 (see Figure 1).

3.2. Sample Description

Table 3(a), presents the sample's demographic data. It shows that there were twice as many women (22) as men (11), a distribution that reflects the trend in the profession. 'Fifty-three per cent of new CAs admitted in the first six months of 2007 are women, up from 51% in 2006' (Tabone, 2007, p. 7). Most students were in their early twenties, 11 in the 21-to-22-year-old range and 13 in the 23-to-24-year-old range. The 25-years-and-over category included nine students. Twenty-one students (63.6%) either had a technical CEGEP diploma[7] in accounting and management (followed by a bachelor's degree in accounting) or had enrolled in a combined CEGEP/bachelor program. The remaining students had completed the two-year CEGEP program before earning an undergraduate degree in accounting. The educational stream chosen, course load taken each term, and extent of work experience before entering university explains the age differences between the students.

Most of the respondents (21, 63.6%) had accounting work experience prior to their graduate program (median of six months), although some had only one month's experience from their CEGEP program. Even limited experience, however, was sufficient for

Table 3. Sample—demographic data.

(a) Sample ($n = 33$ students)			
Gender		Age	
Men	11	21–22 years old	11
Women	22	23–24 years old	13
		25 years and over	9
Technical or combined CEGEP/bachelor		Accounting work experience	
No	12	No	12
Yes	21	Yes	21
		11 in an accounting firm	
		4 in companies	
		6 have both types of experience	
		Duration: Median of 6 months	
		Ranging from 1 month to 10 years	
Cumulative average		Comprehensive case analysis course	
Mean	3.57/4.3	Mean	2.95/4.3
Ranging from 2.95 (B) to 4.29 (A+)		Ranging from 1 (D) to 4.3 (A+)	
(b) Accounting firm offices			
29 assessments by office supervisors in 18 offices of 10 accounting firms in five cities			
Number of students in offices with:			
50 professionals or less	12		
Between 51 and 100	6		
Between 101 and 200	7		
More than 200	4		

them to gain some idea of the work involved and the skills needed, and to make connections between practice and the theoretical knowledge acquired at university.

All students in the sample performed strongly in the bachelor's program, since one of the graduate program's requirements was a cumulative B average (3/4.3); the sample's mean cumulative average (3.57/4.3) was between B+ and A−. Toward the end of their bachelor's program in accounting, students take a Comprehensive Case Analysis course that requires them to solve several complex multi-topic cases as difficult as the cases in the professional examinations. Students likely to underperform in the comprehensive case analysis course may benefit from the VTA program, which exposes them to many complex cases. The sample's mean for this course was B (2.95/4.3). However, individual grades varied widely, from D to A+ (1 to 4.3/4.3).

Twenty-seven office supervisors[8] evaluated the competency levels of 29 students and compared their performance to that of trainees from other universities (Table 3b). A total of 18 offices of 10 different accounting firms were visited in five cities. The offices ranged from small (50 professionals or less) to fairly large (more than 200 professionals).

4. Results and Discussion

This section first outlines the summer questionnaire's results concerning the impact of VTA activities on the development/improvement of competencies. It subsequently examines the results from factor analyses of the competencies investigated and discusses changes in perceptions reported in the winter questionnaire. The accounting supervisors' perceptions of their trainees' competency levels and how they fared in comparison to their peers from other universities are then analysed. Lastly, it reviews students' overall results on the CA uniform examination.

4.1. *Analysis of Student Perceptions—First Administration of the Questionnaire*

Table 4 presents the overall results from the first questionnaire, subdivided into two categories, ethical behaviour[9]/personal attributes (Table 4a) and professional skills (b), and arranged in descending order of mean responses. The means of students' answers to the 32 questions on competencies—ranging from 4.52 to 5.94 on a scale of 7, and averaging a mean of 5.20 for ethical behaviour/personal attributes (a) and 5.38 for professional skills (b)—indicate that they believe VTA activities considerably enhanced the development/improvement of their competencies. Furthermore, all means differ significantly (*t*-tests) from the mid-point of 4, which corresponds to moderately useful. In other words, students believe that the VTA activities benefited all the pervasive qualities and skills investigated in the study.

Apply strategic thinking[10] ranks highest among the ethical behaviour/personal attributes developed by VTA activities (Table 4a). To a lesser but still significantly more than moderate extent, VTA activities developed other personal attributes: ability to identify ethical issues and appropriate conduct, autonomy, ability to adapt to change in the profession, creativity, initiative, and ability to treat others in a professional manner.

Among the professional skills, the five highest ranked competencies are ability to make recommendations, ability to facilitate group processes, ability to present a viewpoint within a group, ability to plan each assignment to meet clients' needs, and ability to evaluate a situation from various perspectives (Table 4b). Ability to analyse and solve problems ranks sixth, followed by ability to organize and delegate tasks in a group and to integrate knowledge.

These abilities are listed as professional competencies in the *CA Candidates' Competency Map* (CICA, 2005) relating to problem-solving, group management, communication, and providing professional services. Among these eight competencies, three ranked among the top five competencies developed/improved by case studies per Weil *et al.* (2004): i.e. ability to evaluate a situation from various perspectives (first), ability to analyse and solve problems (third), and ability to integrate knowledge (fifth). Ability to present a viewpoint within a group, which ranks third in this study, was only in eleventh position in Weil *et al.* (2004). The intensive group work the students did during the VTA program might explain that competency's high ranking in this study.

Two competencies related to managing and supervising rank high among the professional skills—i.e. ability to facilitate group processes (second) and ability to organize and delegate tasks in a group (seventh). By contrast, three other competencies in the same area—i.e. leadership skills (20th), negotiation skills (21st) and ability to motivate members of a team (22nd)—rank among the six professional competencies least developed by VTA activities, even though they involve considerable group work.

The lowest-ranked professional competencies are tied to communication skills—i.e. active listening skills (24th) and appropriate questioning skills (25th). Although both competencies also ranked among the three competencies least developed by the case method in Weil *et al.* (2004), in this study they benefited significantly more than moderately from role play, class discussions, lectures by practitioners, and class presentations. The development of students' ability to communicate appropriately in writing, which ranked last in Weil *et al.* (2004), fares better in this study, ranking fifteenth among the professional skills. The fact that the activities included research projects as well as cases may have influenced this result.

Table 4. Perceptions of the development/improvement of competencies by VTA activities—summer administration of questionnaire

Pervasive qualities/skills[a]	Competencies	Mean[b]	SD	Rank order[c]
(a) Ethical behaviour (EB)/personal attributes (PA)				
PA 3	Apply strategic thinking Q17	5.52	0.94	1
EB	Ability to identify ethical issues and appropriate conduct Q21	5.36	1.34	2
PA 1	Autonomy Q18	5.33	1.24	3
PA 5	Ability to adapt to change in the profession Q19	5.12	1.49	4
PA 4	Creativity Q15	5.03	1.10	5
PA 2	Initiative Q16	5.03	1.26	6
PA 6	Ability to treat others in a professional manner Q20	5.03	1.26	7
	Mean of 7 questions	5.20	0.76	
(b) Professional skills (PS)				
PS 3	Ability to make recommendations Q23	5.94	0.75	1
PS 5	Ability to facilitate group processes Q30	5.91	1.17	2
PS 4	Ability to present a viewpoint within a group Q9	5.76	0.94	3
PS 7	Ability to plan each assignment to meet clients' needs Q29	5.69	1.00	4
PS 2	Ability to evaluate a situation from various perspectives Q4	5.67	0.96	5
PS 2	Ability to analyse and solve problems Q10	5.58	0.94	6
PS 5	Ability to organize and delegate tasks in a group Q32	5.55	1.33	7
PS 2	Integration of knowledge Q6	5.55	1.44	8
PS 3	Ability to consider alternate solutions and apply judgment Q3	5.52	1.03	9
PS 6	Uses technology efficiently Q27	5.50	1.32	10
PS 1	Ability to identify the needs of accounting information users Q22	5.48	1.09	11
PS 5	Ability to plan and carry through professional assignments Q24	5.48	1.30	12
PS 4	Ability to express ideas articulately in an oral presentation Q8	5.45	1.23	13
PS 3	Ability to identify problems Q7	5.42	0.79	14
PS 4	Ability to communicate in writing in an articulate and appropriate manner Q13	5.39	1.17	15
PS 2	Ability to distinguish relevant from irrelevant information Q2	5.33	1.14	16
PS 2	Ability to critically examine and interpret information Q14	5.30	0.98	17
PS 4	Ability to present a viewpoint Q5	5.27	1.13	18
PS 3	Ability to identify problems and their consequences in unstructured situations Q1	5.21	0.93	19
PS 5	Leadership skills Q25	5.12	1.41	20
PS 5	Negotiation skills Q26	5.06	1.11	21
PS 5	Ability to motivate members of a team Q31	4.97	1.13	22
PS 7	Analyse development needs revealed by the assignments Q28	4.97	1.28	23

(Table continued)

Table 4. Continued

Pervasive qualities/skills[a]	Competencies	Mean[b]	SD	Rank order[c]
PS 4	Active listening skills Q12	4.94	1.54	24
PS 4	Appropriate questioning skills Q11	4.52	1.20	25
	Mean of 25 questions	5.38	0.62	

[a]Numbers refer to competencies in each of these three categories in the *CA Candidates' Competency Map* (see Table 1).

[b]All the means are significantly different from the mid-point of 4 at $P = 0$, except Q12, $P = 0.001$, and Q11, $P = 0.019$ (*t*-test, two-tailed). Results are qualitatively similar after the binomial test: $0 \leq P \leq 0.05$, except for Q12 and Q16, $P = 0.082$, and Q11, $P = 1.000$.

[c]Rank order presents the competencies in decreasing order of importance, as per the means obtained after tabulating the summer questionnaire. When the means are identical, the classification has taken standard deviation into account, with a higher rank attributed for a higher SD.

The findings regarding the highest-ranked professional competencies are consistent with the results of numerous previous studies. Students noted the importance of developing/improving their ability to work in groups in Adler and Milne (1997), Berry (1993), Crumbley *et al.* (1998), and Hassall *et al.* (1998), while development/improvement of oral communication skills was described as an important benefit in Adler and Milne (1997), Arquero Montano *et al.* (2004), Ballantine and McCourt Larres (2004), Barsky and Catanach (2005), Crumbley *et al.* (1998), Edmonds *et al.* (2003), Stout (1996), and Weil *et al.* (2004). Students mentioned the development/improvement of their ability to analyse and solve problems in Arquero Montano *et al.* (2004), Edmonds *et al.* (2003), Sawyer (2000), and Weil *et al.* (2004), and integration of knowledge in Hassall *et al.* (1998), Weil *et al.* (2001), and Weil *et al.* (2004). Finally, the development/improvement of the ability to consider alternate solutions has been described in Ballantine and McCourt Larres (2004), Weil *et al.* (2001), and Weil *et al.* (2004).

When students were asked which competency they thought had most improved after VTA activities, oral communication skills were mentioned nine times and project management and group work were mentioned seven times.[11] These improvements were linked to the type of work performed in VTA, i.e. presentations and group work.[12] Personal attributes were mentioned on only six occasions.

4.2. *Factor Analysis of the Competencies and Analysis of Changes in Perceptions—Second Administration of the Questionnaire*

To help organize the results of the numerous competency questions, two separate factor analyses[13] were conducted to derive subscales for ethical behaviour/personal attributes and for the professional skills (Table 5). Two principal components with Eigenvalues above 1 were extracted for ethical behaviour/personal attributes (Table 5a), accounting for 55% of the total variation. The first subscale featured four competencies associated with *values and drive* (Table 5b). Three competencies related to student's *adaptability to situations and persons* were extracted into the second component. The standardized alpha coefficients for these two subscales were 0.64 and 0.68 respectively.

For the professional skills (Table 5c), five subscales accounting for 65% of the total variation were identified using the Eigenvalue above 1 and the Scree-test criteria (Kim and Mueller, 1978). The first subscale featured five competencies related to *analysing* problems; the second subscale, five competencies associated with *making recommendations* (Panel D). The third subscale, *problem identification*, included seven competencies. The

Table 5. Competency subscales from factor analysis

Panel A: Total variance explanation for Ethical Behaviour/Personal Attributes factor analysis

	Initial Eigenvalues (above 1)			**Extraction sums of squared loadings**			**Rotation sums of squared loadings**		
Component competency	Total	% of variance	Cumulative %	Total	% of var.	Cum. %	Total	% of var.	Cum. %
1	2.643	37.750	37.750	2.643	37.750	37.750	2.009	28.698	28.698
2	1.198	17.114	54.865	1.198	17.114	54.865	1.832	26.166	54.865

Panel B: Rotated component matrix for Ethical Behaviour/Personal Attributes factor analysis[a]

	Component	
Competencies	1 Values and drive	2 Adaptability to situations and persons
Initiative Q16	0.786	-
Creativity Q15	0.646	-
Ability to identify ethical issues and appropriate conduct Q21	0.625	-
Autonomy Q18	0.613	-
Ability to treat others in a professional manner Q20	-	0.856
Ability to adapt to change in the profession Q19	-	0.848
Apply strategic thinking Q17	-	0.526

Panel C: Total variance explanation for Professional Skills factor analysis

	Initial Eigenvalues (selected according to the Eigenvalue above 1 and the Scree-Test criteria)			**Extraction sums of squared loadings**			**Rotation sums of squared loadings**		
Component competency	Total	% of variance	Cumulative %	Total	% of var.	Cum. %	Total	% of var.	Cum. %
1	7.815	31.259	31.259	7.815	31.259	31.259	3.802	15.210	15.210

(*Table continued*)

Table 5. Continued

Panel C: Total variance explanation for Professional Skills factor analysis

	Initial Eigenvalues (selected according to the Eigenvalue above 1 and the Scree-Test criteria)			**Extraction sums of squared loadings**			**Rotation sums of squared loadings**		
Component competency	Total	% of variance	Cumulative %	Total	% of var.	Cum. %	Total	% of var.	Cum. %
2	2.489	9.957	41.216	2.489	9.957	41.216	3.495	13.981	29.191
3	2.402	9.607	50.823	2.402	9.607	50.823	3.420	13.681	42.872
4	2.032	8.130	58.953	2.032	8.130	58.953	2.948	11.792	54.664
5	1.510	6.041	64.993	1.510	6.041	64.993	2.582	10.329	64.993

Panel D: Rotated component matrix for Professional Skills factor analysis[a]

	Component				
Competencies	1 Analysing	2 Making recommend-ations	3 Problem identification	4 Team management	5 Presenting ideas
Ability to analyse and solve problems Q10	0.777	-	-	-	-
Uses technology efficiently Q27	0.697	-	-	-	-
Active listening skills Q12	0.690	-	-	-	-
Ability to plan and carry through professional assignments Q24	0.680	-	-	-	-
Appropriate questioning skills Q11	0.505	-	-	-	-
Ability to evaluate a situation from various perspectives Q4	-	0.754	-	-	-
Ability to make recommendations Q23	-	0.739	-	-	-
Ability to consider alternate solutions and apply judgment Q3	-	0.698	-	-	-
Ability to identify the needs of accounting information users Q22	-	0.690	-	-	-
Ability to plan each assignment to meet client needs Q29	-	0.635	-	-	-
Ability to critically examine and interpret information Q14	-	-	0.705	-	-
Analyse development needs revealed by the assignments Q28	-	-	0.661	-	-

Ability to distinguish relevant from irrelevant information Q2	-	-	0.647	-	-
Ability to communicate in writing in an articulate and appropriate manner Q13	-	-	0.596	-	-
Ability to identify problems Q7	-	-	0.557	-	-
Ability to identify problems and their consequences in unstructured situations Q1	-	-	0.524	-	-
Integration of knowledge Q6	-	-	0.461	-	-
Negotiation skills Q26	-	-	-	0.745	-
Leadership skills Q25	-	-	-	0.716	-
Ability to organise and delegate tasks in a group Q32	-	-	-	0.637	-
Ability to facilitate group processes Q30	-	-	-	0.521	-
Ability to motivate members of a team Q31	-	-	-	0.494	-
Ability to express ideas articulately in an oral presentation Q8	-	-	-	-	0.701
Ability to present a viewpoint Q5	-	-	-	-	0.694
Ability to present a viewpoint within a group Q9	-	-	-	-	0.472

[a]Extraction method: principal component analysis; rotation method: varimax with kaiser normalisation.

fourth subscale incorporated five competencies related to *team management*; and the fifth subscale, three competencies needed for *presenting ideas* and viewpoints. The standardized alpha coefficient for the first four subscales ranged from 0.77 to 0.82 and was 0.63 for the fifth subscale.[14]

The subscales obtained from the factor analyses do not correspond to the components of the competency map classification. In fact, contrary to the subscales obtained in this study, the competency map categories were not generated empirically but formulated through *a priori* analysis. The *team management* subscale (Table 5d), however, is very close to the *manages and supervises* component of the competency map (Table 1).

In addition, the questions related to the first three components of the competency map's professional skills subcategory (Table 1), which deal with problem-solving, load on the three subscales of the factor analysis describing the problem-solving process (Table 5d). From a factor analysis of their 15 questions, Weil *et al.* (2004) obtained three subscales, including one containing every question related to *problem-solving*, and one containing the elements that load on the *presenting ideas* subscale used in this study.

Apart from two subscales, the winter results confirmed the questionnaire's initial results (Table 6). First, the students are less convinced that VTA activities enhanced their ability to make recommendations (Table 6b), most likely because they did not apply this competency as anticipated in their capacity as trainees. Second, they are confident that VTA activities greatly enhanced their ability to present ideas (Table 6b), having noted the importance of these skills both in the office and with clients and then put them to the test during their training period. This realisation may have reinforced their understanding of the competency level they had reached and how VTA activities had furthered their development. Overall, since changes were noted on only two subscales, the results indicate that perceptions about the usefulness of VTA activities in developing/improving attributes and competencies had remained relatively stable over time.

Few significant differences ($P \leq 0.05$) were noted by demographic variables—i.e. accounting work experience and prior academic performance in the comprehensive case analysis course (Table 7).[15]

Students with accounting work experience improved their presentation skills more than their counterparts (Table 7a). Their employment might have taught them the importance of presenting ideas articulately in the workplace, leading them to make more efforts to improve related skills through VTA.

In respect of performance in the comprehensive case analysis course (Table 7b), below-average students feel that VTA activities enhanced their ability to identify and analyse problems more than above-average students do. The intensive work with cases, PBL and other pedagogical methods used in VTA were therefore especially helpful to students lacking certain problem-solving skills. Weil *et al.* (2001) found differences for some individual competencies based on prior academic performance, but none for their competency subscales.

4.3. Supervisors' Perceptions of Trainees' Competency

The above analysis shows that students consider VTA activities helpful to competency development. But do their office supervisors feel the same? How did the VTA graduates fare compared to their counterparts? Table 8 answers these questions.

The supervisors reported that the trainees demonstrated very good (19/29) or excellent (4/29) (Table 8a) levels of competency. Only six trainees are rated as good (meaning the novice had attained the office/supervisor's objectives for his/her level), and no one received an unsatisfactory rating.[16] It thus seems clear that VTA activities helped trainees achieve a very high level of competency. However, it should be kept in mind that the

Table 6. Competency subscales of students' perceptions of the development/improvement of competencies by VTA activities

(a) Ethical behaviour/personal attributes

Competency subscales	Summer questionnaire Mean[a] (SD)	Winter questionnaire Mean[a] (SD)	P[b]
Values and drive	5.20 (0.76)	5.11 (0.78)	0.356
Adaptability to situations and persons	5.38 (0.62)	5.36 (0.55)	0.952

(b) Professional skills

Competency subscales	Summer questionnaire Mean[a] (SD)	Winter questionnaire Mean[a] (SD)	P[b]
Problem identification	5.30 (0.78)	5.24 (0.67)	0.326
Analysing	5.19 (0.95)	5.32 (0.58)	0.900
Making recommendations	5.67 (0.74)	5.40 (0.80)	0.025[d]
Team management	5.33 (0.90)	5.28 (0.84)	0.481
Presenting ideas	5.50 (0.84)	5.84 (0.70)	0.004[c]

[a]All the means are significantly different from the mid-point of 4 at $P = 0$ (*t*-tests, two-tailed).
[b]Probabilities are for the Wilcoxon signed ranks test (two-tailed).
[c] and [d] indicate that differences are significant at 1% and 5% levels respectively.

Table 7. Differences in perceptions regarding the impact of VTA activities on the development/improvement of competencies in competency subscales, according to accounting work experience and prior academic performance

(a) Accounting work experience

Competency subscales	Mean/work experience $n = 21$	Mean/no work experience $n = 12$	P[a]
Values and drive	5.12	5.31	0.520
Adaptability to situations and persons	5.43	4.86	0.073
Problem identification	5.39	5.13	0.473
Analysing	5.19	5.20	0.749
Making recommendations	5.70	5.62	0.719
Team management	5.27	5.44	0.984
Presenting ideas	5.75	5.06	0.034[d]

(b) Grade on comprehensive case analysis course

Competency subscales	Mean/below average[b] $n = 16$	Mean/above average $n = 17$	P
Values and drive	5.30	5.09	0.702
Adaptability to situations and persons	5.44	5.02	0.197
Problem identification	5.60	5.04	0.039[d]
Analysing	5.68	4.76	0.007[c]
Making recommendations	5.81	5.54	0.542
Team management	5.28	5.36	0.985
Presenting ideas	5.33	5.65	0.423

[a]All probabilities in the table are for the Mann-Whitney U test (two-tailed).
[b]Sample mean—comprehensive case analysis = 2.95/4.3.
[c] and [d] indicate that differences are significant at 1% and 5% levels respectively.

Table 8. Trainees' competency level and comparative ranking

(a) Trainees' competency level by accounting firm office size

	Number of professionals in accounting firm office				
Competency level[a]	50 or less	Between 51 and 100	Between 101 and 200	More than 200	Total
Good	3	–	1	2	6
Very good	6	6	5	2	19
Excellent	3	–	1	–	4
Total	12	6	7	4	29

Chi-square = 5.762, $P = 0.450$.

(b) Comparative ranking of trainees by accounting firm office size

	Number of professionals in accounting firm office				
Comparative ranking[b]	50 or less	Between 51 and 100	Between 101 and 200	More than 200	Total
Not applicable[c]	7	4	–	–	11
Average	1	1	5	2	9
Above average	3	1	2	2	8
Considerably above average	1	–	–	–	1
Total	12	6	7	4	29

Chi-square = 3.086, $P = 0.379$ (test performed excluding the 'not applicable' classification and after reclassifying the trainee judged considerably above average in the above–average category, 18 trainees).

(c) Trainees' competency level and comparative ranking

	Comparative ranking				
Competency level	Not applicable[c]	Average	Above average	Considerably above average	Total
Good	2	4	–	–	6
Very good	8	5	6	–	19
Excellent	1	–	2	1	4
Total	11	9	8	1	29

Chi-square = 7.091, $P = 0.029$ (test performed excluding the 'not applicable' classification and after reclassifying the trainee judged considerably above average in the above–average category, 18 trainees). For these 18 trainees, spearman $\rho = 0.668$, $P = 0.001$ (one-tailed)

[a]No trainee's competency was judged unsatisfactory.
[b]No UQTR trainee was judged below average or considerably below average compared to trainees from other universities.
[c]Accounting firm offices where all trainees were UQTR students.

supervisors evaluated both the students' generic skills and their specific competencies in performance measurement, assurance, taxation, for example—categories that could not be isolated in the overall assessment. Assuming that both types of competencies are highly correlated, it is possible to link the supervisors' assessment to the development of generic competencies by VTA activities.

Since the students worked in accounting firms of various sizes, the smaller firms may have given the novices more responsibility and thus entertained expectations that the trainees could not reasonably meet. Although no correlation can be established between firm size and novices' competency level (Table 8a), three of the four novices who were rated as excellent worked in a small firm (50 professionals or less), which runs counter to the preceding argument.

The supervisors who oversaw a mixed population of novices characterize the UQTR students as either average compared to novices from other universities (9/18), or above average (9/18), including one who was deemed considerably above average (Table 8b).[17] Several accounting firms were unable to make such comparisons as all their trainees were from UQTR (11/29). There seems to be no correlation between the size of the office and its relative ranking of UQTR trainees.

There is, however, a significant relationship between competency level and relative ranking (Table 8c). The UQTR trainees rated individually as good are classified as only average in comparison with their peers, while those rated individually as excellent are classified as above average or better in comparison. The very good students are ranked in either the average or above-average categories, reflecting differences in supervisors' criteria for these categories.

4.4. Students' Performance on the CA Uniform Evaluation

Students' results on the CA Uniform Evaluation provide another external assessment of their level of competency, both generic and specific. The students who participated in this study took the Uniform evaluation in the autumn of 2007. Of the 31 who sat the examination, 29 were successful, resulting in a 93.5% pass rate. The overall pass rate for students who took the same examination for the first time in the Province of Quebec was 80.3% (OCAQ, 2007). It thus appears that improvement in skills such as problem-solving and the ability to make recommendations helped students in their professional examination, although numerous other factors could have also contributed to this difference.

Summary and Conclusion

The objective of this study was to investigate the usefulness of a mixed teaching approach in developing/improving the generic competencies of accounting students. The skills investigated were selected from the *Canadian CA Candidates' Competency Map* (CICA, 2005), with certain skills also paralleling those studied in the literature (Weil *et al.*, 2001; 2004).

The results show that VTA activities were useful in developing all 32 competencies investigated. Ability to make recommendations, ability to facilitate group processes, ability to present a viewpoint within a group, and ability to analyse and solve problems were among the competencies that VTA activities developed/improved the most. To assess whether the students had changed their views about the effectiveness of their academic program, the survey was administered once again, after they had embarked on their careers. The relatively consistent results of a single questionnaire administered on two separate occasions reveal that the students' perceptions of the contribution of VTA activities remained comparatively unchanged over time.

Some differences in perception were noted by demographic variable particularly that of prior performance in courses involving the resolution of complex case studies. VTA appears to have been more useful in improving problem identification and analysis in below-average students, which could lead to the conclusion that the mixed teaching approach should be advocated as a tool to help below-average students develop certain skills.

The validity of the results concerning the contribution of VTA activities to the development of students' skills and their perceptions of the usefulness of such activities was enhanced by obtaining an independent opinion on competency levels from office supervisors. They reported that VTA veterans mainly had very good or excellent competency levels. Further, when compared to other trainees, office supervisors described UQTR novices as at least average or above average. The excellent performance of the students on the CA Uniform Evaluation, which had a pass rate of 93.5%, also attests to the high level of academic and professional skills of the students who participated in VTA.

Overall, the results of the study support the use of a mixed teaching approach in enhancing personal skills, problem-solving, ability to present ideas, and group work skills. This study and those cited throughout this paper show that academics seeking to develop their students' generic skills should choose teaching methods other than, and in addition to, traditional lectures.

Limitations and Future Research

The current study has the following limitations. First, comparisons among UQTR students on the CA track could not be made because the mock firm was a mandatory part of their CA curriculum, making the inclusion of a control group impossible. Future research should replicate this study and compare VTA students, who are taught using a mixed teaching method, with students in other Quebec universities where the mock firm is not part of the curriculum. Second, replication of this study would also be useful in strengthening the results generally, as they may have been affected by the small sample size. Third, the usefulness of the mixed approach was assessed globally, making it impossible to identify any specific method that best enhanced individual competencies. Future research could focus on assessing students' perceptions of the VTA program's individual components.

The differences in perceptions noted on the basis of students' accounting work experience and prior academic performance may be attributable to learning style, group dynamics or other factors. Personality traits may affect preferences for different learning styles (Hutchinson and Gul, 1997) and therefore their effectiveness. The effort expended in actually performing the learning activities might also be associated with different levels of skills acquisition and thus influence students' perceptions of the activities' effectiveness in enhancing their skills. If future research considers these variables, it may provide additional information on how a mixed teaching approach can develop generic skills.

Acknowledgments

Sylvain Durocher's and Antonello Callimaci's comments on earlier drafts of this paper are gratefully acknowledged.

Notes

[1]In 2007, more than 234 cases had been written. They are available to program instructors on the program's web site.

[2]The Uniform Evaluation is held over a three-day period. On the first day, a five-hour examination on one global multidisciplinary case is administered. On each of the following days, a four-hour examination on three or four multidisciplinary cases is administered.

[3]The first version of the *CA Candidates' Competency Map* was produced for the 2003 uniform evaluation. The map is updated annually, with most of the changes impacting specific competencies.

[4]Depending on the year, between 5% and 8% of students who write the uniform examination in the Province of Quebec are UQTR students.

[5]Working in teams can give students the opportunity to develop their oral skills by defending their ideas. This skill relates to one aspect of the fourth professional skill, 'Shares information and opinions through discussions and presentations' (see Table 1).

[6]Several questions were clarified and two questions from Weil *et al.* (2004) were dropped because students noted similarities with other questions (as evidenced by a very high correlation between both types of questions). The pre-test used a Likert scale of five for one group and seven for the other. The latter was retained as it allowed significantly more variance in the answers.

[7]Quebec students have to take a two-year general course or a three-year technical program in CEGEP after finishing high school and before entering university.

[8]One supervisor had three students to supervise and provided separate evaluations for each of them.

[9]Ethical behaviour relates to personal values and can therefore be combined with personal attributes.

[10]Strategic thinking is defined as the ability to perform an insightful analysis reflecting knowledge of the entity and leading to enhanced decision-making and/or the improvement of organisational performance.

[11]Seven competencies were mentioned only once, while nine competencies were each mentioned twice. Three students mentioned the ability to facilitate group processes, and five, the ability to express ideas articulately in an oral presentation.

[12]That students had a very positive teamwork experience during VTA activities was evident in the means of the eight questions related to group work, all of which were significantly higher than the mid-point of moderately satisfied on a scale of one to seven (*t*-tests, results not presented). Availability, contribution and participation of team members in meetings were quite satisfactory; however, quality of communication seems to have been somewhat less so. Students were satisfied with the quality and contribution of the team members' assignments in report writing and with their overall contribution to the work.

[13]The extraction method was the principal component analysis. The rotation method used was varimax with Kaiser normalization.

[14]Overall, the standardized alpha coefficients obtained for the seven factors are considered sufficient and reliable for a study of this nature (Nunnally, 1978).

[15]As in Weil *et al.* (2004), there were no significant differences ($P \leq 0.05$) on the subscales according to gender (not tabulated). Weil *et al.* (2001), however, obtained differences according to gender on two of their eight subscales. Contrary to Weil *et al.* (2004), there were no significant differences on the subscales according to age (not tabulated).

[16]Supervisors' perceptions of trainee competency did not differ according to gender, age, prior work experience in accounting, or cumulative average (not tabulated).

[17]There was a significant relationship between relative rankings and cumulative averages (not tabulated). Trainees with above-average cumulative averages were always ranked as above average in comparison to their peers, while below-average novices were usually ranked average in comparison.

References

Accounting Education Change Commission (AECC) (1990) Objectives of education for accountants: position statement number one, *Issues in Accounting Education*, 5(2), pp. 307–312.

Adler, R. W. and Milne, M. J. (1997) Improving the quality of accounting students' learning through action-oriented learning tasks, *Accounting Education: an international journal*, 6(3), pp. 191–215.

Albrecht, W. S. and Sack, R. J. (2000) *Accounting Education: Charting the Course Through a Perilous Future* (Accounting Education Series No, 16) (Sarasota, FL: American Accounting Association).

American Accounting Association (AAA) (1986) Committee on the future structure, content and scope of accounting education (The Bedford Committee). Future accounting education: preparing for the expending profession (The Bedford Report), *Issues in Accounting Education*, 1(1), pp. 168–195.

American Institute of Certified Public Accountants (AICPA) (1999) *The AICPA Core Competency Framework for Entry into the Accounting Profession* (New York, NY: AICPA).

Anderson, U., Marchant, G., Robinson, J. and Schadewald, M. (1990) Selection of instructional strategies in the presence of related prior knowledge, *Issues in Accounting Education*, 5(1), pp. 41–58.

Arquero Montano, J. L., Jimenez Cardoso, S. M. and Joyce, J. (2004) Skills development, motivation and learning in financial statements analysis: an evaluation of alternative types of case studies, *Accounting Education: an international journal*, 13(2), pp. 191–212.

Arthur Andersen & Co., Arthur Young, Coopers & Lybrand, Deloitte Haskins & Sells, Ernst & Whinney, Peat Marwick Main & Co., Price Waterhouse and Touche Ross (1989) *Perspective on Education: Capabilities for Success in the Accounting Profession (The White Paper)* (New York, NY: Arthur Anderson & Co. *et al*).

Ballantine, J. A. and McCourt Larres, P. (2004) A critical analysis of students' perceptions of the usefulness of the case study method in an advanced management accounting module: the impact of relevant work experience, *Accounting Education: an international journal*, 13(2), pp. 171–189.

Banning, K. C. (2003) The effect of the case method on tolerance for ambiguity, *Journal of Management Education*, 27(5), pp. 556–567.

Barsky, N. P. and Catanach, Jr A. H. (2005) Motivating student interest in accounting: a business planning approach to the introductory management accounting course, *Advances in Accounting Education: Teaching and Curriculum Innovations*, 7, pp. 27–63.

Berry, A. (1993) Encouraging group skills in accountancy students: an innovative approach, *Accounting Education: an international journal*, 2(3), pp. 169–179.

Blanchette, M. and Brouard, F. (1994) Learning by discovering: using a case in an introduction to accounting course, in: World Association for Case Method Research and Application (Ed.) *The Art of Interactive Teaching*, pp. 121–130 (Needham, MA: World Association for Case Method Research and Application).

Bonner, S. E. (1999) Choosing teaching method based on learning objectives: an integrative framework, *Issues in Accounting Education*, 14(1), pp. 11–39.

Boritz, J. E. and Carnaghan, C. A. (2003) Competency-based education and assessment for the accounting profession: a critical review, *Canadian Accounting Perspectives*, 2(1), pp. 7–42.

Boyce, G., Williams, S., Kelly, A. and Yee, H. (2001) Fostering deep and elaborative learning and generic (soft) skill development: the strategic use of case studies in accounting education, *Accounting Education: an international journal*, 10(1), pp. 37–60.

Breton, G. (1999) Some empirical evidence on the superiority of the problem-based learning (PBL) method, *Accounting Education: an international journal*, 8(1), pp. 1–12.

Canadian Institute of Chartered Accountants (CICA) (1996) *The Inter-Institute Vision Task Force* (Toronto, Ontario: CICA).

Canadian Institute of Chartered Accountants (CICA) (1999) *Securing our Future! Reengineering the CA Qualification Process* (Final Report of the Education Reengineering Task Force) (Toronto, Ontario, CICA).

Canadian Institute of Chartered Accountants (CICA) (2001) *The Canadian CA Competency Map* (Toronto, Ontario: CICA).

Canadian Institute of Chartered Accountants (2005) *The CA Candidates' Competency Map: Understanding the Professional Competencies of CAs* (Toronto, Ontario: CICA).

Canadian Institute of Chartered Accountants (CICA) (2007) *CICA Handbook* (Toronto, Ontario: CICA).

Ciccotello, C. S., D'Amico, R. J. and Grant, C. T. (1997) An empirical examination of cooperative learning techniques and student performance, *Accounting Education: A Journal of Theory, Practice, and Research*, 2(1), pp. 1–8.

Clinton, B. D. and Kohlmeyer, III J. M. (2005) The effects of group quizzes on performance and motivation to learn: two experiments in cooperative learning, *Journal of Accounting Education*, 23(2), pp. 96–116.

Comité consultatif et d'orientation du programme de formation professionnelle (COCOPFP) (1994) *Document de travail* (Working document) (Montreal, Quebec: Ordre des Comptables Agréés du Québec).

Conférence des recteurs et des principaux des universités du Québec/Ordre des comptables agréés du Québec (CREPUQ/OCAQ) (1994) *Rapport du comité conjoint* (Report of the joint committee) (June) (Montreal, Quebec: CREPUQ/OCAQ).

Craig, R. and Amernic, J. (1994) Role playing in a conflict resolution setting: description and some implications for accounting, *Issues in Accounting Education*, 9(1), pp. 28–44.

Crumbley, D. L., Smith, K. T. and Smith, L. M. (1998) Educational novels and students role-playing: a teaching note, *Accounting Education: an international journal*, 7(2), pp. 183–191.

Deppe, L. A., Sonderegger, E. O., Stice, J. D., Clark, D. C. and Streuling, G. F. (1991) Emerging competencies for the practice of accountancy, *Journal of Accounting Education*, 9(2), pp. 257–290.

Dillard-Eggers, J. and Wooten, T. C. (2003) The use of peer tutors in introductory financial accounting, *Advances in Accounting Education*, 5, pp. 55–80.

Easton, G. (1992) *Learning from Case Studies*. (2nd ed.) (London: Prentice-Hall).

Edmonds, C. D., Edmonds, T. P. and Mulig, E. V. (2003) Using problem-based learning to promote skill development in the accounting classroom, *Advances in Accounting Education: Teaching and Curriculum Innovations*, 5, pp. 229–242.

Etter, E. R., Burmeister, S. L. and Elder, R. J. (2000) Improving student performance and retention via supplemental instruction, *Journal of Accounting Education*, 18(4), pp. 355–368.

Fortin, A. and Legault, M. (2006) L'apprentissage au moyen d'une simulation en vérification: Impact sur la performance et les perceptions des étudiants [Learning using an audit simulation: Impact on students' performance and perceptions], *Comptabilité, Contrôle, Audit*, 12(Special Issue) Recherche et pédagogie en comptabilité—contrôle—audit [Research and pedagogy in accounting, control and audit], pp. 39–65.

Gosselin, J. (1998) *Vire, Tuelle & Associés: Guide du personnel professionnel [Vire, Tuelle & Associates: Guide for Professional Employees]* (Quebec: UQTR).

Green, B. P. and Calderon, T. G. (2005) Assessing student learning and growth through audit risk simulations, *Advances in Accounting Education: Teaching and Curriculum Innovations*, 7, pp. 1–25.

Groomer, S. M., Mohrweis, L. C. and Ward, D. D. (1992) An empirical examination of a video simulation for audit instruction, *The Accounting Educators Journal*, 4(1), pp. 40–52.

Grudnitski, G. (2000) The effect of group rewards on obtaining higher achievement from cooperative learning, *Advances in Accounting Education*, 2, pp. 165–177.

Hassall, T., Lewis, S. and Broadbent, M. (1998) Teaching and learning using case studies: a teaching note, *Accounting Education: an international journal*, 7(4), pp. 325–334.

Heagy, C. D. and Lehman, C. M. (2005) Is PBL an improved delivery method for the accounting curriculum? *Advances in Accounting Education: Teaching and Curriculum Innovations*, 7, pp. 221–251.

Hite, P. (1996) A treatment study of the effectiveness of group exams in an individual income tax class, *Issues in Accounting Education*, 11(1), pp. 61–75.

Hutchinson, M. and Gul, F. A. (1997) The interactive effects of extroversion/introversion traits and collectivism/individualism cultural beliefs on student group learning preferences, *Journal of Accounting Education*, 15(1), pp. 95–107.

Hwang, N. R., Lui, G. and Tong, M. Y. J. (2005) An empirical test of cooperative learning in a passive learning environment, *Issues in Accounting Education*, 20(2), pp. 151–165.

Hwang, N. R., Lui, G. and Tong, M. Y. J. (2008) Cooperative learning in a passive learning environment: a replication and extension, *Issues in Accounting Education*, 23(1), pp. 67–75.

International Federation of Accountants (IFAC) (1996) *Prequalification Education, Assessment of Professional Competence and Experience Requirements of Professional Accountants* (International Education Guideline No, 9) (New York, NY: IFAC).

International Federation of Accountants (IFAC) (2003) *International Education Standard for Professional Skills (IES 3)* (New York, NY: IFAC).

Johnstone, K. M. and Biggs, S. F. (1998) Problem-based learning: introduction, analysis, and accounting curricula implications, *Journal of Accounting Education*, 16(3–4), pp. 407–427.

Kern, B. B. (2000) Structuring financial statements analysis projects to enhance critical thinking skills development, *Journal of Accounting Education*, 18(4), pp. 341–353.

Kim, J. and Mueller, C. W. (1978) *Factor Analysis* (Beverly Hills, CA: Sage Publications).

Lancaster, K. A. S. and Strand, C. A. (2001) Using the team-learning model in a managerial accounting class: an experiment in cooperative learning, *Issues in Accounting Education*, 16(4), pp. 549–567.

Libby, P. A. (1991) Barriers to using cases in accounting education, *Issues in Accounting Education*, 6(2), pp. 193–213.

Metrejean, C., Pittman, J. and Zarzesky, M. T. (2002) Guest speakers: reflection on the role of accountants in the classroom, *Accounting Education: an international journal*, 11(4), pp. 347–364.

Milne, M. J. and McConnell, P. J. (2001) Problem-based learning: a pedagogy for using case material in accounting education, *Accounting Education: an international journal*, 10(1), pp. 61–82.

Mohrweis, L. C. (1993) Teaching audit planning and risk assessment: an empirical test of the dermaceutics instructional resources, *Issues in Accounting Education*, 8(2), pp. 391–403.

Nunnally, J. C. (1978) *Psychometric Theory*, Second edition (New York: McGraw-Hill Book Company).

Ordre des comptables agréés du Québec (OCAQ) (1995) *Programme de formation professionnelle des candidats au titre de comptable agréé* [Professional education program for CA candidates] (Montreal, Quebec: OCAQ).

Ordre des comptables agréés du Québec (OCAQ) (2005) *Code of Ethics of Chartered Accountants of Quebec* (Montreal, Quebec: OCAQ). Available at http://ocaq.qc.ca/pdf/ang/2_protection/2_3_deontologie.pdf (accessed 29 May 2008).

Ordre des comptables agréés du Québec (OCAQ) (2007) *Uniform Evaluation*. Available at http://ocaq.qc.ca/exam/2007/pdf/ang/efu2007_statistiques.pdf (accessed 30 November 2007).

Parry, Jr R. W. (1990) The impact of assigned study groups on study effort and examination performance, *Issues in Accounting Education*, 5(2), pp. 222–239.

Ravenscroft, S. P., Buckless, F. A., McCombs, G. B. and Zuckerman, G. J. (1995) Incentives in student team learning: an experiment in cooperative group learning, *Issues in Accounting Education*, 10(1), pp. 97–109.

Ravenscroft, S. P., Buckless, F. A. and Zuckerman, G. (1997) Student team learning-replication and extension, *Accounting Education: A Journal of Theory, Practice, and Research*, 2(2), pp. 151–172.

Ravenscroft, S. P., Buckless, F. A. and Hassall, T. (1999) Cooperative learning—a literature guide, *Accounting Education: an international journal*, 8(2), pp. 163–176.

Sawyer, A. J., Tomlinson, S. R. and Maples, A. J. (2000) Developing essentials skills through case study scenarios, *Journal of Accounting Education*, 18(3), pp. 257–282.

Siegel, P. H., Omer, K. and Agrawal, S. P. (1997) Video simulation of an audit: an experiment in experiential learning theory, *Accounting Education: an international journal*, 6(3), pp. 217–230.

Society for Teaching and Learning in Higher Education (2000) *The Alan Blizzard Award* (Hamilton, Ontario: STLHE).

Stanley, T. and Edwards, P. (2005) Interactive multimedia teaching of accounting information systems (AIS) cycles: student perceptions and views, *Journal of Accounting Education*, 23(1), pp. 21–46.

Stewart, J. P. and Dougherty, T. W. (1993) Using case studies in teaching accounting: a quasi-experimental study, *Accounting Education: an international journal*, 2(1), pp. 1–10.

Stout, D. E. (1996) Experiential evidence and recommendations regarding case-based teaching in undergraduate cost accounting, *Journal of Accounting Education*, 14(3), pp. 293–317.

Tabone, J. (2007) Is the gender gap history? *CAmagazine*, 140(8), p. 7.

Van der Laan Smith, J. and Spindle, R. M. (2007) The impact of group formation in a cooperative learning environment, *Journal of Accounting Education*, 25(4), pp. 153–167.

Watson, S. F., Apostolou, B., Hassell, J. M. and Webber, S. A. (2007) Accounting education literature review (2003–2005), *Journal of Accounting Education*, 25(1–2), pp. 1–58.

Weil, S., Oyelere, P., Yeoh, J. and Firer, C. (2001) A study of student's perceptions of the usefulness of case studies for the development of finance and accounting-related skills and knowledge, *Accounting Education: an international journal*, 10(2), pp. 123–146.

Weil, S., Oyelere, P. and Rainsbury, E. (2004) The usefulness of case studies in developing core competencies in a professional accounting programme: a New Zealand study, *Accounting Education: an international journal*, 13(2), pp. 139–169.

Embedding Generic Employability Skills in an Accounting Degree: Development and Impediments

GREG STONER and MARGARET MILNER

University of Glasgow, UK

ABSTRACT *This paper explores and analyses the views of, and effects on, students of a project that integrated the development of employability skills within the small group classes of two compulsory courses in the first year of an accounting degree at a UK university. The project aimed to build, deliver and evaluate course materials designed to encourage the development of a broad range of employability skills: skills needed for life-long learning and a successful business career. By analysing students' opinions gathered from a series of focus groups spread throughout the year, three prominent skill areas of interest were identified: time management, modelling, and learning to learn. Further analysis highlighted the complex nature of skills development, and brought to light a range of impediments and barriers to both students' development of employability skills and their subject learning. The analysis suggests the need for accounting educators to see skills development as being an essential element of the path to providing a successful accounting education experience.*

Introduction

The embedding of generic or employability skills in the higher education (HE) curriculum has been of interest for many years and, as witnessed by this special edition of *Accounting Education*, continues to be of substantial interest to accounting educators. This exploratory paper reports on students' views and perceptions of the relevance of these skills to their degree studies drawing on a range of issues arising in relation to a skills integration project at a large Scottish university. The project aimed to develop, deliver and evaluate teaching material, in line with the university's strategies of quality enhancement and employability which encouraged students to develop a broad range of generic employability skills: skills needed for life-long learning and a successful business career.

The project embedded skills development within the small group teaching of two compulsory level one courses in an accounting and finance degree programme: a management accounting course and a business statistics course. The course materials made clear and explicit reference to the skills-based intended learning outcomes (ILOs) in addition to the subject-based ILOs. The skills-based ILOs included references to a very broad range of generic skills.[1] The skills selected represent a subset of those identified by previous studies investigating accounting graduates (see, for example, Francis and Minchington, 1999; Gammie *et al.*, 2002; Hassall *et al.*, 2003; Arquero Montaño *et al.*, 2001; 2004; Morgan, 1997; Tempone and Martin, 2003; Zaid and Abraham, 1994). The new learning and teaching material was designed to provide students with opportunities to build their employability profile alongside developing their subject-specific knowledge. This design was intended to encourage students to build their skill base as part of their pathway to higher levels of cognitive development.

The paper looks at three primary themes that arose from the analysis of student focus group transcripts: time management, modelling, and learning to learn. These three issues are prominent in the data and, within this study, are indicative of students' attitudes to skills and their personal development of skills. By focusing on this limited range of issues the paper explores, analyses and brings to light a range of factors that appear to be important barriers, or impediments, to students' skill development within the context of accounting education.

The paper is structured as follows. The next section outlines the background to the project and the motivation for the research, including a review on the nature of the perceived skills gap, and how skills were integrated into the level one compulsory courses. This is followed by a section on research design before the discussion of the principle themes discovered from the focus group data. The paper ends with a discussion of the major issues arising from the results, including how students' skills development relates to the notions of 'threshold concepts': key concepts which, when mastered, transform a learner's understanding of a subject or discipline (Meyer and Land, 2003; Entwistle, 2005; Lucas and Mladenovic, 2007; Jack and McCartney, 2007).

Project Motivation and Background

Recent research in accounting education clearly shows that there is a perceived skills gap when investigating the opinions, attitudes and comments of relevant employers, students and recently-qualified accountants (Arquero Montaño *et al.*, 2001; 2004; Gammie *et al.*, 2002; Hassall *et al.*, 2004; Francis and Minchington, 1999). It is also clear from the literature that the provision of skills is neither easy nor straightforward (Tempone and Martin, 2003). Further, Morgan (1997) refers to the tension between skills development and the provision of support for skills in higher education and notes that this tension is particularly high in vocationally-based degrees. In addition, Milner and Hill (2008) have found that some accounting academics have the attitude that there is 'no time' for skills development in the accounting curriculum, due to the demands of the discipline, accounting research and professional accreditation. Yet experience indicates that many first year students do not appear to develop appropriate learning strategies or possess the necessary skills to deal adequately with the contested nature of the business and accountancy disciplines.

The basic premise of the project was that skills are important for life-long learning and employability, and that addressing the skills gap at an early stage in students' university studies is important in helping students to accelerate their cognitive development and provide the transferable skills required for life-long learning, and by employers. This premise is in line with the current views of professional bodies and significant elements of the higher education establishment (see for example, IFAC, 2003; 2004; 2006; SHEFC, 2005; 2006). The combination of subject-specific elements and generic skills provides *value added* in employability profiles of students (Arquero Montaño *et al.*, 2004). The challenge for academics in higher education is therefore to change what is taught and how it is taught to generate the value added (Tempone and Martin, 2003; Stubbs and Keeping, 2002). This project attempted to do just that: change the small group teaching of two degree courses to facilitate skills development alongside subject learning.

The courses chosen for this project were Introduction to Business Statistics (IBS), delivered in semester one, and Management Accounting 1 (MA1), delivered in semester two, of the 2005–2006 academic session. These courses were chosen primarily because the course coordinators were interested in students' skill development and together these compulsory courses, which are generally taken only by accounting majors, span the whole of the first year. The coordinators attained funding for the development and evaluation of the project from the University's Learning and Teaching Development Fund.[2]

These courses are an integral part of the first year curriculum and provided a variety of different types of learning aims and outcomes. The different subject matter of the courses had an impact on the selection of the employability skills that were emphasized in each course. The different contexts provided the opportunity for students to develop skills from different perspectives whilst illustrating their generic nature. Both courses are often perceived by students as being primarily quantitative. However, both also include a range of more qualitative learning outcomes, including critical analysis and critical thinking skills: vital generic skills that Jack and McCartney (2007) have recently encapsulated in their arguments for the importance of developing 'argumentative accountants'. In this project the development of critical analysis and decision modelling skills was envisaged at least in part as the desire to foster students' ethical and intellectual development (Perry, 1970; Kenefelkamp, 1999): a development process that requires students to move away from dualistic standpoints to learning—where questions tend to be seen as having clear 'right' and 'wrong' answers—towards more relativistic positions, where there is a recognized need towards accepting responsibility to evaluate alternative views and answers in real contexts.

The generic skills of critical analysis and evaluation are important in both statistics and management accounting, as these subjects rarely have definitive right and wrong answers. In statistics this is clearly seen as the discipline moves from the field of descriptive statistics to inferential statistics where understanding and evaluation become important for their understanding. In management accounting the need for critical evaluation becomes apparent in the choice between alternative techniques (for example, between full and marginal costing) in different decision, or reporting, contexts. Similarly, a modelling approach to problem-solving was an integral and fundamental element of each course. The aim of the small group teaching for the business statistics course was to build statistical reasoning by improving students' statistical literacy and by applying statistical concepts and statistical models in problem-solving situations. The management accounting course placed particular emphasis on using a modelling approach to the understanding and critical evaluation of alternative techniques and the choices among them in different contexts.

The employability skills were introduced in a cumulative manner and in association with core subject skills and learning outcomes. Each of the small class learning and teaching activities included multiple, and mixed, skills development tasks. The new learning interventions were designed to encourage students to build these skills and adopt learning strategies and positions that would aid their employability, including developing their intellectual maturity. Further, the skills elements, both those for 'preparatory' and 'in class' tasks, were made explicit within the ILOs and instructions for each tutorial and computer lab activity. The tasks set often included mini-cases or real world data in order to provide the contexts for inference, interpretation and evaluation, and often required students to model either the data or the solution processes. In both courses students were required or encouraged to use spreadsheets to both facilitate their modelling and to help them make their processes explicit in model form.

The next section deals with the approach taken to the evaluation of the project and the methodology adopted for this paper.

Research Design

From the start the project was designed to evaluate qualitatively the newly-developed small group teaching, which was designed to enhance students' employability and life-long learning skills in a variety of ways. This early emphasis on the evaluation of the teaching interventions addresses the criticism that the design and development of teaching is often seen as a separate task (Milton and Lyons, 2003) which diminishes the instructiveness of the feedback and evaluation. Difficulties in the evaluation of the implementation were recognized from the start of the project (detailed in MacIver *et al.*, 2005). Student focus groups, staff and student reflective diaries, interactive questionnaires, and post-intervention debriefing sessions were used in the evaluation. This paper concentrates on the data from the student focus groups, which has proved to be the richest source of information and is recognized as a highly effective means for studying education and training (Field, 2000).

Seven focus group meetings per group were held: with three focus group sessions being scheduled in each semester plus one end-of-year meeting before the degree examination. These meetings were interleaved with the new small group teaching interventions as indicated in Table 1.

As it was recognized that the management of the focus groups would be crucial to the gathering of high quality source data, the University's Teaching and Learning Service

Table 1. Timing and sequence of interventions and focus group meetings: 2005–06.

Week no.	Focus group meeting	Small group interventions	Notes
1			Start of IBS and semester 1
2	October		
3–5		1 and 2	
6	November		
7–10		3, 4 and 5	
11	December		
12			End of IBS teaching and semester one (Christmas break—two weeks)
13			Start of MA1 and semester two
14	January		
14–17		6–9	
18	February		
18–21		10–13	
22	March		End of MA1 teaching and semester two (Easter break—three weeks)
24	April		
26–30			Degree examination period (for courses in both semesters)

(TLS) agreed to manage and facilitate (mediate) the focus group, thus ensuring anonymity between the students and the course staff. This distance of the research team from the focus groups ensured an independent source of student data.

At the start of the academic year all first year students were invited to volunteer for the focus groups during a class session dedicated to explaining the nature of the project. Students were also encouraged to participate in other classes, by e-mail and by virtual learning environment postings. Twenty-four students (25% of the cohort) volunteered, each having given informed consent to their involvement, and were organized into three focus groups. After the first focus group meeting student numbers diminished with seven students attending all semester one meetings, and six students attending all semester two meetings.

The research team supplied the TLS mediator with questions which the mediator delivered in a consistent and, as far as possible, neutral manner across the focus groups (which is another advantage of employing a mediator who was not part of the teaching teams). The questions were intended to prompt students' opinions on, and evaluations of, the small group teaching interventions and employability skills. The focus group sessions were recorded and independently transcribed, with the transcripts exceeding 62 000 words.

There is, of course, the possibility of bias arising in terms of students' participation in the study. It is possible that the students involved in the focus groups were in some way affected by their involvement. However, the use of an independent facilitator, whose research background includes the first year experience and transition to university, was expected to minimize, as much as possible, any such bias. The research team also considered that any such bias arising from participation was likely to be small in comparison with the personal changes which students were likely to go through over the life of the project. It is also possible that there is a degree of self-selection bias in that the students who volunteered to participate may not be representative of the class as a whole. Though attempts were made to minimize this bias by inviting and encouraging all students to participate, this is a recognized attribute of the method used to collect the data. This bias is a recognized limitation of the research and its conclusions and is more than offset by the richness of the data collected, which would not be possible via methods using more representative sampling.

The analysis of the transcript data was qualitatively evaluated in several phases. Initial reading identified themes (Milner and Stoner, 2006). This was followed by free form manual coding in NVivo by a member of the research team who had an informed view but who did not participate in the development of the small group teaching. Finally, the primary researchers repeatedly read and reread the transcripts, using the coding to facilitate the analysis. This mixed strategy was employed to help achieve an appropriate balance of analysis: exploiting the value of purposefully moving between closeness to the data and distance from the data. Closeness promotes familiarity and appreciation of subtle differences, whilst distance facilitates abstraction and synthesis of ideas and concepts (Richards, 1998; Gilbert, 2002; Crowley *et al.*, 2002; Richards, T., 2002; Richards, L., 2002).

Views and Analysis

During the focus groups a large number of issues were raised and addressed: some raised by students, some in response to the facilitator's prompts. Some of these issues related to the subject material and others were of a general nature. This paper looks at three of the most significant and frequently raised employability (generic) skills themes that emerged from the coding and reading of the focus group transcripts. The broad skills areas addressed here being time management skills, modelling and analysis skills, and the overarching skill of learning to learn, with all these skills being considered in the context of students' perceptions of, changing confidence in, and attitudes to, the subjects they were studying.

The following sub-sections address these issues in turn, using interpretations derived from the transcripts along with illustrative quotations of students' comments.[3]

Time Management: Skills and Attitudes

The focus group transcripts include many comments related to students' use and management of their time, sometimes unprompted but also prompted. For example, when asked to indicate what amount of time they were spending on their academic work:

> M: Okay, I'm just trying to get an idea of how much time you are spending outside the lectures on work...?
>
> S: I would say maybe 7 hours per week most. I'll do the work for the tutorials and the workshop say probably 4 hours a week just in Management Accounting, then maybe an hour for Stats, just .... work, maybe half an hour for Finance if anything. ... Economics I will generally spend about an hour on, and then if for any reason I have missed a lecture during the week, then maybe I'll do a bit of reading, but tend to just amalgamate that in with any tutorial workings stuff ... like 6/7 hours. [Feb2]
>
> S: Well my work tends ... is just for the ... If I sit down to do the workshop or tutorial, I tend to do that every week. I try to do the question, it does take about an hour at least ... yeah. If you had to get the right answer at all ... you definitely sitting for an hour, either staring at the page blankly or trying to do something, so yeah... [Feb2]

These and other similar comments indicate fairly modest levels of time given students' class times of between 10 and 14 hours per week. Further, the transcripts do not include claims indicating not having enough time for academic work, except around revision and coursework submission times. This is an interesting observation—particularly when there is concern in universities that economic pressures are forcing students into paid work.

Earlier in the academic year when students were asked about which of a list of skills were important to them, time management was recognized as being relevant and in need of development:

> S: I think maybe like your time management will need to change a [little] bit, because.... have a chapter about it in school, would be a case of I don't know ... but I think it would be a lot shorter. What time you need to set aside to do that chapter in university for that, I mean a university book, to understand it, so it's going to take maybe two or three reads to take it on, whereas in school it is a bit easier for you. It was straightforward enough, just got to adjust your timekeeping, maybe give space a time for it ..., and don't underestimate the things you have to do. [Oct 1]
>
> S: Be able to study and manage your time, take notes in lectures. It's not like school where you get a lot more help. [Oct2]

These quotations illustrate that students recognize that independent study requires more time, as they find it more difficult. Therefore, they are going to have to manage their own time more actively. Further, they realize the need to prioritize for themselves taking leads from feedback from staff, as shown below, rather than having specific direction:

> M: Okay.... you mentioned there about comments on work, what do you think is more important, feedback on your work or the grades?
>
> S: You need the feedback because you want to know what you are doing wrong, what to improve on. What you are doing well and what you are not doing so well, and maybe you can adjust your time doing that, just like come back to time-keeping, adjust your time to what your weaknesses are, and spend more time on those weaknesses. [Oct 1]

At the start of the year students were asked about the skills they would be taught and did not include time management. It appears, from this and other evidence, that students did not see the University to have a role here. Instead, students mentioned a variety of skills: surprisingly high amongst them was social skills, partly in the context of working with others, for example:

S: . . . it's going to be all your presentation skills, and I think one of the big things you learn from university just in a general way is how to get along with a lot of different types of people, and you will find you come across there is so many people you have never interacted with before, and you are sort of forced in your tutorial groups. . . . in your tutorials you might be forced in with people you don't necessarily like, and then to be able to sort of work round that and still produce an effective report at the end of it, . . ., even with somebody you don't particularly like working with, can be really invaluable, especially when you go into the workplace. [Oct 1]

S: Social skills would be quite a big thing . . . [Oct 1]

Such comments are a precursor to the important background issues, or complexities, that students face when developing skills or in their academic work. In the last semester, whilst the mediator was exploring students' preparation for tutorials, students explicitly raised the issue of timetabling tutorial preparation time, and even the possibility of getting staff to introduce a problem then leaving them to prepare for an hour before the formal class (another hour), leading to:

M: so do you prefer the idea of having a two-hour slot, or would you prefer a time beforehand?

S: Either or . . . I just feel that a bit more preparation in groups, like having it a little before or having a time slot, then you should know who you are dealing with and what you are meant to be doing, and what you are aiming for. Having the time before, as long as what we were getting told to do was actually covering it, I wouldn't really mind that, but apart from that. . . . Well just basically that you prepare something that doesn't come up. . .. So if they said, Go and prepare this and then you come into it. . .so wouldn't mind like going away. . . . [Dec 1]

S: Problem being that some in the tutorials don't necessarily know each other that well, so that makes it a little bit difficult. But yeah I suppose so, I mean if you actually even schedule any time . . . it doesn't even need a tutor there, but schedule a time slot where there is a room available for people to go and meet and work on tutorial stuff and so do some preparation work, then that would be useful. [Dec 1]

Here we can see students considering the desirability of staff taking on some of the responsibility for managing students' time and being responsible for specific task direction. Again social skill issues arise. We can see the students' comments are mixed. There are references to difficulties with the amount of instruction, but others suggest the issue is lack of confidence in knowing what is expected or what the 'right' work to do is. This suggests, as before, that time management acts as a mask or a proxy for their lack of confidence or their lack of social skills, and possibly an inability to take responsibility for their work. Further, students appear discontented when they have produced work that is not explicitly reviewed during the class, suggesting they see the work as having no other purpose. They do not mind spending time on work if they feel the work feeds directly into, or is important for, the class. Independent study is not seen to be a priority: it appears not to matter to them.

Later in the year students seem to recognize for themselves that they had used time management as a mask for a lack of confidence or social skills, or even to avoid personal responsibility, as reflected here:

S: I think its been going quite well actually. I don't think the workload's really increased. I think you're probably just more knowledgeable about what you're expected to do, so you maybe put in more work with the likes of the tutorials and the workshops, whereas at the start I think most people were really wondering what was expected of us and really didn't do as much preparations as they might have done. [March 1]

It may well be that students are not spending enough time on their academic work nor possess the skills to allocate their time effectively, including their allocation of time between academic and other activities. Skilfully allocating time demands a degree of confidence and recognition that academic work need not be explicitly specified: that there need not be just one way to do the work. From the analysis of these and other comments of students, it appears that students' development of time management skills only comes when they possess the assurance of knowing the parameters of what they need to do for their academic work and have the confidence that comes with that knowledge.

Modelling: Moving Towards Problem-solving

The project and the newly-designed interventions (tutorials and computer labs) placed particular emphasis on problem-solving and the use of models and the modelling process to support problem-solving as important employability skills. As these skills are also an inherent part of the subjects of the courses they were explicitly introduced in a structured way—more so than the approach taken to developing time management skills, which do not have such a subject-specific emphasis.

From the transcripts it is apparent that the students found it difficult to engage in the modelling process and to recognize that the modelling of data supports problem-solving. Students also found it difficult to move away from their search for 'the correct' answer, which is counter-intuitive to model-building, which emphasizes processes and alternatives (Cleveland, 2005).

In relation to an early business statistics tutorial, students made it clear that they were not happy making decisions on the selection of data for modelling exercises. They had been told to select for themselves variables that they felt could be modelled appropriately from a large dataset. Their reactions included:

M: What sort of guidance were you given for doing the data analysis?

S: I think the only things we were given were 100 firms with lots of data, . . . this massive, massive Excel spreadsheet and you had to pick five firms out of those 100. Analyse some data to do with that. Pick three variables you can discern from that data and then present them in a chart. That was the only guidance we were given, so there was no indication of what sort of variables they're wanting. If they want anything like averages or really sort of more in-depth statistical analysis (you know, the skewness and all that sort of stuff) and how the data's presented and there was no specifics. You could pretty much go away and do whatever you wanted, as long as you had three graphs, three different variables, five firms. (Nov 2)

Rather than seeing the preparation as a modelling exercise the students, here and in other focus groups, seemed to want to approach the tutorial as a suite of instructions, only they saw the instructions as being incomplete. In particular, though they were able to recognize the statistical analysis, there was little appreciation that modelling could be a reiterative process involving choices they had to make. Further, there is an indication that they saw at least part of the objective as looking for the particular variables that those who were in control (the teachers) wanted: showing a reluctance to move away from the notion of 'a correct selection'. Students just 'want to do it'.

Further, rather than being intrigued by the requested analysis and modelling exercise, students seemed annoyed that there were '. . . no specifics' included in the instructions:

S: Well, we were given a . . . a sheet about what each column meant, like the meanings of the headings of the columns, but they didn't really say why you would use that one and why you would choose. [Nov 1]

S: It's perhaps an exercise in interpretation, deciding what the lecturers want, but as far as we're concerned, we're looking for something a bit more specific. To say well, if you want that can we go away and do that rather than you just pick the three easiest. [Nov 2]

The lack of engagement exemplified in the last statement, picking the easiest rather than thinking about what the lecturer intended, emphasizes the unwillingness to make decisions. On prompting from the TLS mediator about the types of models the students were expected to build for their tutorial work, a student commented:

S: Was it not to help with the project? Maybe just at start of the project to get us, familiarize us with everything for the project. That's what I thought. [Nov 2]

As illustrated here the students saw the analytical work as being associated with an assessment rather than as a skill-building or knowledge-building exercise in its own right: a perspective that seems to act as a barrier to the development of their model-building skills.

When the TLS mediator asked about the emphasis of modelling in the second semester interventions, after two interventions that included explicit model building elements (including tutorial ILOs), the students' comments were direct:

M: . . . do you think that the tutorials are covering skills like modelling alternatives and formulating problems?

S: What are modelling alternatives? [Feb 1]

S: What do you mean by models? [Feb 2]

A student who commented above was re-prompted:

M: So do you think you are covering the skill of formulating problems as well as solving them? or . . .

S: Don't know. I don't understand what you mean. . . . [Feb 1]

These statements show a lack of appreciation of the modelling processes and, in conjunction with comments from the first semester, an instrumental and shallow focus towards problem-solving. The joint approach of interventions over both semesters, as well as modelling-based assessed coursework for IBS, does not appear to have materially changed the approach of students to problem-solving and the notion of modelling choices. The need to model the underlying reality of the management accounting problems seems to have been lost on the students, despite the explicit instructions and ILOs. They appear to have failed to see the use of models, modelling processes or model-building as useful for solving business problems.

Another student prompted on modelling alternatives said:

S: Different solutions. . . . That scares me, because I'm confused enough by the first one, then there is [sic] all these other ones you can do. It's just like, my brain explodes. [Feb 2]

There is not just a reluctance to engage in modelling, and the inevitable choices, there is also uncertainty, if not fear.

There were indications of some change over time as indicated by comments in the last focus group in response to the mediator's question about their skills development:

S: I think you have a lot more choice in how you do it here, because I think at school they'd say, 'Oh I think you need this section, this section and this . . .' And here there's that question. . .. [April 1]

S: ... And here.... yeah but... .here just say, 'You are doing a report using what we've covered in lectures and use the dataset', so it's like ... gives you a lot more scope for choice and.... I don't know, I guess you have to do a lot more planning before you can actually start the report, which would have usually been set by the teacher. [April 1]

This notion of choice, which is an integral aspect of an understanding of modelling, is an implicit recognition by the student that there are alternatives: one of the core issues addressed in the next section of analysis.

Learning To Learn: Skills, Attitudes and Perspectives

In the preceding analysis references were made to background issues or complexities that shaped, distorted or inhibited students' skills, attitudes and development. A deeper analysis of the transcripts identifies that these complexities can also be seen as aspects of the 'learning to learn' skills that were considered to be an integral part of the initial project design. These 'learning to learn' skills are a collection of 'higher level' employability skills concerned with students' ability to manage their own learning, including views on the nature of the discipline, their attitudes to learning responsibility, their ability to contextualize their understandings, and their confidence in themselves and in their learning. This is a perspective on learning informed by the notions of students' positioning on Perry's scheme of 'ethical and intellectual development' (Perry, 1970; Kenefelkamp, 1999).

Looking to responsibility, amongst a wide variety of perspectives there are many responses that indicate that students have an understanding that learning is their responsibility and that they expect a change from the school situation;

S: I think one of the biggest things with university is that it's nowhere near as structured as school was. At school you are very much led by the hand ... whereas at university, you are given a lot of information, and there is a lot of additional reading you can do on top of that, so you have to manage what you want to look at ... [Oct 1]

S: So if you didn't turn up, your loss, you don't learn from it. [Mar 1]

Two contrasting ways of expressing a recognition of personal responsibility, at different times of the year. Another focus group dialogue indicates related issues:

M: Okay.... whether you felt that your approach to your learning or your learning styles had changed since you came to university?

S: Yeaaaah.... You have to do sooooo much more on your own and just sort of almost set yourself your homework and things like that, that you were getting set and you just have to have so much more self-motivation, especially reading, so boring. ...

S: Yeah because like here I'm probably working every day or every couple of days sort of extra work just so I know what's going on, but at school I never did anything, like three weeks before the exam, then start going back to the start and going through it all and that worked okay. But the work here I don't like, and I just sort of figured that out now. I think it's especially difficult.... [Feb 2]

The students here display a range of attitudes, including a largely passive attitude at school, but indicate that, whilst accepting some responsibility, they are finding some aspects of the change problematic. Another student indicates a common feeling:

S: Obviously you need to do more stuff yourself, but I feel he should include that in his lecture notes as well. [Feb 1]

An interestingly contradictory statement, supported in the dialogue towards the end of this section of the paper, showing students accepting responsibility to do 'more stuff yourself' but wanting the lecturer to take, or at least share, responsibility by putting more direction in the notes. In terms of intellectual maturity this could be seen as indicative that students don't really accept responsibility but have adopted the notion of acceptance as we—the experts—have told them that is the 'right answer'. This is an interpretation that mirrors our experience that many students, especially first years, attempt to shift the responsibility for their learning to us by demanding 'correct answers'.

There are clear links to the issue of time management. As these students indicate it is not lack of time, *per se*, that is an issue for them; rather it appears that they are not doing work as they have not accepted responsibility for their own learning. This lack of responsibility is also linked to the students' notions in relation to choices in modelling. They appear to want us to make the choices. More positively, however, we see some moves to more relativistic positions, including:

> S: I don't know. I think the problem is that school system at the moment, sort of learning to pass. That's where we sort of get the bad problem-solving and learning to learn skills from, but the way they can improve it is ... I don't really know, ... basically learning to learn is you know you have the knowledge of the subject [as] opposed to memorising the answer, and problem-solving is, you get a certain question, and in your mind some people have the ... the procedure already, and em ... whereas problem-solving you need to adapt and be able to take different routes ... you can't do that with ... I think all these things you learn from experience more than anything. ... Aside from that I can't really I can't see any way of improving how to learning to learn. It's all about just understanding the subject, rather than learning parrot fashion. [Jan 2]
>
> S: I think I'm getting my head round it now. ... whenever I think of anything now, I think, you know don't just think about one thing, you think oh it could be taken from this angle and so on. ... you know it's kind of taken skill to learn from employability type skill you know.... You know if you are going into sort of accounting profession. ...Well if you're dealing with financial accounting, it's all like straight debt rules and so on, but even if you were doing financial accounting and so on ... sort of stuff I've learned from management accounting is...you know, take ideas going round from different angles and so on. So it's quite good to think I've actually taken that and using it in other things, not just management accounting. [Feb 1]

Not only have these students, amongst others, realized the need to accept less dualist modes of understanding; they had also recognized that some subjects are less 'straight' than others. In addition, some students have been able to apply this more mature approach to other disciplines and to contextualize their understandings and to adopt 'deeper' approaches. Whilst this is encouraging, the non-reflection of this maturity in relation to making modelling choices is a concern: a concern possibly related to confidence. There are indications that students see this move away from dualistic notions of understanding uncomfortable, as predicted by Perry (1970).

> M: Okay, well this idea of there being no right and wrong answers, are you happy with this issue of having to make the choices?
>
> S: I don't know ... like for me I think there is total lack of confidence. Just go ahead and put answers in, like you kind of think you hum and haw for ages. Like was that really right... .?
>
> S: ... But then they say there is no right answer, or you've just got to make assumptions and just try and get to an answer and stay at what you assumed, but the you go into tutorial and he'll say, 'What did you get?', and you'll say, 'No, I'm wrong' ... so we are just totally contradicting ourselves. [Feb 2]

Here we can see that the lack of confidence relates to the need to make choices. As Perry's (1970) model shows: the move towards multiplistic notions of reality, and the need to make and justify choices (as in both modelling and critical analysis), is associated with a drop in confidence. This is an important contrast against earlier comments that clearly indicate that students see confidence as being important, and enabling. Yet other students show a degree of acceptance of uncertainty, for example, following a similar prompt:

> S: It's kind of like opened my mind up more. Before when I used to do a question I'd say, that's the answer, argue about it, but as soon as you get the answer you think, but what if you add this or if you add that, so sometimes you get worried – you could end up writing something like eight answers for the same question or something. I think it's OK because he [the lecturer] says as long as you write down a viable explanation as to the assumption you've made, you get marks for it obviously, unless it's a really stupid one. If you kind of argue for the assumption you've made then you should get marks for it. Maybe not all the marks, but you might get a bit of the marks rather than just writing down things without explaining why you've used those figures. [Mar 1]

This could be read as a reflection of the Perry model (1970) prediction that students' moves into the relativistic sphere are associated with increases in confidence. However, another reading might indicate that some of the student's comfort with the notion arises from that student's perception of how assessments are going to be marked, which may be a worrying reference to an instrumental (shallow) approach to learning.

We can see that students' lack of confidence and lack of readiness to accept responsibility are acting as inhibitors, or barriers, to their development of the more commonly addressed employability or generic skills.

In the final focus group, just before the end of year examinations, the moderator asked about skills development and students raised learning to learn, indicating that they were aware that learning to learn is an important skill. The subsequent dialogue illustrates students' interpretation and development of this skill.

> M: What does that mean? [Learning to learn.]
>
> S: Well in school I suppose it's always really structured how you have to learn and you've got a test then and you've got to know this by then and you've got whatever. You've got an exam and you've got estimates[4] and stuff, so, and you are told what's going to be in them and . . . what the questions will be like and . . . so it's all really you are told what to do, but here it's like all this information is thrown at you and you sort of need to work out what's most important and how you yourself can sit down and learn it and understand it so. . . . It's just harder because you have got to push yourself into it because nobody else is going to. . . .

This comment shows some progress towards intellectual maturity and recognition of the need to change in the transition phase of moving to university, especially the increased need to take on responsibility for learning and the need to deal with uncertainty and ambiguity in instructions. The dialogue continues:

> M: So anyone else think they have got the measure of learning to learn?
>
> S: Well I don't think I've got it but . . . (laughter) . . . it's coming slowly, when we first mentioned it we were all like eh? But now. . .. Last term I didn't do any work basically, but then this term I've realized just how much I need to do on my own, and just get down and do it, and I don't know [what] I was doing most of the time.
>
> S: Yeah it's . . . like I did work, but then I've got nothing to show for it and . . . now. . .. Like I think second year will be much better because I'll know the types of things that I need to be doing, and all the reading and stuff. And although like . . . oh this is reading . . . for some reason, you just never really did it. . . .
>
> S: When you know you have not got an exam until you know. . .like eight months away, it doesn't seem important, and I didn't do any of that stuff, and now I'm panicking, it's my own fault, I mean, I'm having . . . I just . . . because we've never had to do anything

like that. I don't think it was really made very clear. I didn't think they had reinforced it very much, because although we're meant to be older and doing stuff on your own, we have ... just ... like a lot of us have just come from school anyway. Like I think a little bit of help would not hurt. [April 1]

Here we see further illustrations of students' change but tinged with caution and a recognition of the slowness, complexity and difficulty in doing so. There is also a positive side, a forecast of hope: that '... second year will be much better'. The last part of the final quotation, however, shows a reluctance to take full responsibility. Although this looks like a contradiction to the earlier statement, it can also be seen, along with other comments, as reflecting a lack in confidence and reflects the complex nature of skills development. On a more positive note, later in the same focus group:

M: And how do you feel about that ... having that freedom, that choice...? [April 1]

S: I like it but then there is also sort of an aspect of uncertainty. You are never sure you are doing it right and you don't know if you are approaching it the right way...but it's good, because it feels like you are doing more. It's more your own project, it's not just ... like ... don't know. At school everything used to be the same, but I don't think that will happen here. [April 1]

This student is showing a preference for choice and relativity, albeit with a slight note of caution, and is seeing uncertainty as a contextual reality rather than as primarily a cause for a lack of confidence.

Discussion and Concluding Remarks

This research has explored and analysed the views of, and effects on, students of a project to integrate employability skills within the first year of an accounting degree by analysing students' opinions gathered from a series of focus groups. There are clearly limitations to this analysis because of the scope of any single case study, the possible selection bias, the nature of longitudinal case study research, and the qualitative nature of the data and analysis. There is therefore the need for more research both on this project and on attempts elsewhere to integrate skills in accounting degrees. The results, however, indicate some important insights into the issues that potentially hinder the attempts of accounting educators to respond to the ever-present demands of government, funding bodies and the profession for us to do so, and indicate important reasons why we ought to persevere in doing so.

The results suggest the students were not able to engage with or develop all of the subset of employability skills the courses emphasized. They reported difficulty in managing their time, in engaging in modelling exercises and problem-solving, and were reluctant to take responsibility for and to have a positive attitude towards learning to learn. The students seem to be lacking in confidence, reluctant to make their own decisions, and appeared to want to shift responsibility for the quality or correctness of their work to others.

Our first observation is that the integration of skills into the curriculum is complicated. Difficulties were expected but not to the extent or of the nature encountered. We were aware, for instance, that students' position on their path of 'ethical and intellectual development' (Perry, 1970) was important to their conception of and approaches to the subject matter of the courses. However, the impact which their stance had on their perceptions and development of skills was unexpected. It is clear that students' lack of confidence about making choices and their reluctance to accept relativistic stances to problems in context has had negative effects on their time management and their modelling skills development. Relating this finding to the idea of 'threshold concept' (Jack and McCartney, 2007; Lucas and Mladenovic, 2007; Entwistle, 2005; Meyer and Land, 2003) we can, therefore, see students' position on the path of intellectual development as a 'threshold concept' in terms or their skills development, as well as being related to their comprehension of the subject. It appears that movement towards relativistic ways of thinking could be seen as an essential prerequisite for both lower and higher level employability skills. This is perhaps unsurprising in relation to the higher level skills such as critical analysis which, by their nature, are related to Perry's stages or positions, but that this sort of intellectual maturity is important to employability skills such as time management and modelling is a new observation. A further implication of this observation is that in this context we could, subject to further research, use the ideas in Perry-inspired work (e.g. Kenefelkamp, 1999) to analyse students who appear to show traits of 'retreat to dualism': a path of student development that is harmful not just to their intellectual development but also to their development of skills.

The analysis also indicates that the use of explicit skills-based ILOs (intended learning outcomes) is problematic in that it appears that students do not use them in the way intended by the course teams. Their inclusion in the documents for each class intervention was intended to add to the information that students would use to guide their work. However, students did not appear to be able to use them to guide their skills development. The focus of ILOs on outcomes does not help students to focus on the activities required to achieve them, a finding which is consistent with the argument of Entwistle (2005). Indeed, there are hints in the analysis that students build reasons for non-preparation in part on this inappropriate focus of the ILOs. So even at the individual learning activity level, the only level at which Hussey and Smith (2008) thought they might have a role, the utility of ILOs is in doubt.

The analysis suggests the need to deploy strategies for building students' capacity to develop relevant skills across their whole degree experience, and that effective strategies need to consider the interrelationships between personal experiences and skills, including the management of confidence, decision-making and handling disparate information. Further, it is important to do this in a way that engages and motivates students to develop their skills, by considering in more detail aspects such as students' social contexts and the need to give students time to develop in environments that are relevant to them.

To an extent also we might see some aspects of skills development as paralleling the needs of students' intellectual development and not as 'merely building skills' (a view of some faculty who believe skills have no place in the higher education curriculum). In this light we need to see skills development not as something that can be ignored in the accounting curriculum, or seen as a 'necessary evil' forced on us by educational bureaucracy and the accounting profession, but an essential element of the path to providing a successful accounting education experience.

Acknowledgements

The authors acknowledge funding from the University of Glasgow Learning and Teaching Development Fund, the help of other members of the initial research team Gillian MacIver, Hok-Leung Ronnie Lo and Mary McCulloch, and the helpful comments of the three anonymous reviewers.

Notes

[1]The skills covered included; taking responsibility for learning; effective team work and work management; effective written, oral and visual communication and presentation skills; IT and data-handling skills; critical analysis of data, theory and sources; model building choices, application and evaluation; critical evaluation of, and searching for, alternative solutions; effective case analysis and contextual learning; and combining

and synthesis of ideas. Further details of the project including details of the skills covered are reported in MacIver *et al.* (2005) and Milner and Stoner (2006).

[2]Details of the courses are available from the Department's web site, at www.gla.ac.uk/departments/accountingfinance/ (accessed 4 March 2008).

[3]Transcript quotations are all from individual students, an interchange or conversation is indicated thus; S indicates student, M indicates mediator (the independent LTS consultant). The month and focus group number are indicated in brackets.

[4]Estimate here refers to the school teachers' estimates or forecasts of the questions and topics that are likely to be set in the public examinations.

References

Arquero Montaño, J. L., Donoso Anes, J. A., Hassall, T. and Joyce, J. (2001) Vocational skills in the accounting professional profile: The Chartered Institute of Management Accountants (CIMA) employers' opinion, *Accounting Education: an international journal*, 10(3), pp. 299–313.

Arquero Montaño, J. L., Jimenez Cardoso, S. M. and Joyce, J. (2004) Skills development, motivation and learning in financial statement analysis; an evaluation of alternative types of case studies, *Accounting Education: an international journal*, 13(2), pp. 191–212.

Cleveland, W. (2005) Learning from data: unifying statistics and computer science, *International Statistical Review*, 73(2), pp. 217–221.

Crowley, C., Harré, R. and Tagg, C. (2002) Qualitative research and computing: methodological issues and practices in using QSR NVivo and NUD*IST, *International Journal of Social Research Methodology*, 5(3), pp. 193–197.

Entwistle, N. (2005) Learning outcomes and ways of thinking across contrasting disciplines and settings in higher education, *Curriculum Journal*, 16(1), pp. 1, 67–82.

Field, J. (2000) Researching lifelong learning through focus groups, *Journal of Further and Higher Education*, 24(3), pp. 323–335.

Francis, G. and Minchington, C. (1999) Quantitative skills: is there an expectation gap between the education and practice of management accountants? *Accounting Education: an international journal*, 8(4), pp. 301–319.

Gammie, B., Gammie, E. and Cargill, E. (2002) Personal skills development in the accounting curriculum, *Accounting Education: an international journal*, 11(1), pp. 63–78.

Gilbert, L. (2002) Going the distance: 'closeness' in qualitative data analysis software, *International Journal of Social Research Methodology*, 5(3), pp. 215–228.

Hassall, T., Joyce, J., Arquero, J. L. and Donoso Anes, J. A. (2003) The vocational skills gap for management accountants: the stakeholders' perspectives, *Innovations in Education and Teaching International*, 40(1), pp. 78–88.

Hussey, T. and Smith, P. (2008) Learning outcomes: a conceptual analysis, *Teaching in Higher Education*, 13(1), pp. 107–115.

IFAC (2003) *International Education Paper IEP 2: Towards Competent Professional Accountants* (New York: International Federation of Accountants, International Accounting Education Standards Board, IAESB).

IFAC (2004) *International Education Standard for Professional Accountants IES 7, Continuing Professional Development: A Program of Lifelong Learning and Continuing Development of Professional Competence* (New York: International Federation of Accountants, International Accounting Education Standards Board, IAESB).

IFAC (2006) *International Education Standard For Professional Accountants IES 8: Competence Requirements for Audit Professionals* (New York: International Federation of Accountants, International Accounting Education Standards Board, IAESB).

Jack, L. and McCartney, S. (2007) The argumentative accountant: or, critical thinking as a threshold concept in financial reporting, paper presented at *BAA Education SIG Conference*, Wales.

Kenefelkamp, L. (1999) Introduction to the 1999 republication of Perry 1970, *Forms of intellectual and ethical development in the college years* (New York: Holt, Rinehart and Winston). (Republished 1999 by John Wiley and Sons Inc.).

Lucas, U. and Mladenovic, R. (2007) The potential of threshold concepts - an emerging framework for educational research and practice, *London Review of Education*, 5(3), pp. 237–248.

MacIver, G., Milner, M. M. and Stoner, G. (2005) Evaluating and embedding skills in undergraduate degree courses: methodological considerations. *Paper presented at the Higher Education Academy, Business, Management, Accounting and Finance Subject Centre conference*, London, April, 2005.

Meyer, J. H. F. and Land, R. (2003) *Threshold concepts and troublesome knowledge: linkages to ways of thinking and practising within the disciplines*, ETL project, Occasional Report 4. Available at http://www.ed.ac.uk/etl/publications.html (accessed 20 December 2007).

Milner, M. M. and Hill, W. Y. (2008) Examining the skills debate in Scotland, *The International Journal of Management Education*, 6(3), pp. 13–20.

Milner, M. M. and Stoner, G. (2006) Embedding skills in undergraduate degree courses. *Paper presented at the British Accounting Association Education Special Interest Group Conference*, London, May, 2006.

Milton, J. and Lyons, J. (2003) Evaluate to improve learning: reflecting on the role of teaching and learning models, *Higher Education Research and Development*, 22(3), pp. 297–312.

Morgan, G. (1997) Communication skills required by accounting graduates; practitioner and academic perceptions, *Accounting Education: an international journal*, 6(2), pp. 93–107.

Perry, W. G. (1970) *Forms of intellectual and ethical development in the college years* (New York: Holt, Rinehart and Winston). (Republished 1999 by John Wiley and Sons Inc.).

Richards, L. (1998) Closeness to data: the changing goals of qualitative data handling, *Qualitative Health Research*, 8(3), pp. 319–328.

Richards, L. (2002) Qualitative computing—a methods revolution? *International Journal of Social Research Methodology*, 5(3), pp. 263–276.

Richards, T. (2002) An intellectual history of NUD*IST and NVivo, *International Journal of Social Research Methodology*, 5(3), pp. 199–214.

SHEFC (2005) *Learning to Work, Enhancing employability and enterprise in Scottish further and higher education* (Scottish Higher Education Funding Council, Edinburgh [now renamed SFC: Scottish Funding Council). Available at http://www.sfc.ac.uk/publications/pubs_other_sfefcarchive/learning_to_work.pdf (accessed 18 December 2006).

SFC (2006) *Employability: Implementation Plan for Learning to Work*, 3 March 2006 SFC/12/2006. Available at http://www.sfc.ac.uk/information/info_circulars/sfc/2006/sfc1206/sfc_12_06.pdf (20 December 2007).

Stubbs, M. and Keeping, M. (2002) Course content and employability skills in vocational degrees: reflections for town planning course content, *Planning Practice and Research*, 17(2), pp. 205–222.

Tempone, I. and Martin, E. (2003) Iteration between theory and practice as a pathway to developing generic skills in accounting, *Accounting Education: an international journal*, 12(3), pp. 227–244.

Zaid, O. and Abraham, A. (1994) Communication skills in accounting education: perceptions of academics, employers and graduate accountants, *Journal of Accounting Education*, 3(3), pp. 205–221.

Knowledge and Skills Development of Accounting Graduates: The Perceptions of Graduates and Employers in Ghana

JOSEPH Y. AWAYIGA*, JOSEPH M. ONUMAH** and MATHEW TSAMENYI†

*Bank of Ghana, West Africa; **University of Ghana Business School, West Africa; †University of Birmingham, UK

ABSTRACT *Accounting education has come under criticism over the past two decades for failing to meet the demands of the changing business environment. This paper presents the results of a survey of accounting graduates and employers from Ghana on the accounting knowledge and skills required by graduates. We examined both the professional and information technology (IT) skill requirements of the graduates. These skills are relevant to preparing the graduates for careers as professional accountants. Analytical/critical thinking was rated as the most important professional skill by both the employers and the graduates. In terms of IT skills, the use of spreadsheet packages was rated by both groups as the most important skill. The only significant differences between the two groups were the IT skills in word-processing and Windows. The findings of the paper have implications for accounting education in Ghana and in other developing countries.*

A. Introduction

The objective of this paper is to investigate the perceived relevance of accounting education in Ghana. For the past two decades, accounting education worldwide has come under criticism for failing to address the skill requirements in today's dynamic business environment. Studies conducted in both the western world (such as the USA, UK and Australia) and the developing/emerging world (such as China) reveals a general dissatisfaction with the quality of accounting graduates (Liebtag, 1987; Nelson, 1989, 1996, 1998; Inman *et al.*, 1989; Gabbin, 2002; Lin *et al.*, 2005; de Lange *et al.*, 2006). In the USA, Albrecht and Sack (2000) found that practising accountants and employers' perceptions of accounting education is that it is outdated or irrelevant and does not meet the demands of the market. The educational model has failed to focus on developing a set of skills for graduates to enable them to pursue successful careers in the accounting profession.

This finding has prompted several researchers to suggest changes to the accounting education curriculum. For example, Hastings *et al.* (2002) argued that, if accountants are to find a value added role in today's dynamic business environment, they must be armed with new skills. Albrecht (2002) identifies skills in analytical and critical thinking, technology, communication and teamwork as being essential to moving the profession into a new era. The Accounting Education Change Commission (AECC, 1990) called for a curriculum where employers could recognize a measurable improvement in the knowledge and skills of accounting graduates. This is imperative because a lot of barriers to information have been drastically reduced by globalization and radical developments in information and communication technology (Albrecht and Sack, 2000).

While the majority of published studies on accounting education have come from the developed world, the issue is now attracting interest from researchers in the developing world (Ahmad and Gao, 2004; Bennett *et al.*, 2004; Devlin and Godfrey, 2004; Dixon, 2004). Lovell and Dixon (2004), for example, argued that research on specific developing countries is necessary since context is important when putting together accounting education programs. In this respect, Ahmad and Gao (2004) studied the development of accounting in Libya and argued that accounting needs to change to support institutional changes from a planned economy to a more private sector involvement in economic activities. Dixon's (2004) study in Kiribati also highlighted the need to contextualize accounting education as some of the Anglo-American business concepts may in fact not be applicable to the country. A study by Bennett *et al.* (2004) on five developing countries—Zimbabwe, Nicaragua, Guatemala, Vietnam and Tanzania—also recognized the need to understand context in the training of finance personnel.

The discussion in this paper contributes to these debates by examining employers' evaluation of the knowledge and skills of accounting graduates in Ghana. For the purpose of our analysis we focus on accounting graduates from the main university in Ghana, the University of Ghana, which produces the majority of the accounting graduates in the country. Both accounting graduates and their employers participated in the survey and the general view was that educators should incorporate the views of both employers and students in any accounting education curriculum development (Albrecht and Sack 2000; Francisco *et al.*, 2003).

The study conducted by Albrecht and Sack (2000) focused on the perceptions of US accounting educators and practitioners concerning skills development and Francisco *et al.*, (2003) examined the perceptions of US accounting students and compared them to those of the educators and practitioners in the Albrecht and Sack (2000) study. The results of the analysis showed that, while there are some disparities between the three groups, these differences are largely insignificant. Only a few skills requirements (such as analytical and critical thinking and computer technology) were rated differently by educators and practitioners on the one hand, and students on the other hand. Between practitioners and students specifically, Francisco, *et al.* (2003, p.4) noted that:

> When the rankings of practitioners were compared to the rankings of accounting students, the two groups were very much in agreement, with variations by only two or fewer positions. It can be inferred from these data that professionals are getting, for the most part, students who have similar views of which skills are the most important for success.

We therefore do not expect any significant differences between the perceptions of the employers and those of the graduates in our study. Instead of focusing on current accounting students as in the Francisco *et al.* (2003) study we decided to focus on accounting graduates since they have an understanding of the university curriculum and have practical experience in an accounting role. Accounting graduates are in a better position to assess the content and relevance of the accounting curriculum than students who are still at university. It will also provide an insight into whether the views of the graduates are similar to or different from those of their employers. The skills examined could generally be classified into professional skills and technology skills (Albrecht and Sack, 2000; Burnett, 2003). As recognized by the AECC (1990), it is not the role of accounting programs to change graduates into professional accountants at the time of entry into the profession. Rather, accounting programs are expected to prepare these graduates to become professional accountants. Thus accounting graduates cannot be expected to possess the same levels of knowledge and skills as professional accountants at the time of their entry into the profession as they will develop these skills through professional training institutions and work place experience. In view of this, our research specifically focuses on the knowledge and skills which graduates acquired from their accounting program at university to prepare them for entry into the profession.

Our study examined two key research questions:

1. What are the professional skills considered important for the current/future career of accounting graduates as perceived by both employers and graduates, and how are the ratings of these skills different or similar between the two groups?
2. What are the technology skills considered important to be possessed by new accounting graduates for entry-level work and career advancement as perceived by both employers and graduates, and how are the ratings of these skills different or similar between the two groups?

The remainder of the paper is organized as follows. The next section provides a brief review of the literature. The next two sections provide an overview of accounting education in Ghana and the structure of professional accounting education in Ghana respectively. This is followed by a brief description of the research methods and survey results. The final section outlines a summary and conclusion.

B. Brief Review of Related Literature

It has been suggested that developments in information technology and globalization of business over the past two decades have significantly changed the business environment (Albrecht and Sack, 2000). Organizations now operate in environments characterized by shorter product life cycles and shorter competitive advantages; a need for better, quicker and more decisive actions by management; outsourcing of essential but non-value adding activities; increased uncertainty, complexity and increased awareness of risk; restructuring of rewards; change in financial reporting and increased regulatory activities, and an increased focus on customer satisfaction (Albrecht and Sack, 2000). Mohamed and Lashine (2003) concluded that these developments in the business environment warrant that the competency level of accountants is improved. This can be achieved by improving the capabilities relating to accounting education.

Various groups and individuals have called for accounting curriculum change in response to these changes in the business environment (AECC, 1990; Albrecht and Sack, 2000; AICPA, 1998; Burnett, 2003). The results of studies carried by various committees (Bedford Committee, 1986; Perspectives on Education, 1989; AECC, 1990; and IEG 9, 1996) reviewing accounting education for instance, pointed out that accounting education has failed to respond to the ever-increasing expectations of students entering the accounting profession.

Prior research examining the issue of knowledge and skills of accounting graduates in comparison to employer expectations (Simons and Higgins, 1993; Bedford Committee, 1986; Perspectives, 1989) consistently found that employers are primarily satisfied with graduates' technical knowledge, but are unhappy with their communication skills and problem-solving ability. We briefly discuss the knowledge and skills required of accounting graduates in the changing business environment as identified by IFAC, 2003 and Perspectives, 1989.

Communication Skills

Communication skills are seen as being imperative for every successful entry-level accountant (Perspectives, 1989). These skills are concerned with the ability to transfer and receive information with ease, and present and defend views through formal and informal, written and oral, presentation. These skills also include listening effectively to gain information and understand opposing points of view, and the ability to locate, obtain and organize information from both human and electronic sources.

Intellectual Skills

These include the ability to identify and solve diverse and unstructured problems in unfamiliar settings and to exercise judgment based on comprehension of an unfocused set of facts; capability for inductive-thought processes and applying a value-based reasoning system to ethical questions, management of stress, prioritizing, and the ability to adapt to change. Simons and Higgins (1993) argued that more emphasis should be placed on developing students' problem-solving skills.

Interpersonal Skills

Interpersonal skills enable accountants to work with others to achieve the objectives of the organization. It involves the ability to interact with culturally- and intellectually-diverse people. Interpersonal skills include the ability to influence others, organize and delegate tasks, motivate, and resolve conflicts (Simons and Higgins 1993). Additionally, it deals with ability to assume leadership positions.

Technical and Functional Skills

Technical and functional skills consist of general skills as well as skills specific to accountancy. They include numeracy (mathematical and statistical applications) and IT proficiency; decision modeling and risk analysis; measurement; reporting and compliance with legislative and regulatory requirements.

Personal Skills

These relate to the attitudes and behavior of accountants. They include self-management; initiative, influence and self learning; the ability to select and assign priorities within restricted resources and to organize work to meet tight deadlines; the ability to anticipate and adapt to change; considering the implications of professional values, ethics, and attitudes in decision-making; and professional skepticism.

Organizational and Business Management Skills

Accounting graduates need to develop a broad business outlook as well as political awareness and a global outlook. Organizational and business management skills include strategic planning, project management, management of people and resources, and decision-making; the ability to organize and delegate tasks, to motivate and to develop people; leadership; and professional judgment and discernment.

IT Skills

The information technology knowledge core should provide accounting students with the knowledge and skills they need to use and evaluate information technology and systems and to provide input into the design and management of those systems. Every accountant must have, prior to qualification, the ability to use a word processing package, a spreadsheet package, a database package and at least one entry-level accounting package (IEG 9, 1996). Boritz (1999) observed that most institutions are adding more IT courses by sacrificing existing elements of the current curriculum. He argued that these sacrifices represent a re-orientation of the accounting curriculum in response to market forces. Knowledge of some accounting packages is no longer a plus; it is a must and it should be emphasized through the university stage (Mohamed and Lashine, 2003).

Perspectives (1989) and IES 3 (2003) also identified the three main knowledge bases of accounting graduates as being general knowledge, organizational and business knowledge, and accounting and auditing knowledge.

General Knowledge

This requires an understanding of history and the sciences, a broad understanding of mathematics and economics, cultural awareness, lifelong learning, and aesthetic sensibility (i.e. 'a broadly educated person').

Organizational and Business Knowledge

This relates to an understanding of the basic internal workings of organizations, and the economic, social, cultural, psychological, and technological forces that affect organizations. It also requires an understanding of interpersonal and group dynamics.

Accounting and Auditing Knowledge

This knowledge should provide a strong fundamental understanding of accounting, auditing and tax, including the history of the accounting profession and accounting thought, as well as the content, concepts, structure and meaning of reporting for organizational operations both for internal and external use. It also includes the methods for identifying, gathering, summarizing, verifying, analyzing, and interpreting financial data. It involves the ability to use the data, exercise judgments, evaluate risks and solve real-world problems.

The research methodology was designed to test the extent to which the accounting graduates and their employers in Ghana perceived these skills and knowledge to be adequately covered in the accounting education curriculum.

C. Overview of the Accounting Education System in Ghana

Accounting education started in Ghana as part of management education and training in January 1952 when the Department of Commerce was founded at the then Kumasi College of Technology (now the Kwame Nkrumah University of Science and Technology). The accounting course was at the time developed entirely based on that of the

Association of Certified and Corporate Accountants in England and Wales. However, after independence in 1957, one of the stated objectives of the government was 'rapid economic development' which was interpreted to mean the 'rapid growth of industry'. This required personnel competent enough to handle the newly-created industries, but the courses offered at the Department of Commerce at the Kumasi College of Technology, especially the accounting course, were not fulfilling this purpose.

Against this background, the Ghana Government in 1959 decided to establish the College of Administration at Achimota to provide training and research in commercial subjects and public administration. The College was responsible for organizing courses in Accounting, Secretaryship, Central and Local Government Administration, and Hospital Administration. These courses led to examinations of United Kingdom statutory bodies including the Association of Chartered Certified Accountants (ACCA), the Chartered Institute of Secretaries and Administrators (CISA), The Corporation of Certified Secretaries (CCS), the Clerical Examinations for Local Government Officers and the Institute of Hospital Administration, London.

Although these courses were useful, they were mainly internationally-oriented and did not fully satisfy the local needs of the country. Additionally, it became established that the study of Administration must be given its proper place in the country's higher education system as was the case in most developed nations. In 1961, the College of Administration made representations to the Committee on University Education for the integration of the College with the University of Ghana, as a School of Administration within the University. The School of Administration was to provide degree courses in Business Management on the basis of curricula approved by the university. Consequently, in October 1962, the Government agreed to this proposal and since then the previous courses, including that of accounting, were phased out. Courses leading to an Honors degree of BSc. Administration were started with accounting being offered as one of the areas of specialization. The name School of Administration was changed in 2004 to the University of Ghana Business School (UGBS) to reflect the current trend in business education globally.

There are other institutions in Ghana also providing accounting education at various levels. The West Africa Examination Council offers examinations in accountancy as part of its business examination scheme under the title General Business Certificate Examinations (GBCE) and the Advanced Business Certificate Examinations (ABCE) leading to the Group Diploma in Accounting. This qualification was previously known as the Royal Society of Arts (RSA), then later as the Ghana Commercial Examinations (GCE). The Institute of Accountancy Training, an institute belonging to the Ministry of Finance, awards a Diploma in Public Finance and Accounting. The Polytechnics award the Diploma in Business Studies (Accounting); and Higher National Diploma in Accounting (HND—Accounting). The universities in the country award various diplomas and degrees in accounting. The University of Ghana, for example, offers courses leading to the Diploma in Accounting; Bachelor Degree in Accounting; Master of Business Administration (MBA) in Accounting; and the Executive MBA in Accounting. Similarly, the University of Cape Coast offers a Bachelor of Commerce Degree in Accounting; and an MBA in Accounting. Accounting degrees are also awarded by the Ghana Institute of Management and Public Administration (GIMPA) and several other new private universities.

D. Professional Accounting Education in Ghana

The Institute of Chartered Accountants, Ghana—ICA(G)—is the officially recognized body responsible to assist in the shaping and direction of accounting education and training in Ghana. The ICA(G) was established by a Legislative Instrument (Act 170) on 19

April 1963. A preamble to the Act 170 states: 'An Act to establish an Institute of Chartered Accounting and to make provision for the conduct of examinations by the Institute and other matters connected with the accountancy profession'. By implication, the ICA(G) has been given the mandate to control the accounting profession in the areas of accounting education and training, examination and award of local qualifications as well as the professional conduct of accountants.

The Act empowered a Council of eleven members to run its affairs, stipulating the following specific objectives:

(a) to conduct or provide for the conduct of the qualifying examinations for membership of the Institute or for registration as a registered accountant under the Act and to prescribe or approve courses of study for such examinations;
(b) to supervise and regulate the engagement, training and transfer of articled clerks;
(c) to specify the class of persons who have the right to train articled clerks and to specify the circumstances under which any person of that class may be deprived of that right;
(d) to maintain and publish a register of chartered accountants and practicing accountants;
(e) to ensure the maintenance of professional standards among the members of the Institute and to take such steps as persons with the methods and practices necessary to maintain such standards;
(f) to maintain a library of books and periodicals relating to accountancy and to encourage the publication of such books; and
(g) to encourage research in the subject of accountancy and general to secure 'the well-being and advancement of the profession of accountants', (ICA(G) Annual Report, 1999, p. 3).

The Institute of Chartered Accountants (Ghana), ICA(G), awards two qualifications, namely the Accounting Technician (AT) and the Chartered Accountant (CA). Table 1 presents the structure of the ICA(G) qualifications.

Table 1. Professional and technician programs of ICA (G)

ICA(G)	AT
Level 1	Part 1
1.1 Accounting Foundations	1.1 Basic Accounting Process and Systems
1.2 Business Management	1.2 Communication Skills
1.3 Economics	1.3 Business Law
1.4 Business Law	1.4 Economics
Level 2	Part 2
2.1 Financial Accounting Practice	2.1 Principles and Practice Financial Accounting
2.2 Management Accounting and Control	2.2 Government of Accounting
2.3 Company and Partnership Law	2.3 Quantitative Analysis
2.4 Taxation	2.4 Information Technology
2.5 MIS and Business Systems	
2.6 Audit and Internal Review	
2.7 Strategic Management	
Level 3	Part 3
3.1 Corporate Reporting Strategy	3.1 Preparation and Audit of Financial Statements
3.2 Assurance and Audit Practice	3.2 Cost Accounting and Budgeting
3.3 Financial Management Strategy	3.3 Preparing Tax Computation and Returns
3.4 Advanced Tax Planning and Fiscal Policy	3.4 Management

Source: Office, ICA (G).

Table 2. Qualified members through ICA(G) (1966–2005)

Period	Number
1966–1970	5
1971–1975	14
1976–1980	27
1981–1985	51
1986–1990	149
1991–1995	169
1996–2000	176
2001–2004	276
2005	135
Total	1002

Source: Office, ICA (G).

In addition to the ICA(G) qualifications, students in Ghana also sit the qualifying examinations of other international professional accounting qualifications, including those of the Association of Certified Chartered Accountants (ACCA), UK (which is the most popular); the Chartered Institute of Management Accountants (CIMA), UK; the Institute of Financial Accountants (IFA), UK, and the Institute of Commercial Management (ICM), UK. These international bodies are attractive to accounting students because they have adequate training resources, both electronic and physical manuals and other educational documentation, which facilitate the learning process and eventual qualification. The relationship between the ICA(G) and these bodies has not been very clear, leaving the membership arrangement of graduates of these bodies into the ICA(G) not well-defined.

The ICA(G) currently has over 7000 students registered for the various stages of its qualifying examinations. However, there are currently only 1002 qualified accountants registered with the ICA(G) (see Table 2).

E. Research Methods

This study solicited the views of accounting graduates and their employers concerning the knowledge and skills that must be possessed by accounting graduates in Ghana. It further analyzes the graduates' views of knowledge and skills required of them by their employers and the extent to which knowledge and skills acquired from their programs are being used at their places of work. It also analyzes the employers' evaluation of the knowledge and skills of the graduates. These analyses are crucial in order to identify the required knowledge and skills for accounting professionals in the current business environment in Ghana. The questionnaires were initially developed based on a review of the literature and examination of the Accounting and Finance degree program document of the University of Ghana Business School. The questionnaires were subsequently revised based on feedback from colleagues at the University of Ghana Business School.

We initially approached the University of Ghana to obtain the destinations of the accounting graduates but we were told that such a database does not exist. In the absence of such a database we decided to contact major employers within the Accra-Tema metropolitan area in order to identify the number and contact details of the accounting graduates.[1] The employers were identified from the area business directory and were contacted by telephone, email and personal visits. A total of 46 major employers were identified and contacted. All the employers provided us with the names and contact details of the accounting graduates. A senior person in Finance and Accounts (in most cases the Finance Director) was nominated in each company to complete the employer

Table 3. Background of the responding graduates

Employment status:	Percentage
Permanent	77%
Temporary	23%
Total	100%
Sector of employment:	
Private	73%
Public	18%
State owned enterprises (SOEs)	9%
Total	100%
Managerial position:	
Senior	13%
Middle	40%
Junior	47%
Total	100%
Year of graduation:	
1987–1992	13%
1993–1998	21%
1999–2004	66%
Total	100%
Industry of employment:	
Manufacturing	13%
Banking	42%
Education	13%
Accounting firms	14%
Public administration	11%
Others[a]	8%
Total	100%

[a]Others include media, hospitality, construction, transport, and IT firms.

questionnaire. A total of 164 graduates agreed to participate in the study. The questionnaires were hand-delivered to all the participants during the month of March, 2005. A similar approach has been used in previous accounting studies in Ghana to enhance the response rate (see for instance, Tsamenyi and Mills, 2003). In all, 131 graduate questionnaires (representing 80% of the graduate sample) and 25 employer questionnaires (representing 54% of the employer sample) were fully completed and collected within a period of four weeks. Several attempts to collect the remaining questionnaires failed. We consider the 80% and 54% response rates from the graduates and employers respectively as being adequate and representative of the population under study.

The background of the respondents is presented in Tables 3 and 4.

The number of accounting graduates employed by the surveyed firms ranged from 1 to 15, with an average of 3 graduates per employer. The responses from the questionnaire were analyzed using SPSS. The statistical techniques conducted are descriptive statistics and *t*-tests. The results are presented in the next section.

F. Survey Results

(i) Professional Skills

Using a five-point Likert scale (1 = not important and 5 = extremely important), respondents were asked to rate the importance of certain professional skills considered significant

Table 4. Background of responding employers

Size-number of employees:	
Less than 100	40%
100 and 1000	44%
Above 1000	16%
Total	100%
Sector:	
Private	84%
Public	12%
State owned enterprises (SOEs)	4%
Total	100%
Industry:	
Manufacturing	8%
Banking and finance	48%
Education	8%
Accounting firms	16%
Public administration	4%
Others[a]	16%
Total	100%

[a]The Accra-Tema metropolitan area is the capital city area of Ghana. Two main reasons motivated limiting the study to this area. First, the majority of businesses in Ghana are located within this area. Second, the hand delivery approach we adopted in distributing the questionnaire acted as a constraint to extend the research to other geographical areas.

for the current/future career of the accounting graduates. This is similar to the Albrecht and Sack (2000) study which asked faculty and practitioners to rate the skills they believe are most important on a one to five scale. The results are presented in Table 5.

The analysis of the mean scores shows that both the graduates and employers perceive that analytical and critical thinking is the most important skill. This is consistent with the average mean ratings by faculty in the Albrecht and Sack study (2000) and the average mean rating by employers (respondent firms) in the Burnett (2003) study. Communication skills and professional demeanor are also rated high by respondents. While there is a general agreement among the respondents in respect of professional demeanor, the graduates rate communication skills higher than the rating provided by their employers. Communication skills were rated second (based on the mean score) by the graduates, which is consistent with the rating given by respondent firms in the Burnett (2003) study. Employers in our study rated this skill fourth. Professionals in studies conducted by Albrecht and Sack (2000) and Burnett (2003) rated communication skills as the most important skill. Computing technology is rated as the second most important skill by employers. Graduates, however, did not rate computer technology as highly as did employers. The possible reason for this may be the lack of computer skills in the accounting education curriculum in Ghana.

The skills rated in the bottom five showed a greater diversity of ratings than the selection of the top rated skills. Those skills in the bottom five that showed the most diversity are intellectual skills, technical and functional skills and interpersonal skills. The respondents rate interpersonal skills and organizational and business management skills the same and are in general agreement as to their importance. Intellectual skills are an area where there is a disparity in responses. In the survey, graduates rate this skill as the fourth most important skill needed for their current or future career. Employers, however, rate intellectual skills next to the last rated skill. There are some differences in the ratings of technical and functional skills. The employers rated these skills higher than did the graduates.

Table 5. Graduates' and employers' perceptions of the professional skills considered important for the current/future career of accounting graduates

Professional skills	Mean (graduates) ($n = 131$)	Mean (employers)($n = 25$)	Average of the mean	Mean difference	T	Df	*P* (sig. 2-tail)
Analytical/critical thinking	4.77	4.80	4.79	−0.029	−0.310	154	0.760
Communication skills	4.41	4.28	4.35	0.132	0.890	154	0.373
Professional demeanor	4.37	4.44	4.41	−0.074	−0.510	154	0.614
Intellectual skills	4.27	4.00	4.14	0.267	1.640	154	0.103
Computing technology	4.25	4.52	4.39	−0.268	−1.810	154	0.072
Interpersonal skills	4.21	3.96	4.09	0.254	1.570	154	0.120
Personal skills	4.06	4.08	4.07	−0.019	−0.120	154	0.904
Organizational and business management skills	4.06	4.08	4.07	−0.019	−0.100	154	0.922
Technical and functional skills	4.01	4.12	4.07	−0.112	−0.620	154	0.539

The graduates also rated interpersonal skills much lower than the ratings provided by their managers/employers.

We used *t*-tests to establish whether or not there are significant differences between the graduates' and their employers' perceptions of the professional skills considered important for the current/future career of accounting graduates. The statistical significance level was set at $P < 0.05$. As indicated in Table 5, there are no statistically significant differences between the graduates' and their employers' perceptions of the relevant professional skills.

(ii) Technology Skills

Table 6 presents the results of the technology skills requirement. Using a five-point Likert scale, the graduates and the employers are asked to rate (1 = not important and 5 = extremely important) how they perceive nine technology skills as important for accounting graduates to have acquired for entry-level work.

An analysis of the mean ratings revealed that spreadsheet package, database package, presentation software, and technology management and budgeting are the top four rated IT skills by the accounting graduates. The employers on the other hand rated spreadsheet package, Windows, technology management and budgeting, and word-processing package as the top four important technology skills. The high ratings of the technology skills suggest that the respondents recognize many of the technology skills identified in the literature as being extremely important. The IEG 9 (1996) states that every accountant must have, prior to qualification, the ability to use a word-processing package, a spreadsheet package, a database package and at least one entry-level accounting package.

We also conducted *t*-tests to establish whether or not there are significant differences between the graduates' and their employers' perceptions of the technology skills to be acquired by accounting graduates for entry-level work and career advancement. The statistical significance level was set at $P < 0.05$ (see Table 6). According to the T-test results, there are statistically significant differences between graduates' and their employers' perceptions with regard to the technology skills of word-processing package (t value of 2.180 and $P = 0.031$) and Windows (t value of 3.460 and $P = 0.001$). The differences between the two groups on the other technology skills are not statistically significant.

Table 6. Graduates' and employers' perceptions on the technology skills to be possessed by new accounting graduates for entry level work

Technology skill	Mean (graduates) ($n = 131$)	Mean (employers) ($n = 25$)	Mean	T	Df	P (sig. 2-tail)
Spreadsheet package	4.74	4.80	−0.060	−0.500	154	0.615
Database package	3.99	3.88	0.112	0.570	154	0.573
Presentation software	3.95	3.72	0.234	1.07	154	0.286
Techno. management and budgeting	3.91	4.04	−0.132	−0.690	154	0.492
Word-processing package	3.65	4.00	−0.351	−2.180	154	0.031
Communication software—Outlook	3.59	3.84	−0.252	−1.500	154	0.135
Electronic commerce	3.57	3.72	−0.147	−0.720	154	0.475
World wide web	3.56	3.80	−0.243	−1.240	154	0.218
Windows	3.40	4.12	−0.715	−3.460	154	0.001

(iii) Knowledge Acquired by the Accounting Graduates

Table 7 presents the results of the importance of the knowledge acquired by the graduates during their study. Using a five-point Likert scale, the graduates are asked to rate (1 = not important and 5 = extremely important) how they perceive the knowledge they acquired during their study in 14 work related tasks and responsibilities.

From the total mean in Table 7, it is evident that knowledge in cost and financial accounting is the highest rated followed by taxation, auditing, and computer applications. Graduates employed in the private sector rated cost and financial accounting, taxation, and auditing in order of importance. Graduates in the public sector rated auditing, cost and financial accounting, and financial management and investment in order of importance. It is surprising to see that the graduates in the public sector did not rate knowledge acquired from public sector accounting very high. Graduates in the State Owned Enterprises (SOEs) rated computer applications, cost and financial accounting, and quantitative methods in order of importance.

We also obtained views from employers regarding the knowledge expected of the accounting graduates at the time of entry. A list of major courses offered under the University of Ghana accounting degree program was presented to employers for them to indicate the extent to which they expected or required graduate employees to be competent in them. Each course was to be rated along a scale of one to five with one being not at all and five to a very high extent. The results are presented in Table 8.

The findings show that areas in which employers require their graduate employees to have knowledge and skills are cost and financial accounting, taxation, auditing, computer applications, quantitative methods, financial management and investments, business communication, and commercial and company law, in descending order of importance. Courses that are least required included social sciences, public administration, marketing, and public sector accounting.

The most interesting finding, which is consistent with the responses of the graduates, is that the skill most highly rated by employers is in cost and financial accounting. Public and SOE employers rated this skill higher than did private employers. This may be due to

Table 7. Means of graduates' perception of use of knowledge and skills acquired during studies by sector of employment

	Private (means)	Public (means)	SOEs (means)	Total (means)
Cost and financial accounting	4.30	4.17	3.67	4.22
Taxation	4.07	3.96	3.58	4.01
Auditing	4.03	4.26	3.25	4.00
Computer applications	4.04	3.83	3.75	3.98
Quantitative methods	3.94	3.96	3.67	3.92
Financial management and investment	3.83	4.17	3.33	3.85
Business communication	3.68	3.78	3.42	3.67
Commercial and company law	3.73	3.35	2.92	3.59
Business policy	3.48	3.57	2.58	3.41
Economics	3.35	3.26	3.50	3.35
Public sector accounting	3.14	2.78	3.00	3.06
Marketing	2.70	3.83	2.00	2.83
Public administration	2.32	3.70	1.75	2.51
Social sciences (psychology, political science, philosophy, etc.)	2.39	2.74	2.42	2.45

Table 8. Means of employers' perception of use of knowledge and skills acquired during studies by sector

	Private (means)	Public and SOEs (means)	Total (means)
Cost and financial accounting	4.67	4.75	4.68
Taxation	4.67	4.50	4.64
Auditing	4.52	4.50	4.52
Computer applications	4.10	4.50	4.16
Quantitative methods	4.19	4.00	4.16
Financial management and investment	4.14	4.00	4.12
Business communication	4.05	4.25	4.08
Commercial and company law	4.24	3.25	4.08
Business policy	3.90	4.00	3.92
Economics	3.86	3.50	3.80
Public sector accounting	3.38	3.75	3.44
Marketing	3.19	4.00	3.32
Public administration	2.90	3.75	3.04
Social sciences (psychology, political science, philosophy, etc.)	2.57	2.50	2.56

the fact that few graduates find themselves in the public sector given the higher salary levels in the private sector, hence contributing to the shortage of this skill in the public sector.

(iv) Areas that are Perceived to be Important but not currently Covered in the Accounting Degree Program

The graduates were asked to list areas or topics that they believe are very important but which are not covered in their degree program. The answers contain only the topics that are believed to be very important to the respondents in terms of list not scale. A long list of topics and areas was compiled from the responses and this is summarized in Table 9. The results are grouped under three five-year periods: 1987–1992, 1993–1998, and 1999–2004. This is to enable us to assess whether the views of the graduates have changed over the years.

Computer skills/spreadsheet application is the area mentioned by most of the graduates (see Table 9). It is quite understandable that graduates are finding themselves lacking in computing skills given the technological developments in that area. The university offers only two introductory courses on computer applications which do not prepare graduates adequately for the job market. In addition, it lacks the necessary equipment and facilities to cope with the current student population. Accounting information systems and accounting software training is ranked second by accounting graduates. This is evidenced by the fact that the accounting program does not have any course in this area. These findings correspond highly with those of the employers who indicate that 76% of the graduates did not possess any accounting-related IT skills when they were first hired (see Table 10). Entrepreneurship and SME management was ranked third, an indication that the program did not contain the relevant courses to prepare graduates adequately to become self-employed. It is possible that the more recent graduates (14% from the 1993–1998 group, and 9% from the 1999–2004 group) identified entrepreneurship and SME as an important area not covered in their program because it requires

Table 9. Important areas not covered by the accounting degree program (per cent)

	Year of graduation			
	1987–1992	1993–1998	1999–2004	Total
Computer skills/spreadsheet applications/business information management	26	18	18	20
Accounting information systems/accounting software training	14	9	16	12
Entrepreneurship and SME's management	6	13	9	10
Management accounting	6	13	3	8
French/ second language	11	0	3	4
Project management and project audit	0	9	3	4
Practical attachment/training course	0	4	5	3
Seminar presentations/forum with practitioners	0	5	3	2
Fundamentals of insurance accounting	0	5	2	2
Leadership skills	5	0	2	2
International business	5	0	2	2
Financial management	0	5	1	2
Banking laws	0	5	1	2
Report writing and communication skills	0	0	5	1
VAT laws and The Ghana Free Zones Acts	4	0	1	1
Taxation/tax management and planning	0	0	3	1
Case studies	0	0	3	1
Strategic business management	0	0	2	1
Social responsibility accounting	0	0	1	1
Securities and exchange laws	5	0	0	1
Project and trade finance	4	0	0	1
Presentation skills	0	0	3	1
Presentation and professional outlook	0	4	0	1
Philosophy (logic)	0	0	1	1
Organizational behavior	0	0	1	1
Office management	0	5	0	1
Negotiation skills	0	0	1	1
Introduction to NGO's accounting	0	5	0	1
Introduction to financial systems and markets	0	0	1	1
Internet research on accounting related issues	0	0	1	1
International accounting	0	0	1	1
Foreign currency transactions	0	0	1	1
Financial modeling	0	0	1	1
Environmental accounting	0	0	2	1
Decision Analysis	5	0	0	1
Credit management of banks	0	0	1	1
Corporate Finance	4	0	0	1
Computerized budgeting and its applications	5	0	0	1
Business plan writing	0	0	1	1
Business ethics and corporate governance	0	0	2	1
Total	100	100	100	100

skills for starting up their own business, as employment in the public sector had been declining over time. The current effort of the University of Ghana in making entrepreneurship a compulsory course in the first year, therefore, is a step in the right direction.

Table 10. Employers' perceptions of accounting-related IT skills of accounting graduates when first hired by sector (per cent)

	Employer	
	Private sector	Public/SOEs
General knowledge	67%	25%
Organizational and business knowledge	62%	100%
Accounting, finance and auditing knowledge	90%	100%
Information technology knowledge	38%	0%

The graduates also mentioned other areas that they believed were important but not covered in the program which included management accounting, French, project management and project audit, practical training, fundamentals of insurance accounting, and leadership. Management accounting is included in this list because several of the accounting graduates are of the view that the current cost accounting course lacks the managerial issues that they are faced with in their jobs. The 1997–1998 year graduates mentioned the deficiency in the management accounting course because most of them were directly involved in making managerial decisions.

(V) Assessment of Knowledge and Abilities of the Accounting Graduates

Using a scale of one to five (with one representing very bad and five representing very good), employers were asked to assess the accounting graduates in terms of their general knowledge, organizational and business knowledge, accounting, finance and auditing knowledge, and information technology knowledge. The results are presented in Table 10.

The responses in Table 10 indicate that the majority of the employer respondents from the private sector rated the graduates as being very good/good in general knowledge (67%), in organizational and business knowledge (62%), and in accounting, finance and auditing knowledge (90%) but only 38% rated them as being very good/good in information technology. All the employer respondents from the public sector rated the graduates as being very good in organizational and business knowledge, and in accounting, finance and auditing knowledge. However, only 25% rated them as being very good/good in general knowledge and none rated them as being very good/good in information technology.

(vi) Future Services for Accounting Graduates

Albrecht and Sack (2000) argue that, if accounting education is to keep up with changes occurring in the business world, educators must understand what types of services their graduates will perform in the future. We asked both the graduates and their employers the kinds of services that would be needed of accounting graduates in five years time on a scale of one (less important) to five (very important). The results are presented in Table 11.

The analysis of the responses shows that the graduates perceived financial reporting, and audit and assurance to be the most important services in the future, while employers perceive strategic consulting as the most important service in the future. The only significant difference between the graduates and employers relate to strategic consulting which was

Table 11. Independence group *t*-test between accounting graduates' and their employers' perceptions of future accounting skills and services

Future services	Graduates	Employers	T	df	Sig. (2-tail)	Mean difference
Audit and assurance	4.46	4.48	−0.15	154	0.8786	−0.022
Financial analysis	4.33	4.46	−1.586	154	0.1147	−0.272
E-commerce consulting	3.75	3.72	0.16	154	0.8744	0.028
Financial planning	4.45	4.44	0.07	154	0.9406	0.01
Systems consulting	3.73	3.8	−0.38	154	0.7053	−0.067
Tax consulting	4.21	4.32	−0.67	154	0.5042	−0.106
Financial reporting	4.56	4.68	−0.86	154	0.3908	−0.123
Strategic consulting	4.31	4.76	−2.61	154	0.0099[a]	−0.447

[a]*P*-value <0.05

rated higher by the employers (a mean score of 4.76) than the graduates (a mean score of 4.31). A possible explanation for this is that as the business environment is becoming more competitive, employers perceive a higher need for people with the ability to undertake strategic analysis.

G. Summary and Conclusion

Recent studies (Albrecht and Sack, 2000; Gabbin, 2002; Hastings *et al.*, 2002; Lin *et al.* 2005) have suggested that accounting education lags behind developments in the business environment. These studies have therefore called for accounting education to be aligned with developments in the business environment. For example, it has been suggested that accounting education needs to change from knowledge acquisition to a process of learning (AECC, 1990). This will enable accounting education to provide students not only with the required knowledge and skills, but also with the ability to apply those skills throughout life. The role of accounting education programs is to prepare graduates for the workplace and develop their skills to enable them to pursue a career in the accounting profession.

Our study was therefore designed to examine the knowledge and skill requirements of accounting graduates in Ghana at the time of entry to the profession. Based on a survey questionnaire we have elicited the perceptions of both accounting graduates and employers about the knowledge and skill levels of the accounting graduates. Analytical/critical thinking has been rated by both the employers and the graduates as being the most important professional skill. The two groups are also largely in agreement about the other professional skill requirements though there were some small variations in the ratings of some of these skills. For example, the least important skills as rated by the graduates are technical and functional skills while the employers rated interpersonal skills as being the least important. However the average ratings of the technical and functional skills by the graduates (4.01) and the average ratings of the interpersonal skills by the employers (3.96) are still high enough to suggest that these skills are very important The differences in the overall mean ratings provided by the two groups are not statistically significant as shown in Table 5. This conclusion is in line with some previous studies (Albrecht and Sack, 2000; Francisco *et al.*, 2003; Burnett, 2003).

In terms of IT skills, spreadsheet packages are rated by both groups as being the most important. The least rated IT skill by the graduates is Windows while Presentation software and Electronic Commerce are equally rated as being the least important IT skills by the employers. Overall, there are only two IT skills which showed statistically significant differences (Table 6) between the two groups. These are word-processing packages and Windows for entry-level work. The higher level of importance attached to word-processing package and Windows by the employers is indicative of the essence of these two skills among the basic IT skills required by every accounting graduate aspiring to be a successful accounting professional.

The findings and conclusions in the paper should provide empirical and relevant input for assessing the content and delivery means of the existing accounting programs and facilitate the design of the curriculum to develop the required knowledge and skills for 21st century accountants in Ghana and in other developing countries. In particular, we encourage developing countries to reconsider their accounting education process, and introduce necessary changes required to focus on skill development, especially the need to introduce industrial attachment, encourage practicing accounting firms to forge links with academic institutions so as to assist in infusing accounting practical training with classroom theory.

The study also adds to the limited body of evidence on accounting education in developing countries (Ahmad and Gao, 2004; Bennett *et al.*, 2004; Devlin and Godfrey, 2004; Dixon, 2004). A significant number of graduates from Ghana and other developing countries go on to study postgraduate and/professional accounting programs in institutions in the Western world (mainly the UK, USA, Canada, and Australia). In addition, a significant number of Western companies are investing in Ghana and in other developing countries. Western educators and investors will find the findings reported in the study useful. Our findings suggest that the skills and knowledge requirements of accounting graduates in Ghana are no different from those required in advanced countries (see for instance Albrecht and Sack, 2000; Francisco *et al.*, 2003; Burnett, 2003). This would suggest that there are some generic issues in accounting curricula design. The call to understand accounting education could therefore be construed as a global problem. Thus, accounting education faces similar problems whether it is in the Western world (May *et al.*, 1995; Morgan, 1997; Gammie *et al.*, 2002; de Lange *et al.*, 2006) or in other emerging and developing countries (Hove, 1986; Wijewardena and Yapa, 2005; Lin *et al.*, 2005).

Ghana's accounting education system is relatively strong compared to those reported in some other developing countries such as Armenia (Bloom *et al*, 1998), Kiribati (Dixon, 2004), and Libya (Ahmad, and Gao, 2004). Similar to other Commonwealth developing countries (Briston, 1978; Hove, 1986; Wijewardena and Yapa, 2005), Ghana's accounting system is based largely on the British system (see for instance Ghartey, 1978). However, we observe that the content of the accounting degree program has not changed significantly over the years. The same courses have been taught over the years with none or only minor changes. This problem clearly needs addressing. The University of Ghana Business School has recently recognized this problem and attempts are currently being made to review the content of the accounting degree program.

While our study focused on only one institution—the University of Ghana—we believe this is not a major problem as the University of Ghana is the largest and oldest tertiary institution in Ghana and has the highest number of accounting students compared to any other tertiary institution in the country. However, we are currently planning future research to extend the study to other tertiary institutions in the country. We also see future opportunities for a comparative study with other developing countries. Our study is also limited because it relies predominantly on survey data. Future research that adopts a data triangulation approach by combining both quantitative and qualitative data would enrich the results. Interviews, observations and focus groups could provide additional sources of rich data. Our research did not investigate transferable and managerial skills (see for instance, Gammie *et al.*, 2002 and de Lange *et al.*, 2006). We plan to investigate these as part of the future research we have identified above.

Note

[1]The Accra-Tema metropolitan area is the capital city area of Ghana. Two main reasons motivated limiting the study to this area. First, the majority of businesses in Ghana are located within this area. Second, the hand delivery approach we adopted in distributing the questionnaire acted as a constraint to extend the research to other geographical areas.

References

Accounting Education Change Commission (AECC) (1990) Objectives of education for accountants: position statement number one, *Issues in Accounting Education*, 6(2), pp. 307–319.

Ahmad, N. and Gao, S. (2004) Changes, problems and challenges of accounting education in Libya, *Accounting Education*, 13(3), pp. 365–390.

Albrecht, S. W. (2002) Accounting Education on the Edge, *BizEd*, (March–April), pp. 40–45.

Albrecht, S. W. and Sack, R. J. (2000) *Accounting Education: Charting the Course through a Perilous Future*, Accounting Education Series Vol. No. 16 (Florida: American Accounting Association).

American Institute of Certified Public Accountants (AICPA) (1998) CPA vision project identifies top five issues for the profession, *The CPA Letter*, 1, p. 12.

Bedford Committee (1986) Future accounting education: preparing for the expanding profession. Committee on the future structure, content, and scope of accounting education, American Accounting Association (AAA), *Issues in Accounting Education*, 1(1), pp. 168–195.

Bennett, M., Bouma, J. J. and Ciccozzi, E. (2004) An institutional perspective on the transfer of accounting knowledge: a case study, *Accounting Education: an international journal*, 13(3), pp. 329–346.

Bloom, R., Fuglister, J. and Myring, M. (1998) The state of accounting in Armenia: A case, *The International Journal of Accounting*, 33(5), pp. 633–654.

Boritz, J. E. (1999) *The Accounting Curriculum and IT*, Working Paper, School of Accountancy University of Waterloo, Waterloo, Ontariol; Canada, M6C 1T1.

Briston, R. J. (1978) The evolution of accounting in developing countries, *International Journal of Accounting Education and Research*, 14(2), pp. 105–120.

Burnett, S. (2003) The future of accounting education: a regional perspective, *Journal of Education for Business*, 78(3), pp. 129–134.

de Lange, P., Jackling, B. and Gut, A. (2006) Accounting graduates' perceptions of skills emphasis in undergraduate courses: an investigation from two Victorian Universities, *Accounting and Finance*, 46(3), pp. 365–386.

Devlin, P. J. and Godfrey, A. D. (2004) Still awaiting orders: reflections on the cultural influence when educating in Albania, *Accounting Education: an international journal*, 13(3), pp. 347–364.

Dixon, K. (2004) Experiences of an accounting educator in Kiribati, *Accounting Education: an international journal*, 13(3), pp. 311–327.

Francisco, B., Parham, A. G. and Kelly, A. (2003) Skills Development in Accounting Education, *American Institute of Certified Public Accountants (AICPA), Members in Education*, April Issue. Available at http://www.aicpa.org/members/div/career/edu/index.htm (accessed 15 January 2006).

Gabbin, A. L. (2002) The crisis in accounting education, *Journal of Accountancy*, 193(4), pp. 81–86.

Gammie, B., Gammie, E. and Cargill, E. (2002) Personal skills development in the accounting curriculum, *Accounting Education: an international journal*, 11(1), pp. 63–78.

Ghartey, A. (1978) A new perspective for accounting education in Ghana, *The International Journal of Accounting Education and Research*, 14(l), pp. 121–132.

Hastings, C. I., Philip, R. and Lannie, S. (2002) The state of accounting curriculum: where it is and where it needs to be. Arizona State University, Working Paper, pp. 1–31.

Hove, M. R. (1986) Accounting practices in developing countries: Colonialism's legacy of inappropriate technologies, *International Journal of Accounting Education and Research*, 22(1), pp. 81–100.

IEG 9 (1996) *Prequalification Education, Assessment of Professional Competence and Experience Requirements of Professional Accountants*. IFAC first issued 1991, revised 1996.

IEG 11 (2003) *Information Technology for Professional Accountants*. IFAC (issued in January). Available at http://www.ifac.org.

IES 1 (2003) *Entry Requirements to a Program of Professional Accounting Education*. IFAC (issued in October).

IES 2 (2003) *Content of Professional Accounting Education Programs*. IFAC (issued in October).

IES 3 (2003) *Professional Skills*. IFAC (issued in October).

IES 4 (2003) *Professional Values, Ethics and Attitudes*. IFAC (issued in October).

IES 5 (2003) *Practical Experience Requirements* IFAC), (issued in October).

IFAC (2003) *Framework for International Education Statements.* (Published in October). Available at http://www.ifac.org (accessed 20 January 2006).

IFAC (2003) *Introduction to International Education Standards.* (Published in October). Available at http://www.ifac.org/ (accessed 11 February 2006).

Inman, B. C., Audre, W. and Peter, D. W. (1989) Square pegs in round holes: are accounting students well-suited to today's accounting profession? *Issues in Accounting Education*, 4(1), pp. 29–47.

Liebtag, B. (1987) News feature—compensation curves, *Journal of Accountancy*, 164(4), pp. 75–79.

Lin, Z. J., Xiong, X. and Liu, M. (2005) Knowledge base and skill development in accounting education: evidence from China, *Journal of Accounting Education*, 23(3), pp. 149–169.

Lovell, A. and Dixon, K. (2004) Editorial: experiences of the transfer of accounting education (based upon Anglo/American notions of accounting and education) into less-developed economies, *Accounting Education: an international journal*, 13(3), pp. 285–288.

May, G., Windal, F. W. and Sylvestre, J. (1995) The need for change in accounting education: an educator survey, *Journal of Accounting Education*, 13(l), pp. 21–43.

Mohamed, E. K. A. and Lashine, S. (2003) Accounting knowledge and skills and the challenges of a global business environment, *Managerial Finance*, 29(7), pp. 4–16.

Morgan, G. (1997) Communication skills required by accounting graduates: practitioner and academic perceptions, *Accounting Education: an international journal*, 6(2), pp. 93–107.

Nelson, A. T. (1989) The human resource dilemma in accounting, *Journal of Accountancy*, 168(2), pp. 46–52.

Nelson, I. T. (1996) A Tetrahedral view of accounting education: how can we improve the quality of our graduates? *Journal of Accounting Education*, 14(2), pp. 227–236.

Nelson, I. T. (1998) What's happening in the job market? *New Accountant*, March/April, pp. 19–24.

Perspectives on Education (1989) *Capabilities for Success in the Accounting Profession* (New York, NY: Arthur Andersen & Co., Arthur Young, Coopers & Lybrand, Deloitte Haskins & Sells, Ernst & Whinney, Peat Marwick Main & Co., Price Waterhouse, and Touche Ross (The Big Eight)).

Simons, K. and Higgins, M. (1993) An examination of practitioners' and academicians' views on the content of the accounting curriculum, *Accounting Educators' Journal*, 8(2), pp. 24–34.

Tsamenyi, M. and Mills, J. (2003) A survey of perceived environmental uncertainty, organizational culture, budget participation and managerial performance, *Journal of Transnational Management*, 8(1&2), pp. 17–52.

Wijewardena, H. and Yapa, S. (2005) Colonialism and accounting education in developing countries: the experiences of Singapore and Sri Lanka, *The International Journal of Accounting*, 33(2), pp. 269–281.

The Acquisition of Generic Skills of Culturally-diverse Student Cohorts

MONICA KENELEY* and BEVERLEY JACKLING**

*Deakin University, Australia **Victoria University, Australia*

This article was originally published in *Accounting Education: an international journal*, volume 20, issue 6 (December, 2011).

ABSTRACT *The changing nature of higher education and the structure of graduate labour markets have increased emphasis on employability and graduate outcomes. Universities have responded to this changed environment by embedding generic skills in the curriculum. This paper examines the generic skills that students perceived they acquired in their accounting studies in preparation for graduate employment. Given the changed background profiles of students studying accounting degree in Australia, and the employment difficulties they encounter on graduation, the study specifically addresses the perceptions of students from diverse cultural backgrounds. The findings demonstrate that, overall, students believed that their accounting course assisted in developing generic skills, while differences in perceptions were identified between different cultural cohorts. The research highlights the need to develop educational practices which embed generic skills development in the curriculum in a way that maximises the opportunities for culturally-diverse student cohorts to enhance their employment outcomes on graduation.*

Introduction

Debate over the types of skills and attributes required in the workplace has been ongoing for several decades. It is an issue that crosses national borders and which has become a focus of university educators in developed and emerging economies (Moreau and Leathwood, 2006; Awayiga, Onumah and Tsamenyi, 2010). The changing nature of higher education and the structure of graduate labour markets have increased emphasis on employability and graduate outcomes, reflecting structural problems in graduate and professional labour markets. These problems have become of greater interest to policy makers since the so called 'massification' of higher education.

Within the accounting discipline, increased complexity and rapid change in the professional role of the accountant has prompted the review and evaluation of university accounting courses (e.g. in Australia, Mathews, Jackson and Brown, 1990; and in the USA, AECC, 1990; Albrecht and Sack, 2000). A greater emphasis on graduate outcomes has occurred as part of a growing trend, particularly in OECD countries. In the UK, it is reported that debate about the employability of graduates is becoming an increasingly prominent matter for public comment (Moreau and Leathwood, 2006). Canada, USA, New Zealand and Denmark have all introduced measures to promote an accepted set of generic skills. In the USA, Albrecht and Sack (2000) argued that the conventional accounting curriculum taught in American universities was too narrow and outdated, and that students were not being prepared adequately for employment in the modern business environment.

Discussion over the desired type and level of skills expected of accounting graduates has been motivated by the shifting role of accountants as 'knowledge professionals' in the international business environment (Howieson, 2003). A better mix of technical and generic skills is seen as being necessary to address the diversity of business challenges. Prior studies have indicated that the successful acquisition of particular skill sets within a tertiary degree is related to students' perceptions of the importance of these competencies in the work environment (Usoff and Feldman, 1998; Arnold, Loan-Clark, Harrington and Hart, 1999; Rainsbury, Hodges, Burchell and Lay, 2002).

Given the emphasis placed on generic skills in the employment market, the aim of this study is to understand the generic skills that undergraduate students perceive they acquire in their studies to prepare them for graduate employment. The study specifically distinguishes between international and local cohorts of students to identify whether there are differences in perceptions of skill development in undergraduate accounting studies (Birrell and Healy, 2008).

Identification of the perceptions of differing cohorts of students has become important with the increased growth in international student numbers in universities in many Western countries. In Australia, as part of a skilled migration program, international students have been encouraged to complete degrees that are linked to occupations where there are identified skill shortages. International students completing these degrees have traditionally been given additional points towards any application for permanent residency (PR) in Australia (Birrell, 2006). This policy has been linked to the substantial growth in the number of international students enrolled in accounting courses in Australia. International students now make up approximately 51% of all commencing students in the management and commerce field of study in the higher education sector (Department of Education, Employment and Workplace Relations, DEEWR, 2010). Approximately 83% of international student enrolments in Australia come from Asia, principally from China and India (DEEWR, 2010). The Asian cohort of international students has been growing nationally at a rate which is in excess of 10% per annum with an average overall annual growth rate of 5.7% since 2005 (DEEWR, 2010).

The increased proportion of international students in Australian higher education has raised concerns about the employability of these accounting graduates, particularly given the opportunities provided via the migration policy to remain in the country. Of specific concern has been whether international students acquire the range of generic skills which are embedded in accounting courses and which are expected by employers of accounting graduates (Birrell, 2006; Watty, 2007).

Bui and Porter (2010), in referencing the difference in expectations of employers and the performance of graduates, have constructed a framework which indentifies the elements contributing to an expectations-performance skills gap. One constraint affecting the development of skills required by employers was students' perceptions of the accounting profession, their ability and aptitude. The current study examines the extent to which accounting students perceive that they develop generic skills in their degree programme.

More specifically, the study distinguishes between the perceptions of international and local students in the development of generic skills. With high numbers of international students expected to enter the Australian workforce on completion of accounting degrees, it is important to determine whether these students perceive that their accounting course contributes to the acquisition of a broad range of skills required of accountants. In addition, this study also provides an understanding of the extent to which the embedding of generic skills in the curriculum has narrowed the performance gap identified in studies such as Bui and Porter (2010).

Accordingly two research questions are investigated:

RQ1 To what extent do students perceive that their undergraduate accounting degree studies have contributed to the development of their generic skills?
RQ2 Are there differences in the perceptions of skill development between local and international students?

The next section of the paper commences with a review of the literature on the scope of generic skills, their development in the university curriculum and the skills expected of graduates entering the workforce, with an emphasis on international graduates. The section that follows explains the research method adopted, the data collection methods and analysis techniques employed. The fourth section discusses the results of the analysis and their importance for accounting education. The paper concludes with recommendations for future research and possible directions for educators and professional accounting bodies in preparing accounting students to meet the needs of a changing global business environment.

Literature Review

Professional accounting bodies in Australia, New Zealand and the UK have sponsored studies designed to identify the desired competencies of professional accountants (e.g. in Australia and New Zealand, Birkett, 1993; in the UK, the ICAEW, 1996). These studies have identified that professional accountants require technical skills as well as a range of more generic behavioural and cognitive skills. Generic skills have become an important component of professional practice and curriculum design. Hence, initially the literature review will focus broadly on the importance of generic skills before considering generic skill classification, generic skill integration into the curriculum as well as key stakeholders' perceptions.

Over the past two decades there has been a shift in emphasis in university education away from the concept of 'graduateness' to that of employability. 'Graduateness' refers to the deeper knowledge and understanding that comes with study for a university qualification. Employability is associated with the enhanced prospects for employment and career progression from degree studies. With this shift has come a growing emphasis on a broadening of the skill base to include personal skills, which will prepare graduates for the workplace (Glover, Law and Youngman, 2002; Walsh and Kotzee, 2010).

In the UK, the Dearing Report (National Committee of Inquiry into Higher Education, NCIHE, 1997) recommended the development of communication, numeracy, technology and 'learning how to learn skills' at a higher level within all subjects. These generic skills are further defined in the subject benchmark statements released by the UK's Quality Assurance Agency for Higher Education (QAA, 2007). In Australia, universities now require that graduates acquire a 'generally accepted' set of generic skills as part of their studies. The development of these skills has been typically embedded within degree courses across each university. This type of university-wide policy demonstrates the desire of universities to develop generic skills which encompass lifelong learning, technical training, oral, written and interpersonal skills, as well as exposure to organisational and information technology skills.[1]

Broadening the skill base in university teaching programs to meet a set of generally accepted graduate attributes has been proposed to provide more competent practitioners who are adaptable to a constantly changing work environment. In the 1990s, professional accounting bodies advocated the inclusion of generic skills in university teaching programs. In the USA, the Accounting Education Change Commission (AECC, 1990) set out the desired capabilities which accounting courses should develop in students. The AECC argued that accounting degrees should prepare graduates *to become* (not to *be*) professional accountants when first entering the workforce. They emphasised fostering broadly-based communication and interpersonal skills (AECC, 1990). Australian and New Zealand accounting bodies agreed on a similar approach. A study commissioned by the major accounting bodies in Australia and New Zealand formed the basis of the development of the competency requirements of accounting graduates (Birkett, 1993). The key professional accounting bodies in Australia now require generic skills to be incorporated in the accounting curriculum of universities (ICAA/CPA Australia, 2009). Sin, Jones and Petocz (2007) indicate that generic skills have been promoted consistently by employers and academic boards across Australia and New Zealand.

Arguments put forward for incorporating generic skills in the curriculum have been prompted by concerns regarding the employability and work-readiness of graduates. The re-evaluation of higher education systems (which many universities have undertaken since the 1990s) suggests that this is just one of several reasons for the increasing emphasis on skills-based educational outcomes (Nunan, Rigmor and McCausland, 2000; Bowden, Hart, King, Trigwell and Watts, 2000). Employers, educators and graduates have acknowledged the need for educational processes to encourage the development of well-rounded, socially-responsible graduates. Employers have increasingly called for a broadening of the graduate skill base. Employers in both the UK and Spain viewed the development of non-technical (generic) skills as being essential for the practice of management accounting (Hassall, Joyce, Arquero Montãno and Donaso Anes, 2005). Employers also believed it was the responsibility of universities to develop these skills within the student body. Studies of the views of graduates also indicate an awareness of the importance of generic skills in enhancing career prospects (Rainsbury, Hodges, Burchell and Lay, 2002).

Debate over what constitutes the skill base an accounting graduate should have acquired during university study is compounded by the lack of distinction between capabilities and competencies (Rainsbury *et al.*, 2002). Competencies derive from a more vocational approach to education. Definitions of what constitutes a competency-based approach vary, but a common thread is the focus on workplace outcomes (Boritz and Carnaghan, 2003). The International Federation of Accountants (IFAC) defines competence as the ability to perform a work task to a defined standard with reference to real working environments (IFAC, 2001). Capabilities, on the other hand, relate to knowledge, skills and personal qualities needed to perform specific tasks. This interchange of terms has blurred understanding of the nature of skill development (Boritz and Carnaghan, 2003). In this respect, knowledge of differing perceptions of skill requirements can provide insights into the outcomes of the shift in educational emphasis to employability.

The classification of generic skills

Although there is widespread debate on what constitutes the generic skills of a university graduate (e.g. Barrie, 2006; Bridgstock, 2009; Fallows and Stevens, 2000), categorisation of the main features of skills brings us closer to a common understanding. Nunan *et al.* (2000) identified four main categories of skills:

- First, the discipline-specific knowledge which underpins the course of study.
- Second, the understanding which derives from applying, communicating and evaluating that body of knowledge.
- Third, the dimensions of service which follow from the graduate's appreciation of broader community and social responsibilities.
- Fourth, the development of personal skills and the capacity for employment.

> In basic terms, generic skills are those skills which are required if one is to be deemed competent in the discipline, in more general analytical and problem-solving skills, in appreciative skills which reflect broader social value frameworks, and in personal skills which reflect the employability of the graduate in his/her chosen field (Nunan *et al.*, 2000).

The classification proposed by Nunan *et al.* (2000) reflects the skills requirements adopted by accounting bodies such as CPA Australia. This organisation has identified a comprehensive list of skills required of accounting graduates. These skills are divided into cognitive skills and behavioural skills; and then further classified into five sub categories - routine skills, analytic skills, appreciative skills, personal skills, and interpersonal skills (ICAA/CPA Australia, 2009). Figure 1 provides an overview of the skill categories expected to be developed in university accounting courses accredited by CPA Australia. The cognitive skills include routine skills (report and essay writing and computer literacy), analytic/design skills (problem solving, analytical reasoning and interpretation of data) and appreciative skills (making complex and creative judgments, thinking and acting critically).

The generic skills that relate to behavioural skills include personal skills (handling oneself in different situations, acting strategically, and focusing on outcomes) as well as interpersonal skills (people skills, listening, communication and empathy, understanding group dynamics). Although communication skills are not listed as being a separate skills area, they are incorporated into many other areas. It is acknowledged by the professional body that the ability to communicate clearly and precisely is highly valued by employers and by professional accounting bodies worldwide (ICAA/CPA Australia, 2009).

A consideration in the generic skills debate is how these skills are developed in courses of study. Bowden *et al.* (2000) argued that the acquisition of a skill set involves a process in which students become increasingly accomplished over time. This implies a holistic

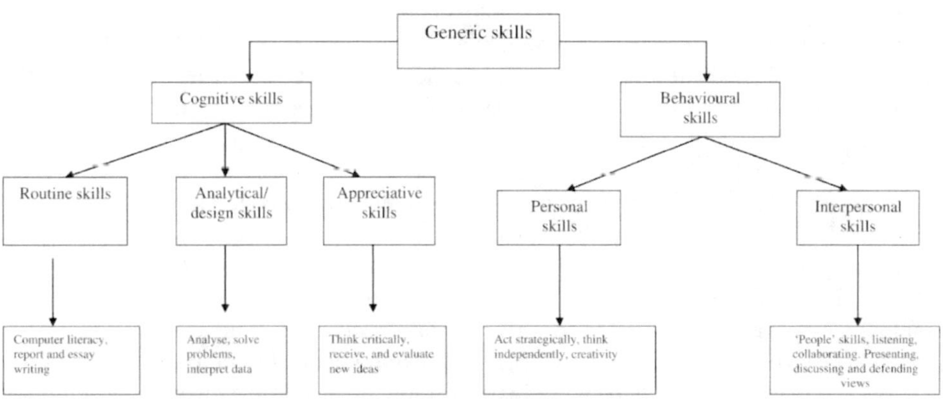

Figure 1. Generic skills hierarchy (ICAA/CPA Australia, 2009).

approach to their degree studies in which skill development is fully integrated into the educational process as students progress through their course. Alternative approaches include the 'bolting on' of modules designed to foster specific skills, and the parallel development of skills outside the specific course curriculum (Cranmer, 2006).

A key argument for embedding skill development into the teaching unit is that the development of such skills is more relevant when placed within the context of the discipline under study (e.g. Clanchy and Ballard, 1995; Bowden *et al.*, 2000; Barrie, 2004; Hancock *et al.*, 2009b). Increasingly, there has been recognition that technical skills need to be accompanied by non-accounting skills to 'enable the professional accountant to make successful use of the knowledge gained through education' (IFAC, 1996, p. 16). Therefore, in preparing accounting graduates for employment, the curriculum should incorporate a range of technical and generic skills.

In Australia, professional accounting bodies (such as CPA Australia) expect generic skills to be integrated into the core curriculum of accounting courses. This is a requisite of the course accreditation processes undertaken by university accounting departments. The message which professional associations have conveyed to university educators is that generic skills are a requirement of competent professional practice and that they are highly valued by employers (ICCA/CPA, 2009). Typically, such skills have been developed in units of study via case studies, small group discussion, debates, group assignments, problem-solving tasks, and simulated decision-making in complex and ambiguous situations.

Stakeholders' Perceptions about Generic Skill Development

One particular issue that has a direct bearing on the success of university programs in fostering skill development and positive graduate employment outcomes are the perceptions of generic skill development (Hancock *et al.*, 2009a). University courses which successfully foster skills development have a high probability of narrowing what De Lange, Jackling and Gut (2006) refer to as an expectation gap. They assert that an expectation gap occurs between graduates and employers in terms of the types of skills that each group believes is required to pursue a successful career in accounting. For example, a UK study of management students found that they had positive perceptions of generic skill development. However, their perceptions of the value placed on specific skills differed from those of employers (Arnold *et al.*, 1999). A study of accounting undergraduates at an American college found that, although students recognised the importance of generic skills, they did not rank them as highly as technical skills (Usoff and Feldman, 1998). An Australian study conducted by Kavanagh and Drennan (2008) found that, whilst there was some agreement between students and employers in terms of skills required in the workplace, the importance which each group placed on specific skills differed. Further, a national study of graduates, employers and academics which sought feedback about the employment skills set of business graduates identified that the greatest area of skill deficiency expressed by the three stakeholder groups was the development of team skills (Oliver, Whelan, Hunt and Hammer, 2011).

Awareness of skill competency also differs between student cohorts. A study of recent graduates from Australian universities found that international students rated their level of competency in generic skills lower than that of local graduates (Graduate Careers Australia, 2008). The study also showed that international students were less confident over obtaining employment in their chosen profession, given their perceived level of generic skills.

Differences in perceptions of generic skill requirements for employment between employers and graduates lead to labour market problems such as the inability of graduates to gain employment. This has been the case recently in Australia, where university students from differing educational and cultural backgrounds have found it difficult to acquire employment, often because employers perceive that they lack the required standard of generic skills. Birrell (2006) has reported that recent accounting graduates who were former international students struggle to find positions as accountants largely because they are perceived as lacking some generic skills, specifically communication skills. Reconciling the different perceptions held by various stakeholders (e.g. employers and graduates) has strong potential to provide a greater understanding of the problems associated with synchronising skill requirements for employment.

This paper contributes to the literature and adds a further dimension to the debate about skills and skills levels, by investigating the extent to which undergraduates perceive that their studies specifically aid the development of generic skills.

Research Method

Development of Generic Skills in the Accounting Curriculum

Feedback from students undertaking a second year course at an Australian university was sought. The focus of the project was on students' views midway through their course in order to gauge the perceptions of those currently undertaking a program which had embedded generic skill development in the curriculum. Other research has considered the perceptions of graduates and employers (De Lange *et al.*, 2006; Jackling and De Lange, 2009).

This unit of study involved was one of six accounting units included in the undergraduate accounting degree program accredited by CPA Australia.[2] To ensure a comprehensive coverage of generic skill development throughout the degree course, the Programme Director (in consultation with unit coordinators), ensures that each unit covers a range of the specified generic skills. The university in question also has an explicit operational policy requiring that a set of generic skills be incorporated into all academic programs. A further requirement is that these skills and attributes must be documented and communicated to students in each unit of their study. This unit is the second accounting unit studied by students undertaking an accounting major. The technical content incorporates introductory financial reporting (income, statement of financial position (Balance Sheet) and Cash Flow Statements), double entry accounting, journals, ledgers, balance day adjustments, closing entries, together with an overview of the conceptual framework which underpins the International Financial Reporting Standards (IFRS).

Integrated in the curriculum of the three year accounting degree programme is a set of generic skills, consistent with the requirements for professional accounting accreditation. It is not anticipated that each unit of study in the accounting course addresses all core curriculum generic skills areas shown in Figure 1. Instead, it is envisaged that the skills development will be integrated across the three years of the undergraduate degree course. The course (via the nature of assessment tasks), anticipates that students will develop a commitment to ethical behaviour, enhance their capacity to think and act independently, improve their ability to think creatively, and improve flexibility in new/different situations. Tutorial classes emphasising presentation skills are not included in this unit. The cognitive skills include analytic/design skills and appreciative skills, with a focus on problem-solving and the interpretation of data, and reports interwoven with the technical aspects of the curriculum. Assessment tasks incorporate several of these skills. For example, analytic skills and appreciative skills form part of the formal testing process of progressive assessment and in final examinations. The behavioural skills are assessed more subtlety via students' ability to organise their study schedules to meet deadlines, and adaptation of learning to meet the challenges of a relatively independent teaching model. This approach to learning differs from that experienced in prior studies at secondary school and alternate entry pathways to university.[3]

Data Collection

The data were collected via questionnaires completed by 437 students undertaking the second unit in the accounting major as part of their undergraduate studies in an Australian bachelor's degree. The questionnaire collected background information relating to gender, entry pathway, and country of permanent residence.[4] The focus of the questionnaire was on students' perceptions of the contribution of their undergraduate accounting studies to the development of generic skills. The selection of generic skills was further informed by prior research (De Lange *et al.*, 2006; Hellier, Keneley, Carr and Lynch, 2004). The methodology also draws on work undertaken by the Australian Chamber of Commerce and Industry (2002) which developed an employability skills framework which summarises the generic skills that employers expect of university graduates. Further refinement of the questionnaire was undertaken following interviews with employers and accounting graduates in Australia, China, Hong Kong and Taiwan.

A series of specific generic skills were listed and students were asked to rate the extent to which they believed that their studies contributed to the development of these skills. Skills referred to decision-making, problem-solving, adaptive and teamwork competencies, as well as to critical thinking and reasoning skills. Issues related to ethical and moral judgment were also included (see Appendix 1 for relevant components of the questionnaire). The selected items were broadly based on the accreditation requirements for generic skill development set by professional accounting bodies in Australia (e.g. ICAA/CPA Australia, 2009).

The questionnaire was completed in the final week of the semester for the unit of study. All students surveyed undertook the unit at the same time. This timing of distribution enabled students to reflect on the contribution of their studies to the development of generic skills, taking into consideration all aspects of the course, including delivery of content and various assessment tasks. The analysis of the contribution of undergraduate study to the development of generic skills involved the collection of descriptive statistics. A one-way analysis of variance was used to test for differences in perceptions of generic skill development between local and international students.

Descriptive Statistics

The 437 responses represented a response rate of approximately 64 per cent, based on the number of students sitting the final examination in the unit surveyed. This level of response is typically seen as being acceptable when employing a survey method (Sekaran, 1992; Zikmund, 2000). Two hundred and seven respondents were male and 227 female (three respondents did not identify their gender). Of the 437 respondents, 30% (133) were local students and 70% (303) international students with one non-identified. Table 1 shows that the majority of international students were from China (43.9%), Hong Kong (14.5%) and Sri Lanka (9.9%). The high representation of international students from China is typical of undergraduate courses in Australia. Of the 303 international students who participated in the survey, 284 responded to the question about intention to seek permanent residency in Australia. Of these 284, there were 237 (78.2% of all international students) who indicated that they intended to seek permanent residence in Australia once they have completed their studies. This result demonstrates that this

Table 1. Descriptive statistics $n = 437$

	Frequency	Per cent
Gender		
Male	207	47.4
Female	227	51.9
No response	3	0.7
Residence		
Australia	133	30.4
Overseas	303	69.3
Missing	1	0.2
Country of permanent residence—overseas ($n = 303$)		
China	133	43.9
Hong Kong	44	14.5
Indonesia	23	7.6
Sri Lanka	30	9.9
Other Asian countries	43	14.1
Other non Asian countries	18	6.0
Missing	12	4.0
Intention to seek permanent residence—overseas ($n = 303$)		
Yes	237	78.2
Missing	19	6.3
Entry pathway—first year studies		
First year university	155	35.5
Alternative pathways (credit transfers)	279	63.8
Missing	3	0.7

pathway to permanent residency under the existing migration laws was important for international students undertaking undergraduate accounting studies.

Table 1 also details the characteristics of the respondents, including entry pathway. Given the different pathways provided to university study, only 35% of the sample entered the second year of study from the traditional pathway (i.e. from having studied first year accounting at the university where the study was conducted). International students typically enter university—and specifically accredited accounting courses—via diverse pathways (see end note 3) and, to a lesser extent, via direct entry to first year university courses. Further analysis (not shown in this study) indicated that international students were highly represented in alternative entry pathways.

Since the introduction of government measures making the study of accounting more attractive to overseas students, the commerce and management enrolments as a proportion of all enrolments in universities by international students have grown exponentially (DEEWR, 2010). The country of origin of international enrolments in business degrees in Australian universities has also shifted to reflect changes in motivation to study accounting. The traditional markets for recruiting international students to study in Australia (for example, Malaysia and Singapore) have typically experienced a decline in enrolments. These students have been replaced by growing enrolments from China, India and South Korea (Birrell and Rapson, 2005). The country of origin of international students surveyed was typical of that experienced in the recent influx of overseas students studying accounting in Australia. The proportion of students from China (43.9% of international students in this sample) is representative of the blend of international students studying at the undergraduate level. International students from India and to some extent South Korea are more highly represented in postgraduate accounting degree courses in Australia.

While non-response bias is always a concern, a comparison of broader university students' profile descriptors and respondents' demographics suggest that responses captured a 'typical' population of undergraduate accounting students studying at the second year level in several Australian universities. This conclusion is supported by the research of Birrell (2006) who has highlighted the expansion of overseas student enrolments in accounting degrees in Australia.[5]

Results

Students' perceptions of the extent to which their undergraduate accounting studies have promoted the development of various generic skills were measured in this study. A five-point Likert-type scale was used. Students were asked to rate whether their degree studies had contributed to the development of the skills listed. Ratings varied from a score of 1 = 'no contribution' to generic skill development to a score of 5 = 'great contribution' to skill development, with a mid-point score of 3 indicating neutrality. Table 2 shows, in descending order, the results of the initial analysis for the mean scores for each of the generic skills in total, for all respondents. The results suggest that, on average, students perceive that their studies contribute to generic skill development.

Table 2 shows that respondents perceive their accounting studies had made the greatest contribution to the development of the generic skill 'thinking and reasoning logically' with an overall mean score of 3.91 out of a possible score of 5. Other generic skills ranked highly by respondents were the ability to 'solve problems' (mean of 3.87) and 'be open to new ideas and possibilities' (3.81). For the most part, the generic skills that were more highly rated linked with the technical content of the curriculum of the unit of accounting study. For example, thinking and reasoning logically, solving problems and adapting knowledge to new situations reflects the nature of the tasks completed by students in classrooms. Students complete set problem-solving tasks in tutorial groups and in lectures. Behavioural skills were overall perceived by students to be less well developed in their studies to date. For instance, their responses suggest that students did not believe that team working skills were developed to an acceptable level in their studies and were the lowest ranked skill with a mean of 3.4.

Table 2. Descriptive statistics: Perceptions of generic skill acquisition

Generic skill item	*n*	Mean[a]	Std deviation
Think and reason logically	430	3.91	0.772
Solve problems	432	3.87	0.779
Adapt knowledge to new situations	433	3.82	0.821
Open to new possibilities	430	3.81	0.826
Make decisions	432	3.75	0.791
Work with minimum supervision	428	3.73	0.927
Think creatively	431	3.67	0.886
Make and take responsibility	431	3.66	0.886
Understand ethical implications of decisions	432	3.54	0.890
Question accepted wisdom	430	3.48	0.833
Work in a team	434	3.41	0.974

[a]In descending order.

The difference in perceptions of international and local students was tested with reference to the generic skills built into the curriculum of the unit of study of the undergraduate accounting course. The generic skills were broadly categorised according to the framework shown in Figure 1. This categorisation, based on the earlier Birkett (1993) framework, helped facilitate discussion of the skills between the two student cohorts consistent with the accreditation guidelines of the professional accounting bodies. Table 3 shows the differences in means between the two groups within each of the two main categories, cognitive skills and behavioural skills, as outlined in Figure 1.

A one-way analysis of variance was used to test for the significance of differences in the means for each of the items related to perceptions of generic skill development for local and international students. The independent variable was residence. Local students were categorised as '0' and international students as '1'. The analysis of variance was based on the null hypothesis that there was no significant difference in the perceptions of generic skill development between local and international students. Table 4 shows the results of the one-way analysis of variance for each of the items that were classified as either behavioural or cognitive type generic skills.

Table 4 reveals that there were significant differences between perceptions of the development of two of the four cognitive type generic skills between local and international students: thinking and reason logically ($F = 4.278$ df 1 $P < 0.05$) and decision-making skills ($F = 3.796$, df 1, $P = 0.05$). Table 3 shows that the means for 'think and reason logically' and 'making decisions', was higher for international students when compared with local students (local student mean = 3.80, international student mean = 3.97; local student mean = 3.64; international student mean = 3.80).

In terms of behavioural skills, Table 4 shows that there were significant differences between local and international students on four of the six skill types: questioning accepted

Table 3. Comparison of generic skill development: Local and international students

		n	Mean	Std deviation
Cognitive skills				
Think and reason logically	Local	133	3.80	0.900
	International	296	3.97	0.696
Make decisions	Local	133	3.64	0.882
	International	298	3.80	0.738
Solve problems	Local	133	3.80	0.874
	International	298	3.90	0.725
Adapt knowledge to new situations	Local	133	3.77	0.910
	International	299	3.85	0.773
Behavioural skills				
Understand ethical implications of decisions	Local	132	3.48	0.928
	International	299	3.58	0.869
Question accepted wisdom	Local	132	3.30	0.971
	International	297	3.57	0.746
Open to new possibilities	Australia	132	3.73	0.917
	International	297	3.84	0.783
Work in a team	Local	133	3.27	1.009
	International	300	3.48	0.952
Think creatively	Local	133	3.38	0.983
	International	297	3.80	0.804
Make and take responsibility	Local	133	3.47	0.942
	International	297	3.74	0.849

Table 4. Analysis of variance re. generic skills: International and local students.

		Sum of Squares	df	Mean square	F	Sig.
Cognitive skills						
Think and reason logically	Between groups	2.501	1	2.501	4.278	0.039
	Within groups	249.644	427	0.585		
	Total	252.145	428			
Make decisions	Between groups	2.341	1	2.341	3.796	0.052
	Within groups	264.596	429	0.617		
	Total	266.937	430			
Solve problems	Between groups	0.886	1	0.886	1.479	0.225
	Within groups	257.095	429	0.599		
	Total	257.981	430			
Adapt knowledge to new situations	Between groups	0.519	1	0.519	0.776	0.379
	Within groups	287.461	430	0.669		
	Total	287.979	431			
Behavioural skills						
Understand ethical implications of decisions	Between groups	0.940	1	0.940	1.194	0.275
	Within groups	337.835	429	0.787		
	Total	338.775	430			
Question accepted wisdom	Between groups	6.839	1	6.839	10.129	0.002
	Within groups	288.312	427	0.675		
	Total	295.152	428			
Open to new possibilities	Between groups	1.198	1	1.198	1.753	0.186
	Within groups	291.744	427	0.683		
	Total	292.942	428			
Work in a team						
	Between groups	3.910	1	3.910	4.160	0.042
	Within groups	405.092	431	0.940		
	Total	409.002	432			
Think creatively	Between groups	16.042	1	16.042	21.542	0
	Within groups	318.723	428	0.745		
	Total	334.765	429			
Make and take responsibility	Between groups	6.387	1	6.387	8.267	0.004
	Within groups	330.673	428	0.773		
	Total	337.060	429			

wisdom, working in a team, thinking creatively, and making and taking responsibility. In each instance where there were significant differences, the mean score for international students was higher than for local students (see Table 3). Of particular note is the difference between means for the items questioning accepted wisdom (local student mean = 3.30; international student mean = 3.57) and think creatively (local student mean = 3.38; international student mean = 3.80). These differences suggest that the curriculum design results in different learning experiences for the two cohorts, which exposes international students to behavioural skills which may not have featured in their previous educational experiences. In contrast, local students have had prior learning experiences in first year university studies and/or in secondary school studies which are aligned more closely to the development of these types of skills. Thus, the results suggest that the accounting curriculum tends to produce different learning experiences for local and international students in terms of generic skills.

Discussion

In the decade and a half since major reviews into accounting education recommended a change in emphasis, university curricula have evolved to incorporate generic skill development as a core objective. Until recently there has been little assessment of stakeholders' perceptions of such skill development. This study has assessed one aspect of stakeholders' perceptions—namely, how students view the skills they acquire in their accounting studies.

The results indicate that students perceive that their accounting degree studies contribute to the development of generic skills. However, some skills are perceived to be integrated more intensively into the curriculum than others. A number of cognitive skills were ranked highly e.g. think and reason logically (mean = 3.91), solve problems (mean = 3.87), and adapt knowledge to new situations (mean = 3.82). Behavioural skills such as open to new possibilities (mean = 3.81) was also ranked highly. Overall, however, behavioural skills were ranked lower than cognitive skills. These differences may have significance in terms of labour market expectations. De Lange *et al.* (2006) found that behavioural skills were ranked very highly by employers in Australia. If students do not perceive that they are acquiring these skills, they may be unable to demonstrate effectively the required degree of competency to prospective employers. In the present study it would appear that students perceive that behavioural skills are important, with international students in particular identifying that their accounting studies contributed to this area of skill development. A related aspect is the impact of students' perceptions on their motivation to learn. Kavanagh and Drennan (2008) suggest that students' motivation to learn and acquire skills is influenced by their perceptions of the relevance of specific skills. The degree of skill acquisition may be influenced by the fact that students perceive some skills to be more important than others, particularly if certain skills form some part of the assessment process. If this is the case it has further implications for the successful integration of generic skills into the curriculum.

Overall, analysis of the contribution of undergraduate studies to the development of generic skills suggests that international students perceive that their course aids development of generic skills more so than local students. Two main reasons are proposed to explain this difference. First, international students tend to enter their studies at the second year level. Consequently, the curriculum content in these pathways may have varying degrees of emphasis on the development of generic skills when compared with the traditional university curriculum. Second, the results—at least in part, can be explained by the potential differences in the education models of the two cohorts which produce different learning environments. Given that a large proportion of the international students originated from China and Hong Kong (58.4%), the Chinese setting for their prior studies will have contributed to the differences in the findings for international students when compared with local students. Prior research indicates that Chinese teachers typically concentrate on passing technical knowledge on to students and make little attempt to develop students' learning abilities and skills (Xiao and Dyson, 1999). Xiao and Dyson (1999) suggest that techniques to develop generic skills, such as small group discussion, student presentations and group work assignments are rarely used in China, although case studies and essay writing are becoming more popular.

The Western teaching environment which international students, particularly those from China, encounter in their studies in Australia assists in explaining the significant differences in their perceptions of skill development. The items within the factor 'behavioural skills', including the development of the questioning of accepted wisdom, thinking creatively, thinking and reasoning logically, serve to demonstrate the contrast from the traditional Chinese learning environment that many students may have undertaken prior to the commencement of their studies in Australia.

In some aspects of their evaluation of the contribution of their studies to developing cognitive generic skills such as problem-solving and adapting knowledge to new situations, no significant differences were found between international and local students. However, in both instances the mean for the international cohort was greater than for the local cohort, which indicates that the learning environment was still an influential factor.

Conclusion

The outcomes of the current study indicate that, from an overall perspective, students have positive perceptions about the way in which the accounting curriculum fosters generic skill development. This supports earlier findings such as that of Arnold *et al.* (1999). However, there is a suggestion that students perceive that their accounting studies have contributed more to the development of some types of generic skills than others. Results also indicate a difference in perceptions between local and international students—particularly in relation to behavioural skills. In general, international students believe that their studies are contributing more to the development of these skills than is the case for local students. This finding is important given that prior studies (e.g. De Lange *et al.*, 2006) have highlighted that behavioural skills are highly regarded by employers in Australia when recruiting accounting graduates.

The findings from this study provide a basis for further extension of inquiry which would provide educators and professional bodies with a more complete picture of skill integration into the curriculum. For example, further investigation of the level of generic skills displayed by recent graduates is warranted. This would provide useful feedback for accounting educators on the contribution that undergraduate studies make to the development of these skills as a preparation for employment. Similarly, a study of employers' perceptions of graduate competence, particularly international graduate competence, would indicate the degree to which graduates are able to integrate their learning into the work environment. In future studies, accounting educators should consider using structured interactive feedback based on small group discussion in each year level, (along the lines proposed by Lizzio, Wilson and Simons, 2002) to monitor the changes in students' perceptions of the development of generic skills.

The preceding findings are subject to various limitations, including that the study was conducted in one university at one point in time. In addition, the study indicates students' perceptions of generic skills partway through their university studies of accounting but not taking into account the number of units each student has undertaken. The separation of the sample into sub-samples based on the number of accounting units undertaken may provide better insights into whether different levels of progress in the accounting course leads to different levels of skills development. Furthermore, a pre-test and post-test of students' perceptions would have provided a superior measure of perceived skill development. It is also acknowledged that students develop generic skills in a range of units of study and from their own experiences, particularly from work experience opportunities. The study also assumes that local students are a relatively homogeneous group accustomed to a Western educational environment. Similarly, international students are grouped together although high proportions are from Asian cultural backgrounds and, as a consequence, are less likely to have been exposed to Western educational approaches. These limitations need to be taken into account when interpreting the results, and are worthy of consideration in terms of the design of future studies addressing generic skill development.

Despite these limitations, the results of this study indicate that, overall, the incorporation of generic skills into the accounting education course is positively perceived as being successful by students. However, the study has highlighted that students perceive some deficiencies in their acquisition of generic skills. Additionally, the differences in perceptions of skill development between international and local students suggest that international students perceive the academic environment to be an important source of generic skill development. Therefore, it is critical that accounting educators consider curriculum development initiatives which maximise opportunities for diverse student cohorts to develop skills that are required to compete in global graduate employment markets.

Acknowledgements

The authors should like to thank Professor Russell Craig (University of Canterbury, New Zealand) and Dr Riccardo Natoli (Financial Education Research Unit, Victoria University, Australia) for their advice and feedback on early drafts of this paper. Additionally, the authors thank the anonymous referees and the Editor for their helpful comments and constructive feedback on the paper.

Notes

[1]Many alternative terms are used to describe generic skills. In the USA generic skills are some times referred to as transferable skills or 'workplace know-how'. In the UK terms such as core skills or personal skills are terms used more frequently to denote generic skills. Hancock *et al.* (2009a, p. 28) has a more comprehensive listing of alternate names for generic skills based on country of usage.

[2]CPA Australia is one of three professional bodies in Australia. The other professional bodies, Institute of Chartered Accountants in Australia (ICAA) and the Institute of Public Accountants (formerly known as the National Institute of Accountants (NIA)) have similar requirements for the professional recognition of undergraduate accounting courses for entry to the professional body as associate members. On completion of requisite additional requirements (including work experience and completion of units of study), associate members become qualified accountants. Students would typically take one unit of accounting in their first year, two units in the second year and three units in the third year.

[3]Alternative pathways include completion of equivalent first year studies with technical and further education colleges, completion of one-year diploma courses with registered private providers, twinning programmes with partnered universities off-shore. These educational experiences are generally in small classrooms, in contrast to the large lecture environment at second year university.

[4]Country of permanent residence was used to distinguish Australian residents ('local' students) from students from other countries (classified as 'international' students).

[5]It is impossible to obtain from DEEWR the number of students commencing studies in accounting. Data are collected more broadly by field of education study (i.e. 'Management and Commerce'). Typically,

accounting has attracted a higher proportion of international students than other discipline areas in this broad field of study given it is a discipline area that appears on the Critical Skills List for migration purposes. The proportion of international students (70%) is therefore higher in a sample of accounting students compared with the national average of 51% for the field of study reported by DEEWR (2010).

References

Accounting Education Change Commission (AECC) (1990) Objectives of education for accountants: position statement number one, *Issues in Accounting Education*, 5(2), pp. 307–312.

Ahmad, N. and Gao, S. (2004) Changes, problems and challenges of accounting education in Libya, *Accounting Education: an international journal*, 13(3), pp. 365–390.

Albrecht, W. S. and Sack, R. J. (2000) *Accounting Education: Charting the Course Through a Perilous Future*, Accounting Education Series, Volume Number 16. (Florida: American Accounting Association).

Arnold, J., Loan-Clarke, J., Harrington, A. and Hart, C. (1999) Student perceptions of competence development in undergraduate business-related degrees, *Studies in Higher Education*, 24(1), pp. 43–59.

Australian Chamber of Commerce and Industry (ACCI) (2002) Employability skills: an employer perspective, *ACCI Review*, 88, pp. 1–6.

Awayiga, J., Onumah, J. and Tsamenyi, M. (2010) Knowledge and skills development of accounting graduates, the perceptions of graduates and employers in Ghana, *Accounting Education: an international journal*, 19(1), pp. 139–158.

Barnett, R. (1990) *The Idea of Higher Education* (Bristol: Society for Research into Higher Education and Open University Press).

Barrie, S. (2004) A researched-based approach to generic skills graduate attributes policy (editorial), *Higher Education Research and Development*, 23(3), pp. 261–275.

Barrie, S. (2006) Understanding what we mean by the generic attributes of graduates, *Higher Education*, 51(2), pp. 215–241.

Bennett, M., Bouma, J. and Ciccozzi, E. (2004) An institutional perspective on the transfer of accounting knowledge, a case study, *Accounting Education: an international journal*, 13(3), pp. 329–346.

Birkett, W. P. (1993) *Competency Based Standards for Professional Accountants in Australia and New Zealand* (Sydney: Institute of Chartered Accountants in Australia and the New Zealand Society of Accountants).

Birrell, B. and Rapson, V. (2005) *Migration and the Accounting Profession in Australia,* Report prepared for CPA Australia (Melbourne: Centre for Population and Urban Research, Monash University).

Birrell, B. (2006) *The Changing Face of the Accounting Profession in Australia,* Report prepared for CPA Australia Centre for Population and Urban Research (Melbourne: Monash University).

Birrell, B. and Healy, E. (2008) Migrant accountants—high numbers, poor outcomes, *People and Place*, 16(4), pp. 9–16.

Boritz, J. E. and Carnaghan, C. A. (2003) Competency-based education and assessment for the accounting profession: a critical review, *Canadian Accounting Perspectives*, 2(1), pp. 7–42.

Bowden, J., Hart, G., King, B., Trigwell, K. and Watts, O. (2000) *Generic Capabilities of ATN University Graduates*, Final report to Department of Education, Training and Youth Affairs (Melbourne: ATN Teaching and Learning Committee).

Bridgstock, R. (2009) The graduate attributes we've overlooked, enhancing graduate employability through career management skills, *Higher Education Research and Development*, 28(1), pp. 31–44.

Bui, B. and Porter, P. (2010) The expectation-performance gap in accounting education: an exploratory study, *Accounting Education: an international journal*, 13(3), pp. 23–50.

Clanchy, J. and Ballard, B. (1995) Generic skills in the context of higher education, *Higher Education Research and Development*, 14(2), pp. 123–136.

Cranmer, S. (2006) Enhancing graduate employability: best intentions and mixed outcomes, *Studies in Higher Education*, 31(1), pp. 169–84.

De Lange, P., Jackling, B. and Gut, A. (2006) Accounting graduates perceptions of skills emphasis in undergraduate courses: an investigation from two large Victorian Universities, *Accounting and Finance*, 46(3), pp. 365–386.

Department of Education and Employment and Workplace Relations (DEEWR) (2010) *International Student Enrolments in Higher Education in 2009.* Available at http://aei.dest.gov.au/AEI/PublicationsAndResearch/Snapshots/Default.htm (accessed 16 August 2010).

Fallows, S. and Stevens, C. (Eds) (2000) *Integrating Key Skills in Higher Education* (London: Kogan Page).

Glover, D., Law, S. and Youngman, A. (2002) Graduateness and employability: student perceptions of the personal outcomes of university education, *Research in Post Compulsory Education*, 7(3), pp. 293–306.

Graduate Careers Australia (2008) *University and Beyond 2007—International Students.* Available at http.// www.graduatecareers.com.au/content/view/full/3282 (accessed 16 August 2010).

Hancock, P., Howieson, B., Kavanagh, M., Kent, J., Tempone, I. and Segal, N. (2009a) *Accounting for the Future, More than Numbers.* Volume 1: Strategies for embedding non-technical skills into the accounting curricula (Sydney: Australian Learning and Teaching Council). Available at http://www.altc.edu.au/.../ DS7619Accountingforthefuture.Finalreport2009.Volume 1.pdf (accessed 16 August 2010).

Hancock, P., Howieson, B., Kavanagh, M., Kent, J., Tempone, I. and Segal, N. (2009b) *Accounting for the Future, More than Numbers.* Volume 2: Strategies for embedding non-technical skills into the accounting curricula (Sydney: Australian Learning and Teaching Council). Available at http://www.altc.edu.au/.../ DS7619Accountingforthefuture.Finalreport2009.Volume2.pdf (accessed 16 August 2010).

Hassall, T., Joyce, J., Arquero Montãno, J. L. and Donaso Anes, J. A. (2005) Priorities for the development of vocational skills in management accountants, a European perspective, *Accounting Forum*, 29(4), pp. 379–394.

Hellier, P., Keneley, M., Carr, R. and Lynch, B. (2004) Towards a market oriented approach: employer requirements and implications for undergraduate economics programs, *Economic Papers*, 23(3), pp. 213–233.

Higher Education Council (HEC) (1992) *Achieving Quality, Australian Government Publishing Service* (Canberra: HEC). Available at http.//www.dest.gov.au/sectors/training_skills/publications_resources/ind exes/documents/92_37_pdf.htm (accessed 17 August 2010).

Howieson, B. (2003) Accounting practice in the new millennium, is accounting education ready to meet the challenge?, *British Accounting Review*, 35(2), pp. 69–104.

Institute of Chartered Accountants in Australia and CPA Australia (2009) *International Accreditation Guidelines for Accounting Degree Programs* (Melbourne: CPA Australia).

Institute of Chartered Accountants in England and Wales (ICAEW) (1996) *Added-Value Professionals, Chartered Accountants in 2005: A Consultation Document* (London: ICAEW).

International Federation of Accountants (IFAC) Education Committee (1996) *Pre-qualification Education Assessment of Professional Competence and Experience Requirement* (New York: IFAC).

International Federation of Accountants (IFAC) Education Committee (2001) Competence-based approaches to the preparation and work of professional accountants, draft discussion paper (New York: IFAC).

Jackling, B. and De Lange, P. (2009) Do accounting graduates' skills meet the expectations of employers? A matter of convergence or divergence, *Accounting Education: an international journal*, 18(4–5), pp. 369–385.

Kavanagh, M. and Drennan, L. (2008) What skills and attributes does an accounting graduate need? Evidence from student perceptions and employer expectations, *Accounting and Finance*, 48(2), pp. 279–300.

Lizzio, A., Wilson, K. and Simons, R. (2002) University students' perceptions of the learning environment and academic outcomes, implications for theory and practice, *Studies in Higher Education*, 27(1), pp. 27–52.

Mathews, R., Jackson, M. and Brown, P. (1990) *Accounting in Higher Education: Report of the Review of the Accounting Discipline in Higher Education:* (1) (Canberra, ACT: Australian Government).

Moreau, M. and Leathwood, C. (2006) Graduates' employment and the discourse of employability, a critical analysis, *Journal of Education and Work*, 19(4), pp. 305–324.

National Committee of Inquiry into Higher Education (NCIHE) (1997) Higher education in the learning society—The Dearing Report (London: HMSO).

Nunan, T., Rigmor, G. and McCausland, H. (2000) Implementing graduate skills at an Australian University, in: S. Fallows and C. Stevens (Eds) *Integrating Key Skills in Higher Education*, pp. 57–66 (London: Kogan Page).

Oliver, B., Whelan, B., Hunt, L. and Hammer, S. (2011) Accounting graduates and the capabilities that count: perceptions of graduates, employers and accounting academics in four Australian universities, *Journal of Teaching and Learning for Graduate Employability*, 2(1), pp. 2–27.

Quality Assurance Agency for Higher Education (QAA) (2007) Honours Benchmark Statement, Accounting. Available at http://www.qaa.ac.uk/academicinfrastructure/benchmark/honours/default.asp (accessed 19 November 2008).

Rainsbury, E., Hodges, D., Burchell, N. and Lany, M. (2002) Ranking workplace competencies, student and graduate perceptions, *Asia Pacific Journal of Co-operative Education*, 3(2), pp. 8–18.

Sekaran, U. (1992) *Research Methods for Business: A Skill-Building Approach* (Singapore: Wiley).

Sin, S., Jones, A. and Petocz, P. (2007) Evaluating a method of integrating generic skills with accounting context based on a functional theory of meaning, *Accounting and Finance*, 47(1), pp. 143–163.

Usoff, C. and Feldman, D. (1998) Accounting students' perceptions of important skills for career success, *Journal of Education for Business*, 73(4), pp. 215–220.

Walsh, A. and Kotzee, B. (2010) Reconciling 'graduateness' and work based learning, *Learning and Teaching in Higher Education*, 4(1), pp. 36–50.
Watty, K. (2007) Quality in accounting education and low English standards among overseas students: is there a link?, *People and Place*, 15(1), pp. 22–29.
Xiao, Z. and Dyson, J. (1999) Chinese students' perceptions of good accounting teaching, *Accounting Education: an international journal*, 8(4), pp. 341–361.
Zikmund, W. (2000) *Business Research Methods* (Chicago: Dryden Press).

Appendix

Extract from Questionnaire

- Use BLOCK LETTERS
- Mark only ONE BOX, unless instructed otherwise
- Use a DARK pen

Section A: About you

Q1. Your Gender? Male Female
Q2. Where is your permanent home residence? Australia Overseas
In what country is your permanent home?
Q3. If you indicated in response to question 2 that your permanent residence is overseas, do you intend to seek
Permanent Residence in Australia on completion of your qualification? Yes No
Q4. Have you completed Year 12 Accounting as part of your studies towards the Victorian Certificate of Education, (V.C.E.)? Yes No
Q5. Where did you study the first unit in accounting or equivalent?

☐ XXX
☐ XXX (Private provider)
☐ XXX Tafe
☐ Another Tafe
☐ Other (please specify)

Section A: Your Studies

Q1. Generic skills
From your studies in accounting so far, cross one number on each line below to indicate the degree to which your studies have contributed to your development of the generic skills listed below. 1 = no contribution, while 5 = great contribution.

The ability to:

a. Work in a team
b. Make decisions
c. Solve problems
d. Adapt knowledge to new situations
e. Work with minimum supervision

f. Understanding the ethics and social/cultural implications of decisions
g. Question accepted wisdom
h. Be open to new ideas and possibilities
i. Think and reason logically
j. Think creatively
k. Make and take responsibility in moral, social & practical matters
l. Other (please specify)

*__Please note:__ A student will collect your completed questionnaire and seal it in an envelope. The questionnaires will be locked away securely until the results in this unit are finalised. This will ensure that students completing the questionnaire can be confident that their completion of the questionnaire in no way influences their result in the unit.

*This statement is consistent with the requirements of the Ethics approval for the research project.

Index

Page numbers in *Italics* represent tables.
Page numbers in **Bold** represent figures.

For Product Safety Concerns and Information please contact our EU representative GPSR@taylorandfrancis.com Taylor & Francis Verlag GmbH, Kaufingerstraße 24, 80331 München, Germany